D1097720

No man
is an island

No man is an island

A selection from the prose of John Donne

Selected, edited and introduced by Rivers Scott

London
The Folio Society

1997

© The Folio Society Ltd 1997

Second printing 1998

Set in Monotype Caslon by
Gloucester Typesetting Services
Printed on Ibis Wove paper
at St Edmundsbury Press, Bury St Edmunds
and bound in Lorenzo vellum
by Hunter & Foulis, Edinburgh.

Designed by Bernard Roberts

Contents

List of Illustrations

Introduction

In the churchyard of old St Paul's Cathedral in London—
that is, of the dilapidated medieval edifice burnt down in the
Great Fire of 1666 and replaced by Wren's cool and seem-
ingly indestructible masterpiece—stood 'a pulpit cross of
timber, mounted upon steps of stone and covered with lead,
in which are sermons preached by learned divines every
Sunday in the forenoon'. Up those steps and into that pulpit,
on Sunday 24 March 1617, climbed for the first time a man
already being hailed as the most studiously learned and most
charismatic preacher of his age, the Reverend John Donne,
D D, former wit, former poet, now a noted controversialist,
renegade from his childhood faith, and the greatest 'catch'
for the Church of England of that or any other time.

His task that morning was a patriotic and heart-warming
one—to preach on the commemoration, then annually kept,
of the death of Queen Elizabeth and the accession of her
cousin and successor James I. Paul's Cross, London's most
famous open-air pulpit, was often used for 'political' sermons
(later Donne would be commanded by the King to preach
there in defence of an unpopular 'gagging' decree) and the
turn-out could match the event. This time, looking down on
the cluster of grandees assembled to hear him, even Donne
must have been pleased. Sir Francis Bacon, then newly
created Lord Keeper, the Lord Privy Seal, the Earl of
Arundel, the Earl of Southampton, the Master of the Rolls
and the Archbishop of Canterbury were all present, as well
as the usual mixed throng of Londoners—civic dignitaries,
merchants and their families, clerks, journeymen, tramps and
whores—and though a contemporary letter-writer, in con-
descending vein, described the sermon as no more than
'daintie', Donne's clerical career was well and truly under
way. He may still have had a few of the preacher's arts to
perfect—he had only been ordained two years—but four
years later he had been made Dean of St Paul's; and when he
died after ten years in that office, on 31 March 1631, in a
blaze of macabre and personally stage-managed glory, it was
natural enough that both he and his congregation should
assume that what he would be remembered for in the future
would be his sermons, not his poems.

But all this was soon to change. By 1633 a first volume of

his verse, 'pirated' from manuscripts that had long been circulating, was already before the public; and in 1635 there
followed a fuller collection, overseen by his biographer and
'convert' Izaak Walton with the help of others, and group-
ing the poems very much in the order in which they are still
presented to us today. So the works of his youth and the
works of his age—the works of 'Jack Donne' and the works
of the grave 'Dr Donne'—were now both before the public,
and the public applauded them both. This immediately made
the distinction which he himself had so strongly insisted
upon less easy to sustain, and critics, who of course know
much more about writers than writers know about themselves, have long since dismissed it as nonsense. What they
cannot dismiss is the split within the man himself, or deny
that this split occurred at the deepest level, the level of his
faith. Whether that split was ever healed, whether he wished
it to be healed, has been argued more hotly than anything to
do with his art. And yet it intimately involves his art.

'The first thing to remember about Donne is that he was a
Catholic; the second, that he betrayed his Faith', writes
Professor John Carey in his astringent *John Donne: Life,
Mind and Art*—thereby blowing out of the water, with one
resounding salvo, the rotting hulk of obsequious pseudo-
piety which was threatening to make the man into a lifeless
plaster saint. Far from being any such thing, Donne retained,
even in his most deanishly respectable days, the soul of the
showman and chancer he had always been, though one of the
brightest, best-educated showmen and chancers who have
ever walked this earth. When younger, there was no crooked
statesman he would not crawl to for worldly advancement,
and after his ordination the establishment, not then so called,
could hardly have wished for a more obedient servant. To
say this is in no way to disparage his superb gifts. No great
artist is required to be a saint, and very few have been. To
see Donne for what he was, in so far as that is ever possible,
can only make one wonder all the more at what he achieved,
and increase one's gratitude for what he has bequeathed to us.
    John Donne was born in 1572—when Queen Elizabeth's
reign still had thirty-one years to run—into a family not just
of devoted Catholics, but of extremely distinguished ones.
Sir Thomas More was an ancestor. A great-uncle, Thomas
Heywood, had been martyred for his faith. Two uncles were
Jesuit priests. All this was on his mother's side. His father, a
prosperous ironmonger, who died when the boy was four,

Izaak Walton, Donne's friend and biographer. The engraving is the frontispiece to his *Compleat Angler*

appears to have been no less firm in his faith, but to have known how to keep out of trouble.

Donne and his brother Henry, because of their religion, had imposed on them the advantages of a cosmopolitan education. Both were clever enough to be sent up to Hart Hall, Oxford, at what would now seem to us an extremely tender age. (Donne was twelve when he matriculated.) Then both entered first Thavies and then Lincoln's Inn, the inns of court in that era being often referred to as England's third university, but with more play and less work involved than at the other two. There Henry Donne gave refuge to a seminary priest, a capital offence in those days. Both men were arrested but, mercifully for him, Henry died of the plague in Newgate before he could be brought to trial. The priest, William Harrington, was hung, taken down, and disembowelled alive, in the usual disgusting manner, to the delight of the crowd and of the Queen's chief torturer Topcliffe, whom he denounced from the scaffold and who continued to shout insults at him until he was too near death to hear them.

It might well be concluded that, with this horrible example before him, it would have been astonishing if Donne had *not* lapsed. What has to be asked is why he not only lapsed, but went so far to the other side. He always spoke and wrote of his father with reverence. He was extremely proud of his connection with Sir Thomas More. And he must have known that his Jesuit uncles, Ellis and Jasper Heywood, however much he (and indeed most English Catholics) may have disapproved of their intransigent line, were personally both brave and sincere. Yet he hated Jesuits with special bitterness.

To understand what was going on one has to remember that, politically and internationally, England really did feel under threat—a small Protestant island surrounded by large Catholic states, her Queen excommunicated by Pope Pius V, her people longing for unity and as afraid of popish spies as a later age was of Reds under the bed. Personally therefore, nothing could have been more sensible than to keep one's head below the parapet. Why make a martyr of oneself— literally? But, equally, why transfer to a fortress occupied by the enemy?

The short answer to this is, first, Donne's overriding ambition: better to reign in Hell than serve in Heaven; second, his seduction by money and the good life. It did not have to be spelt out to this exceedingly gifted man that no public advancement was open to those of his faith. You could prosper quietly, as his father had done before him, or, more often, you could fail to prosper, at home; alternatively, if your tastes lay that way, and your financial resources could somehow be made to stretch to it, you could wander about abroad. Donne came into money—through his share of his father's estate. He could now lead an entertaining and an intellectually stimulating life, hold down a good job and hobnob with the likes of Ben Jonson—if he kept quiet about his beliefs.

But pleasures of this sort also exact their price, and the price they exacted from Donne can be glimpsed from a passage in the autobiography of Sir Toby Mathew, son of an Archbishop of York (and former Bishop of Durham), who became a Catholic in Florence in 1606, thereby creating a considerable scandal, then foolishly returned to England, was imprisoned in the Fleet by the order of the Archbishop of Canterbury, and was finally packed off into exile. Writing of the people who visited him in his confinement, he reports that 'both Donne and Martin [a mutual friend] were very full of kindness to me at that time, though it continued not to be hearty afterward. By their discourses with me, when I was in prison, I found that they were mere libertines in themselves.' Mathew was a sort of cleaned-up version of the late Guy Burgess, a man who, in exile, longed to be back at home but who had denied himself that possibility by placing a set of principles and beliefs above party and even country. Unlike Burgess, however, Donne had to equip himself with a new set of beliefs *after*, not before, the event.

Consider the timing. When he paid his visit to Mathew in the Fleet he was thirty-five years old. Ten years earlier, in 1597–98, he had entered the service of Sir Thomas Egerton, later Lord Ellesmere and Viscount Brackley, a legal vulture of the first water and invaluable as a fixer to both Elizabeth and James I. Here he had a behind-the-scenes view of many high matters and appeared to have his foot on the ladder of success until, in 1601, at the age of twenty-nine, he contracted a secret marriage to a girl who was probably the only woman he ever truly loved, Anne More, daughter of an extremely rich Surrey landowner whose sister had recently become Egerton's second wife. 'John Donne, Anne Donne, Un-done', her new husband famously wrote to her, and so indeed the case appeared. Egerton sacked him, refused to take him back, and fifteen years of straitened circumstances and frantic job-hunting followed.

If Egerton, himself an apostate, would not have countenanced a return by Donne to the practice of his faith while he was in his employ, as must certainly be supposed, even less would it have been possible for Donne, once married, to say to his angry father-in-law, not to mention his distressed wife, 'I'm sorry, I'm now going back to being a recusant'. The die was long since cast, and the date (if any) on which he formally declared his adherence to the Anglican creed is immaterial. So when Walton waxed lyrical in his admiring and beautiful *Life* over the years Donne spent reading up the religious arguments for and against the Roman Catholic faith, he was surely deceiving himself. Donne, with his sharp intellect and natural dislike of being shown to be in the wrong, simply had to find ways of justifying his position. He was, therefore he thought. And helpful though his studies were to prove when it came to taking Anglican orders, they were, in themselves, nothing better than the creation of an elaborate alibi. Thomas Morton, later Bishop of Durham, the shrewd and courteous Anglican controversialist who employed Donne during his lean years, sensed this and clearly saw what should be done with him. He urged him to become an Anglican priest.

While all this was going on and the Donnes were living, first, with Mrs Donne's cousin, Sir Francis Wolley, at Pyrford in Surrey, and later in a cottage in Mitcham with a growing number of mouths to feed, the poet still managed to slip up to London from time to time (indeed he took lodgings there), see his friends, keep in touch with the great world, and also write letters to a wide circle of correspondents. This, however, was a sad, restricted time, and though the cottage at Mitcham was by no means as wretched as Donne's letters imply, it was an interlude of deep frustration in a life otherwise characterised by almost incessant activity. In youth he had been, as a contemporary described him, 'a great visitor of ladies, a great frequenter of plays, a great writer of conceited verses'. He had been a soldier, taking part in two military expeditions—one to Cadiz with Essex in command, the other the 'Islands' expedition to the Azores— during which two incidents—a storm and a calm—became the subject of two of his poems. He took part in more than one diplomatic mission, probably did a bit of spying, and was twice an MP: all this before James I took matters out of his restless and dissatisfied hands and virtually ordered him into the Anglican Church.

In short, in most respects he was a true Renaissance man, paradoxical, thrusting, litigious as was his age (at one period he was conducting a heated feud with the actor-manager

Edward Alleyn, who had married his eldest daughter, Constance), volatile, proud, yet obsequious to the great. He was also, however, possessed of enormous charm, a real talent for friendship, and a loyalty to his family which no personal doubts, differences in faith with his mother, or disappointments at his children's behaviour were able to affect.

And, once ordained, with his fence-sitting days over, he was rightly jealous of his new status, hurt when somebody suggested that he had exaggerated an illness to get out of preaching, and furious when a young man whom a friend had asked him to fix up with a living implied at a disastrous interview that really there was nothing very much to Donne's job; he (the youth) could stand in for him any day. 'You know the ticklishness of London pulpits', he tartly and memorably wrote to the friend, Mrs Cockayne, who had pressed the youth's claims, as he thought, rather too hard. All these traits are reflected in his prose, even more than in his verse.

Today one would imagine Donne not so much in a 'ticklish' pulpit as in an equally ticklish television studio, where, as a pundit of genius, a sort of Malcolm Muggeridge plus, he would make religion and morality topics of burning interest, mediate ideas, sometimes outrageous, sometimes abstruse, boost his allies, demolish his opponents, and be ready with an opinion on any issue of the hour, from beggars to birth control, as indeed he was in his life.

On one matter only would we still think him over the top, and that is the manner of his death. Those who know nothing else about Donne know about this: how, first, he preached his last sermon, afterwards named 'Death's Duel', before the King at Whitehall, looking like death and nearing it; how then, at the Deanery, when even nearer his end, he ordered a plinth, wrapped himself in a shroud, then stood on the plinth while an artist made a life-size sketch of him, in preparation for his marble monument. So vivid are the facts that they have almost become legend, to the point where some believe that he appeared in the pulpit in his shroud. (This version is even found, surprisingly enough, in that charming volume *Life in English Literature*, co-authored with Monica Redlich by the cultivated and knowledgeable L. A. G. Strong and published before the war for the instruction of the young.) Fact or legend, one has to remember that Donne was conforming, with his own special brand of panache, to a custom of his time, which dictated that if you had lived like Someone you took care to go out like Someone—like Sir Thomas More, Sir Philip Sidney, or the Earl of Essex, to name but three. And

A detail from an Italian engraving of Catholic martyrdom at Tyburn in 1535. Religious persecution had been experienced by members of Donne's own family, his Jesuit uncles Ellis and Jasper Heywood. *Below*, an exterior view of St Paul's, with the classical porch which was added by Inigo Jones in the 1640s

perhaps now, with showbiz personalities and others to the fore, we are not so far from returning to that time-honoured style.

It is on Donne's supreme aliveness, on the interest, appositeness and up-to-dateness of much of his work, when the pedantry and props of the time have been stripped away, that my selection has tried to concentrate. To this end I have modernised both spelling and punctuation. Sir Edmund Gosse, in his double-decker study *The Life and Letters of John Donne*, much mocked by later scholars on account of its frequent inaccuracies but none the less a landmark in the Donne revival on its first publication in 1899 (and an enjoyable read still), wrote in his preface: 'I do not think that "to join with you to move his Lordship to withdraw it" is made more luminous by printing it, "to joyne wth yo^w to moue hys Lp to wthdrawe ytt".' With this I agree. While scholars have not been wasting their time in establishing Donne's authentic texts, and while one comes to acclimatise oneself to, and even enjoy, Donne's and his printers' archaic spellings and punctuation, these can also act as a barrier to readers who want to get straight to the author's sense, as it is my hope that in this book they will. With the same end in view I have been fairly free with my cutting. Nothing that contradicts the essential logic of the thought in a particular passage is omitted without an indication of the fact. But, elsewhere, the shortenings are silent. There are other plagues to be feared and avoided besides those which raged in the late sixteenth and early seventeenth centuries, and one of them is the plague of dots.

I have also omitted two of Donne's works entirely, *Pseudo-Martyr* and *Ignatius His Conclave*. Both made an impact on the public in their time; and *Ignatius* was considered what would now be called a hilarious send-up. They remain necessary sources for historians of religion and scholars tracing in detail the ins and outs of Donne's self-doubt, but for the rest of us they just echo battles long ago that we are glad enough to forget. These apart, I have included at least some extracts from virtually all Donne's other prose works, on which here are a few comments.

Paradoxes and Problems

Shakespeare was twenty-eight when he collaborated on *Henry VI* and wrote, on his own account, *Richard III* and *Venus and Adonis*. Donne may have been no more than eighteen when he first started circulating his *Paradoxes*, with a selection of which this anthology starts; and barely more—though the dating here is highly disputable—when he set to work on his *Songs and Sonnets*, with many of which they seem to be connected in mood. The Paradoxes are joke productions, albeit of a learned kind. They tickle the fancy and are great fun to read (those of them of which the subjects have not gone out of date) because they represent Donne in his happier, more carefree years, before unwise matrimony and other troubles had started to weigh him down. The Problems, in the same section, which do spring from that time—that is, from the first decade of the seventeenth century—are more serious but hardly sad. Cheerfulness keeps breaking in, and again we can watch a precocious and erudite mind playing with a form as ancient as classical Greece.

Biathanatos

Biathanatos, the first English treatise on suicide, and written about 1607 or 1608, is another matter. Donne was anxious about it, fearful of what its unorthodox line might do for his prospects if ever good fortune should come his way again but unwilling to see it destroyed. The puzzle is, why did he write it? Was he so gloomy at Mitcham as to wish to do away with himself? Who was he addressing? What exactly did he wish to prove? Was he merely writing it to put to some use his extensive knowledge of civil and canon law? The work is divided into three sections—on the Law of Nature, of Reason and of God—but the reader need not make too much of these headings. Donne's son, also John Donne, published the work in 1644 and was much criticised, then and later, for his mercenary behaviour in so doing. In fact, we should thank him for preserving for us a work which, odd though it is, has never lost its fascination.

Letters

Donne's *Letters* also carry a special cachet deriving from the fact that a larger collection of his personal correspondence has survived than that of any other writer of importance up to that time. They were models of letter-writing—literally, for some readers—and while not 'newsy' or scandalous they show Donne in all his moods. They are a real treat, if one has never come across them before, and all one can say to the reader is, dip in.

Devotions

Devotions Upon Emergent Occasions, or *The Devotions* as they are generally called, must be one of the most peculiar hybrids in English or any other literature, an amalgam of religion, medical reportage and current affairs, given coherence by the power and strangeness of one man's temperament.

In late November 1623, at the age of 51, and about eight years after his ordination into the Anglican priesthood, Donne fell seriously ill. He had always been an arch hypochondriac and moaner. Now he had something to moan about. The disease he contracted was then called 'spotted fever'. It has since been identified as epidemic typhus, and more often than not it proved fatal. Some patients would have slumped back, said their prayers, and hoped for the best. Donne adopted a different course. He certainly slumped. And he certainly prayed—at length. But he also watched with obsessive fascination every changing manifestation of his illness, compared what was going on in his own body with what he could observe of the body politic outside, and wrote the lot down.

The illness itself lasted approximately fourteen days, the period of convalescence a little over three months, according to the latest authority on the subject. By the end of that time the book was in the hands of the printer and was published the following year, Donne having, to quote the same scholar, turned 'an exhausting human experience into a complicated artefact' and added a dedication to 'the most excellent prince, Prince Charles', soon to reign as Charles I.

The work is divided into twenty-three sections, each of them in turn divided into three parts: first, a 'meditation' charting the course of the sickness and triggering reflections on the spiritual health of both the patient and the world at large; then an 'expostulation', a sort of extended discussion with God elaborating the theme of the meditation preceding it. (For instance, Meditation 6 starts off with the heading 'The physician is afraid', so Expostulation 6 addresses God on the subject of fear.) Finally comes a prayer, a little sermon in itself, the reverse of the short, simple 'lifting of the mind and heart to God' which most spiritual guides suggest is what pleases Him best. Donne was much better at lecturing God than listening to him, a not uncommon feature of his age, and it is tempting to imagine on the part of the Almighty a certain wearied resignation, if not a distinct impatience, every time the words 'O my God', or 'O Eternal and most gracious God' came wafting up from the Dean's chamber. The whole work is prefaced by twenty-two lines of Latin verse, called 'Stationes', summarising the twenty-three stages of the disease. In the original, these, with an English translation or adaptation, are reprinted at the head of each set.

This is an astonishingly innovative work. Why did Donne write it—and how did he choose its form? Some see it as echoing the 'Spiritual Exercises' of St Ignatius Loyola, with their tripartite structure of memory, understanding and will. Some find links with earlier attempts at spiritual auto-biography, from St Augustine onwards. Some call Donne 'morbid', some accuse him of 'showing off'. One point to remember, however down-to-earth, is that Donne was in the public eye—a continual outpouring of work was expected of him as it is of any top performer. This too was the moment at which the ground for secular, as opposed to purely re-ligious, autobiography was just starting to be prepared. It can be argued quite simply that Donne stepped instinctively into it, the first great writer to do so, and that the outcome was a piece of both personal and religious self-searching that still ranks as unique.

In this selection I have, except for two short passages, omitted the 'Expostulations' in their entirety, as being hard going nowadays unless one is making a considered study of the whole work, but I have made brief extracts from a num-ber of the prayers, which I hope may be found of some use and consolation, even by patients in hospital wards today. (I have also added three prayers, similarly shortened, from *Essays in Divinity*). The 'Meditations' themselves seem to me to become more haunting and absorbing at every re-reading and it has been difficult to stop them encroaching beyond what seemed their allowable length.

Sermons

James I thought Donne's verses were like 'ye peace of God, they passed all understanding'. Yet neither he nor his sub-jects, however lowly their estate, seem to have found the slightest difficulty in following his sermons, and it was left to the eminent Henry Hart Milman, one of Donne's nine-teenth-century successors in the Deanery of St Paul's, to express the astonishment of later generations at the pulling power of these orations—at how vast congregations would listen,

John Heywood was a poet and Donne's maternal grandfather. The portrait is from his own book *The Spider and the Flie* of 1556

not only with patience but with absorbed interest, with unflagging attention, even with delight and rapture, to these interminable disquisitions, to us teeming with laboured obscurity, false and misplaced wit, fatiguing antitheses. However set off, as by all accounts they were, by a most graceful and impressive delivery, it is astonishing to us that he [Donne] should hold a London congregation enthralled, unwearied, unsatiated.

But that is what he did.

If, as on the occasion already mentioned, he was preaching at Paul's Cross, the rain might start, and if it turned into a downpour the crowd would scatter, just as they did at the playhouse. Indeed, with a preacher of Donne's quality on his feet, these performances were as good as the playhouse, and free with it. The roof over the pulpit, when it was added, was enough to shelter the preacher, but sometimes the whole gathering was obliged to call it a day and move into the cathedral itself.

Here a different set of obstacles had to be contended with, for while divine service was held in the choir, the nave was put to less religious purposes. To quote from Evelyn M. Simpson, in the monumental ten-volume edition of *The Sermons of John Donne*, this space had become

> the great meeting place of Londoners. Merchants wearing their hats transacted business in the aisles, and lawyers received their clients. Gallants walked up and down in their finery, while masterless servingmen sat on a bench waiting to be engaged to a new master.

Protest was usually vain—one miscreant, when rebuked for his rowdy activities, replied that he was sorry, he didn't realise it was a church—and sometimes the air of disturbance penetrated to the choir itself. Once Donne had a man committed to Newgate for refusing to kneel down. Another nuisance in churches in the City of London, and doubtless in St Paul's as well, was the howling of stray dogs, which had to be whipped out of the buildings by the sexton or put down by specially paid dog-killers.

Besides St Paul's and Paul's Cross, Donne preached regularly at the Court and at Whitehall, well away from the hurly-burly but not from the sharp and critical ears of his theologically-inclined monarch. Before his appointment as Dean he had had a happy five years as Divinity Reader for

Lincoln's Inn, where his sermons, addressed to old friends and new, gave pleasure to both sides. He preached at the Spital (or Spittle), which was rather like Paul's Cross, but situated in the churchyard of St-Mary-Without Bishopsgate. Here the Lord Mayor and Aldermen, arrayed 'in their scarlets', would assemble after Lent, as would the boys of nearby Christ's Hospital, of which Donne was a governor, in a 'large house' specially built for them—perhaps the only members of those numerous congregations who found the occasions too long. Donne also received the livings of a number of country parishes—including Sevenoaks in Kent, where he would stay with the Dorsets at Knole—and would preach in them on his rare visits. Last, and most prominent, was St Dunstan-in-the-West. Here he became very much the parish priest, and here he delivered a number of his finest sermons, including, most memorably, one in 1624, celebrating the first return of himself and his parishioners after the terrible plague of that year.

Of course Dean Milman was quite right in his listing of what puts us off now; a great deal of Donne's eloquence is buried for modern readers beneath the rubble of outworn forms of scholarship and ways of thought, which even in his own time harked back to the medieval. Walton, in his *Life*, describes his hero's method of work:

> As he usually preached once a week, if not oftener, so after his sermon he never gave his eyes a rest till he had chosen out a new text, and that night cast his sermon into a form, and his text into divisions.

In other words, his sermons are schematised: first, a close linguistic analysis of the text, studded with Latin translations and appeals to the early Fathers; then an announcement of how the sermon will be laid out; and then a daunting plod (as it would be for us) through those various parts, which we fancy we would be silently counting off on our fingers as we count off the pages of an inexperienced lecturer's typescript. But of course we wouldn't, because Donne wouldn't address us like that. His pedantry, though it exists, is the time-bound part of him. His format too is of his period. Embedded in it are the timeless nuggets.

Donne's age was sermon-mad. Each sermon would normally last an hour, perhaps much longer (the hour-glass by his side is several times mentioned by Donne), and people would sometimes attend two or even three in a day, hanging onto

the preacher's words and dissecting them at length afterwards. They expected to have sermons at banquets and city
feasts (which the frivolous thought was too much). They also
followed their favourite preachers round from church to
church, a practice Donne affected to deplore.

So what, after the passage of nearly four centuries, do we
principally retain and treasure? The cadences of course, and
the showers of telling phrases: 'Death is an old man's door';
'He kisses in a biting kiss' (of Judas); 'The air is not so full
of motes, of atoms, as the Church is of mercies.' (To extract
its full savour, all Donne's prose needs to be read aloud.) Then
the vivid illustrations from everyday life: Donne was a Lon-
doner born and bred, lovingly familiar with every sight and
sound of his city, from its taverns to its River Thames; he
knew business and the law, and he draws on the whole scene
to ram home his spiritual points. Here are misers and usurers
cheating each other and the poor; here are adulterers creeping out under cover of night, making their way to houses of
ill-fame, only to find the doors boarded up because of the
plague. Then there is humour, and the odd humorous trick
of the trade. In one delightful sermon, preached at Whitehall, he begins on a bland and apparently innocuous note,
well calculated to lull the courtiers into a sense of false security, then suddenly pounces—hey, you at the back there, star-
ing out of the window, what are you thinking about? Not what
I'm saying, I'll warrant! He also, very vividly, describes his
own distractions at prayer—how the creaking of a door, the
noise of a wheel in the street, is enough to put him off.

A poet's tongue and a lawyer's brain combine in the sermons
to make theology luminous. A heavenly disquisition on
angels, a masterly catalogue of everything you always wanted
to know about the mechanics of the general Resurrection but
weren't sure whom to ask—take your choice. But what lay
behind it all? How much was sincere, how much was mean-
ingless rhetoric? T. S. Eliot, who one suspects had a nose for
a fraud, found it hard to take seriously Donne's repentance
for his former sins, but reading today his sublimest passages,
those impassioned descriptions of the joys of the life to come,
or even the tenderer passages in some of his letters, it is hard
to believe that they did not proceed from the heart. That his
doubts continued well after his ordination is evident from a
number of hints in his prose and also (I believe) from the
beautiful sonnet 'Show me dear Christ, thy spouse, so bright
and clear'. Perhaps they persisted. Perhaps they went away.

Or perhaps he was, in modern parlance, the ultimate existentialist, making his life as he went along and making it so well that he finally deceived himself.

If so, what did he think, if anything, in those very last moments when the play-acting was over and even the praying had had to stop? Nobody can tell, but every lover of English prose can be grateful for the legacy this exemplar of the paradox in life as in literature bequeathed. In a telling passage in *Biathanatos* he wrote: 'Not to pray for them which die without faith is a precept so obvious to every religion that even Mahomet hath inhibited it. But to presume impenitence because you were not by and heard it is an usurpation.' It is a charitable judgement, and a fitting thought on which to end.

RIVERS SCOTT

Paradoxes and Problems

Both these forms date back to classical times, both were on their last legs by the time Donne took them up. There is some dispute about Paradox 6, 'A Defence of Women's Inconstancy', which the latest authority on the subject, Dr Helen Peters, thinks was not written by Donne. But it goes on being quoted and attributed to him, no doubt on account of its sparkle, and is included here for the same reason. The majority are given in full. See the Introduction for further comments.

Paradoxes

1. That Women Ought to Paint Themselves

Foulness is loathsome—can that be so too which helps it? Who forbids his beloved to gird in her waist, to mend by shoeing her uneven lameness, to burnish her teeth or to perfume her breath? Yet that the face be more precisely regarded, it concerns more. For as open, confessing sinners are always punished, but the wary and concealed, offending without witness, do it also without punishment, so the secret parts need less respect. But of the face, discovered to all surveys and examinations, there is not too nice a jealousy. Nor doth it only draw the busy eye, but also is most subject to the divinest touch of all: to kissing, the strange and mystical union of souls.

If she should prostitute herself to a more worthy man than thyself, how earnestly and how justly wouldst thou exclaim! Then for want of this easy and ready way of repairing, to betray her body to ruin and deformity, the tyrannous ravishers and sudden deflowerers of all women, what a heinous adultery is it! What thou lovest most in her face is colour, and this painting gives that. But thou hatest it not because it is, but because thou knowest it.

Fool, whom only ignorance makes happy! The stars, the sun, the sky which thou admirest, alas have no colour, but are fair because they seem coloured. If this seeming will not satisfy thee in her, thou hast good assurance of her colour when thou seest her lay it on. If her face be painted upon a board or a wall, thou wilt love it, and the board, and the wall. Canst thou loathe it then, when it smiles, speaks and kisses, because it is painted? Is not the earth's face in the most pleasing season new painted? Are we not more delighted with seeing fruits and birds and beasts painted than with the naturals? And do we not with pleasure behold the painted shapes of devils and monsters, whom true we durst not regard?

We repair the ruins of our houses, but first cold tempest warns us of it and bites us through it. We mend the wrack and wash the stains of our apparel, but first our eye and other body is offended. But by this providence of women this is prevented. If in kissing or breathing upon her the painting fall off, thou art angry. Wilt thou be so if it stick on? Thou didst love her. If thou beginnest to hate her, then it is because she is not painted. If thou wilt say now, thou didst hate her before, thou didst hate her and love her together. Be constant in something, and love her who shows her great love to thee by taking these pains to seem lovely to thee.

2. That Old Men Are More Fantastic than Young

To be fantastic in young men is a conceitful distemperature and a witty madness, but in old men, whose senses are withered, it becomes natural, therefore more full and perfect. For as, when we sleep, our fancy is most strong, so it is in age, which is a slumber of the deep sleep of death.

They tax us with inconstancy, which in themselves young they allowed, so that, reproving that which they did approve, their inconstancy exceeds ours because they have changed once more than we. Yea, they are more idly busied in conceiting apparel than we, for we, when we are melancholy, wear black; when lusty, green; when forsaken, tawny: pleasing our own inward affections, leaving them to others indifferent. But they prescribe laws and constrain the noble, the scholar, the merchant and all estates to certain habits.

The old men of our time have changed with patience their own bodies, much of their laws, much of their language, yea their religion; yet they accuse us. To be amorous is proper and natural in a young man, but in an old man most fantastic. And that riddling humour of jealousy, which seeks and would not find, which enquires and repents his knowledge, is in them most common, yet most fantastic. Yea, that which falls never in young men is in them most fantastic and natural, that is, covetousness—even at their journey's end to make great provision. Is any habit in young men so fantastic as in the hottest seasons to be double gowned and hooded, like our elders? Truly, as amongst philosophers the sceptic which doubts all is more contentious than either the dogmatic which affirms or academic which denies all, so are these uncertain elders, which both call them fantastic which follow others' inventions and them also which are led by their own humours' suggestions, more fantastic than either.

3. That a Wise Man Is Known by Much Laughing

Ride si sapis o puella ride: girl, if thou beest wise, laugh. For since the powers of discourse and reason and laughter be equally proper to only man, why shall he not be most wise which hath most use of laughing, as well as he which hath most of reasoning and discoursing? I always did and shall understand that adage, By much laughter thou canst know a fool, that by much laughing thou mayst know there is a fool: not that the laughers are fools, but that among them there is some fool at whom wise men laugh. Which moved Erasmus to put this as the first argument in the mouth of his Folly, that she made beholders laugh. For fools are the most laughed at, and laugh least themselves, of any. And Nature saw this faculty to be so necessary in man that she hath been content that by more causes we should be importuned to laugh than to the exercise of any other power. For things in themselves utterly contrary beget this effect. For we laugh both at witty and absurd things. At both which sorts I have seen men laugh so long and so earnestly that at last they have wept that they could laugh no more.

And therefore the poet, having described the quietness of a wise, retired man, sayeth in one that we have said before in many lines: *Quid facit Canius tuus? ridet* (What is your friend Canius doing? He is laughing). We have received that even the extremity of laughing—yea, of weeping also—hath been accounted wisdom; and Democritus and Heraclitus, the lovers of these extremes, have been called lovers of wisdom. Now, amongst our wise men, I doubt not that many would be found who would laugh at Heraclitus's weeping, none which would weep at Democritus's laughing. At the hearing of comedies or other witty reports I have noted some which, not understanding the jests, have yet chosen this as the best means to seem wise and understanding, to laugh when their companions laugh, and I have presumed them ignorant whom I have seen unmoved.

A fool, if he comes into a prince's court and sees a gay man leaning at the wall, so glistering and so painted in many colours that he is hardly discerned from one of the pictures in the arras hangings, his body like an ironbound chest girt in, and thick-ribbed with broad, gold laces, may, and commonly does, envy him. But alas, shall a wise man, which may not only not envy this fellow, but not pity him, do nothing at this monster? Yes: let him laugh. And if one of these hot, choleric firebrands, which nourish themselves by quarrelling and kindling others, spit upon a fool but one spark of disgrace, he, like a thatched house quickly burning, may be angry. But the wise man, as cold as the salamander, may not only not be angry with him, but not be sorry for him. Therefore let him laugh. So shall he be known a man, because he can laugh: a wise man that he knows at what to laugh, and a valiant man that he dares laugh.

For who laughs is justly reputed more wise than at whom it is laughed. And hence I think proceeds that which in these later, formal times I have much noted: that now, when our superstitious civility is become but a mutual tickling flattery of one another, almost every man affects a humour of jesting and is content to deject [debase] and deform himself, yea to become fool, to none other end that I can spy but to give his wise companions occasion to laugh, and to show themselves wise. Which promptness of laughing is so great in wise men that I think all wise men (if any wise men do read this paradox) will laugh both at it and me.

4. That Good Is More Common than Evil

I have not been so pitifully tired with any vanity as with silly old men's exclaiming against our times and extolling their own. Alas, they betray themselves. For if the times be changed, their manners have changed them. But their senses are to pleasure as sick men's tastes to liquors. For indeed no new thing is done in the world: all things are what and as they were. And good is as ever it was, most plenteous, and must of necessity be more common than evil because it hath this for nature and end and perfection—to be common. It makes love to all creatures and all affect it, so that in the world's early infancy there was a time when nothing was evil.

But if this world shall suffer dotage in the extremest crookedness thereof, there shall be no time when nothing shall be good. It dares appear and spread and glister in the world, but evil buries itself in night and darkness and is suppressed and chastised when good is cherished and rewarded. And as embroiderers, lapidaries and other artisans can by all things adorn their works—for by adding better things they better them so much, by equal things they double their goodness, and by worse they increase their show and lustre and eminency—so good doth not only prostitute her own amiableness to all, but refuseth no aid—no, not of her utter contrary, evil—that she may be more common to us.

For evil manners are parents of good laws, and in every evil there is an excellency which, in common speech, we call good. For the fashions of habits, for our movings in gestures, for phrases in our speech, we say they were good as long as they were used—that is, as long as they were common. And we eat, we walk, we sleep only when it is, or seems, good to do so. All fair, all profitable, all virtuous, is good; and these three things I think embrace all things but their utter contraries, of which also foul may be rich and virtuous, poor may be virtuous and fair, vicious may be fair and rich. So that good hath this good means to be common, that some subjects she can possess entirely, and in subjects poisoned with evil she can humbly stoop to accompany the evil. And of indifferent, many things are become perfectly good only by being common, as customs by use are made binding laws. But I remember nothing that is therefore ill because it is common but women; of whom also they which are most common are the best of that occupation they profess.

5. That It Is Possible to Find Some Virtue in Some Women

I am not of that seared impudency that I dare defend women, or pronounce them good. Yet when we see physicians allow some virtue in every poison, alas, why should we except women, since certainly they are good for physic at least so as wine is good for a fever. And though they be the occasioners of most sins, they are also the punishers and revengers of the same sins. For I have seldom seen one which consumes his substance or body upon them escape diseases or beggary.

And this is their justice. And if to give to each his own be the fulfilling of all civil justice, they are most just, for they deny that which is theirs to no man. And who may doubt of great wisdom in them that doth but observe with how much labour and cunning our justices and other dispensers of the laws [strive] to entrap them, and study how zealously our preachers dehort [dissuade] men from them, only by urging their subtleties and policies and wisdom which are in them —yea, in the worst and most prostitute sort of them. And who can deny them a good measure of fortitude, if he consider how many valiant men they have overthrown and, being themselves overthrown, how much and how patiently they bear?

Necessity, which makes even bad things good, prevails also for them, and we must say of them as of some sharp, punishing laws: if men were free from infirmities, they were needless.

6. A Defence of Women's Inconstancy

That women are inconstant I with any man confess, but that inconstancy is a bad quality I against any man will maintain [argue]. For everything, as it is one better than another, so is it fuller of change. The heavens themselves continually turn, the stars move, the moon changeth, fire whirleth, air flieth, water ebbs and flows, the face of the earth altereth her looks, time stays not; the colour that hath most light will take most dyes. So in men. They that have the most reason are the most alterable in their designs, and the darkest and most ignorant do seldomest change.

Therefore women, changing more than men, have also more reason: they cannot be immutable, like stocks, like stones, like the earth's dull centre. Gold that lieth still, rusteth; water corrupteth; and air that moveth not, poisoneth. Then why should that which is the perfection of other things be imputed to women as greatest imperfection? Because thereby they deceive men? Are not your wits pleased with those jests which cozen your expectation? You can call it pleasure to be beguiled in trifles, and in the most excellent toy in the world you call it treachery. I would you had your mistresses so constant that they would never change, no, not so much as their smocks; then should you see what a sluttish virtue constancy were.

Inconstancy is a most commendable and cleanly quality, and women in this quality are far more absolute than the heavens, than the stars, than moon or anything beneath it; for long observation hath picked certainty out of this mutability. The learned are so well acquainted with the stars' signs and planets that they make them but characters to read the meaning of the heaven in his own forehead. Every simple fellow can bespeak the change of the moon a great while beforehand. But I would fain have the learnedest man so skilful as to tell when the simplest woman meaneth to vary. Learning affords no rules to know, much less knowledge to rule, the mind of a woman. For as philosophy teacheth us that light things do always tend upwards and heavy things decline downwards, experience teacheth us otherwise—that the disposition of a light woman is to fall down, the nature of women being contrary to all art and nature.

Women are like flies which feed amongst us at our table, or fleas sucking our very blood, who leave not our most re-tired places from their familiarity. Yet for all their fellowship

ANNO DNI. 1591.
ÆTATIS SVÆ·18·
ANTES MVDADO
MVERTO QVE

This was for youth, Strength, Mirth, and wit that Time
Most count their golden Age; but t'was not thine.
Thine was thy later yeares, so much refind
From youths Drosse, Mirth, & wit; as thy pure mind
Thought (like the Angels) nothing but the Praise
Of thy Creator, in those last, best Dayes.
    Witnes this Booke, (thy Embleme) which begins
    With Love; but endes, with Sighes, & Teares for sins.

Will: Marshall .sculpsit.   IZ:WA:

A youthful portrait of Donne on the frontispiece to his *Poems*, published
1635

will they never be tamed, nor commanded by us. Women are like the sun, which is violently carried one way yet hath a proper course contrary. So though they, by the mastery of some overruling, churlish husbands, are forced to his bias, yet have they a motion of their own which their husbands never know of. It is the nature of nice and fastidious minds to know things only to be weary of them. Women, by their sly changeableness and pleasing doubleness, prevent even the mislike of those, for they can never be so well known but that there is still more unknown.

Every woman is a science, for he that plods upon a woman all his life long shall at length find himself short of the knowledge of her. They are born to take down the pride of wit and ambition of wisdom, making fools wise in the adventuring to win them, wise men fools with conceit of losing their labour, witty men stark mad being confounded with their uncertainties. Philosophers write against them for spite, not desert, that having attained to some knowledge in all other things, in them only they know nothing, but are merely ignorant. Active and experienced men rail against them because they love in their liveless and decrepit age, when all goodness leaves them. These envious libellers ballad against them because, having nothing in themselves able to deserve their love, they maliciously discommend all they cannot obtain, thinking to make men believe they know much because they are able to dispraise much, and rage against inconstancy when they were never admitted into so much favour as to be forsaken. In my opinion such men are happy that women are inconstant, for so they may chance to be beloved of some excellent woman—when it comes to their turn—out of their inconstancy and mutability, though not out of their own desert.

And what reason is there to clog any woman with one man, be he never so singular? Women had rather—and it is far better and more judicial—to enjoy all the virtues in several men than but some of them in one, for otherwise they lose their taste like diverse sorts of meat minced together in one dish. And to have all excellences in one man (if it were possible) is confusion, not diversity. Now who can deny but [that] such as are obstinately bent to undervalue their worth are those that have not soul enough to comprehend their excellence: women being the most excellent creatures, in that man is able to subject all things else, and to grow wise in everything, but still persists a fool in woman. The greatest scholar, if he once take a wife, is found so unlearned that he must begin his hornbook, and all is by inconstancy.

To conclude, therefore: this name of inconstancy, which hath been so much poisoned with slanders, ought to be changed into variety, for the which the world is so delightful, and a woman for that the most delightful thing in the world.

'Thou hast good assurance of her colour when thou seest her lay it
on . . .' — a seventeenth-century portrait of a woman at her toilet

Problems

1. Why Die None for Love Now?

Because women are become easier? Or because these later times have provided mankind of more new means for the destroying themselves and one another: pox, gunpowder, young marriages, and controversies in religion? Or is there in truth no precedent or example of it? Or perchance some do die, but are therefore not worthy the remembering or speaking of.

2. Why Have Bastards Best Fortune?

Because Fortune herself is a whore? But such are not most indulgent to their children. The old natural reason—that these meetings in stolen love are most vehement, and so contribute more spirit than the easy and lawful—might govern me, but that I see now that mistresses are become domestic and in ordinary, and they and wives wait but by turns and agree as well as if they lived in the Ark. The old moral reason —that bastards inherit wickedness from their parents, and so are in a better way of preferment by having a stock beforehand than those that must build all their fortune upon the poor, weak stock of original sin—might prevail with me, but that since we are fallen into such times as, now, the world might spare the Devil because we could be bad enough without him, I see men scorn to be wicked by example or to be beholden to others for their damnation.

It seems reasonable that, since laws rob them of succession and civil benefits, they should have something else equivalent. As Nature, which is law's pattern, having denied women constancy to one, hath provided them with cunning to allure many, so bastards *de jure* should have better wits and abilities. But (besides that by experience we see many fools amongst them) we should take from them one of their chiefest helps to preferment if we should deny them to be fools. And that (which is only left) that women choose worthier persons than their husbands, is false *de facto*.

Either then it must be that the Church, having removed them from all place in the public service of God, they have thereby better means than others to be wicked, and so fortunate; or else because the two greatest powers in the world, the Devil and princes, concur to their greatness, the one giving bastardy, the other legitimation, as Nature frames and conserves great bodies of contraries.

Or perchance it is because they abound most at Court, which is the forge where fortunes are made, or at least the shop where they are sold.

3. Why Venus Star Only Doth Cast a Shadow

Is it because it is nearer the Earth? But they whose profession it is to see that nothing be done in Heaven without their consent (as Kepler says in himself of all astrologers) have bid Mercury to be nearer. Is it because the works of Venus need shadowing, covering and disguising? But those of Mercury need it more. For eloquence, his occupation, is all shadows and colours. Let our life be a sea, and then our reason, and even passions, are wind enough to carry us whither we should go, but eloquence is a storm and tempest that miscarries us. And who doubts that eloquence (which must persuade people to take a yoke of sovereignty and then beg and make laws to tie them faster, and then give money to the invention [institution], repair and strengthen it) needs more shadows and colourings than to persuade any man or woman to that which is natural; and Venus's markets are so natural that when we solicit the best way (which is by marriage) our persuasions work not so much to draw a woman to us as, against her nature, to draw her from all others besides.

And so, when we go against nature and from Venus's works (for marriage is chastity) we need shadows and colours, but not else. In Seneca's time it was a coarse and un-Roman and a contemptible thing, even in a matron, not to have had a love besides her husband, which, though the law required not at their hands, yet they did it zealously, out of the counsel of the custom and fashion, which was venery of supererogation. Horace, because many lights would not show him enough, created many images of the same object by wainscotting his chamber with looking-glasses. So then Venus flies not light so much as Mercury, who, creeping into our understanding in our darkness, were defeated if he were perceived. Then either this shadow confesseth that same dark melancholy repentance which accompanies it; or that so violent fires need some shadowy refreshing and intermission; or else light, signifying both days and youth, and shadow both night and age, she pronounceth by this that she professeth all times and persons.

4. Why Is Venus Star Multinominous and Called Both Hesperus and Vesper?

The Moon has as many names, but not as she is a star but as she has diverse governments [powers]. But Venus is multi-nominous to give example to her prostitute disciples who so often, either to renew or refresh themselves towards lovers, or to disguise themselves from magistrates, are to take new names. It may be she takes many names after her many functions, for as she is supreme monarch of all love at large (which is lust), so is she joined in commission by all mythologists with Juno, Diana and all others for marriage. It may be, because of the diverse names of her affections, she assumes diverse names to herself.

For her affections have more names than any vice, to wit Pollution, Fornication, Adultery, Lay Incest, Church Incest, Rape, Sodomy, Masturbation, and a thousand others. Perchance her diverse names show her appliableness to diverse men, for Neptune distilled and wept her into love, the Sun warmed and melted her, Mercury persuaded and swore her, Jupiter's authority secured, and Vulcan hammered her. As Hesperus she presents you with her *bonum utile*, because it is wholesomest in the morning; as Vesper, with her *bonum delectabile* because it is pleasantest in the evening. And because industrious men rise and endure, with the Sun, their civil business, this star calls them up a little before, and remembers them again a little after, for *her* business.

5. Why Does the Pox So Much Affect to Undermine the Nose?

Paracelsus perchance says true, that every disease has its exaltation in some certain part. But why this in the nose? Is there so much mercy in this disease that it provides that one should not smell his own stink? Or has it but the common fortune that, being begot and bred in the obscurest and secretest corner, because therefore its serpentine crawlings and insinuations be not suspected or seen, it comes sooner to great place, and is abler to destroy the worthiest member than a disease better born. Perchance as mice defeat elephants by gnawing their proboscis, which is their nose, this wretched [West] Indian vermin practises to do the same upon us. Or as the ancient furious custom and connivance of some laws (that one might cut off their noses whom he deprehended in adultery) was but a type of this, and now that more charitable laws have taken away all revenge from particular hands, this common magistrate and executioner is come to do the same office invisibly. Or by withdrawing this conspicuous part, the nose, it warns from adventuring on that coast (for it is as good a signal to take in a flag as to hang one out).

But because, by consent of all, there is an analogy and proportion and affection between the nose and that part where this disease is first contracted (and therefore Heliogabalus chose not his minions in the bath but by the nose, and Albertus [Albert the Great] had a knavish meaning when he preferred great noses, and the licentious poet was *Naso Poeta*), I think this reason is nearest truth, that the nose is most compassionate with that part. Except this be nearer, that it is reasonable that this disease should in particular men affect the most eminent and conspicuous part, which amongst men in general doth affect to take hold of the most eminent and conspicuous men.

Biathanatos

The first work in English on the subject of suicide, *Biathanatos* was probably written between 1607 and 1608 and was published by Donne's son in 1644. The wording of the title page, reproduced here, shows the younger Donne's apprehensiveness as to how it would be received, and also Donne's own attempt, when he originally circulated copies, to deflect any criticism by categorising it as a 'Paradox'. This has prevented anyone, either in his own day or since, from being quite sure what he was about.

Preface

Beza,* a man as eminent and illustrious, in the full glory and noon of learning, as others were in the dawning and morning when any the least sparkle was notorious, confesseth of himself that only for the anguish of a scurf which overran his head he had once drowned himself from the Miller's Bridge in Paris if his uncle by chance had not then come that way. I have often such a sickly inclination. And whether it be because I had my first breeding and conversation with men of a suppressed and afflicted religion, accustomed to the despite of death and hungry of an imagined martyrdom, or that the Common Enemy find that door worst locked against him in me, or that there be a perplexity and flexibility in the doctrine itself, or because my conscience ever assures me that no rebellious grudging at God's gifts, nor other sinful concurrence, accompanies these thoughts in me, or that a brave scorn, or that a faint cowardliness, beget it: whensoever any affliction assails me, methinks I have the keys of my prison in mine own hand, and no remedy presents itself so soon to my heart as mine own sword. Often meditation of this hath won me to a charitable interpretation of their action who die so, and provoked me a little to watch and exagitate [scrutinise] their reasons which pronounce so peremptory judgements upon them.

A devout and godly man hath guided us well, and rectified our uncharitableness in such cases, by this remembrance: Thou knowest this man's fall, but thou knowest not his wrestling, which perchance was such that almost his very fall is justified and accepted of God. For to this end, saith one, God hath appointed us temptations that we might have some excuses for our sins, when he calls us to account.

Contemplative and bookish men must of necessity be more quarrelsome than others, because they contend not about matters of fact, nor can determine their controversies by any certain witnesses nor judges. But as long as they go towards peace—that is, truth—it is no matter which way. The tutelary angels resisted one another in Persia, but neither resisted God's revealed purpose. Jerome and Gregory seem to be of opinion that Solomon is damned, Ambrose and Augustine that he is saved: all Fathers, all zealous of God's glory. At the same time when the Roman Church canonised Becket, the

* A 16th-century Calvinist theologian.

schools of Paris disputed whether he could be saved: both Catholic judges, and of reverend authority. And after so many ages of a devout and religious celebrating the memory of St Jerome, Causeus hath spoken so dangerously that Campion says he pronounces him to be as deep in Hell as the Devil.

But in all such intricacies, where both opinions seem equally to conduce to the honour of God, his justice being as much advanced in the one as his mercy in the other, it seems reasonable to me that this turn the scales, if on either side there appear charity towards the poor soul departed. The Church in her hymns and antiphons doth often salute the nails and cross with epithets of sweetness and thanks. But the spear which pierced Christ when he was dead it ever calls *dirum mucronem.*

This pity, I protest again, urges me in this discourse. And therefore, without any disguising or curious and libellous concealing, I present it to all of candour and indifference. For as, when Ladislaus took occasion of the Great Schism to corrupt the nobility in Rome and hoped thereby to possess the town, to their seven Governors, whom they called *Sapientes*, they added three more, whom they called *Bonos*, and confided in them; so do I wish, and—as much as I can—effect, that to those many learned and subtle men which have travelled in this point, some charitable and compassionate men might be added.

If therefore of readers, which Gorionides observes to be of four sorts—sponges which attract all without distinguishing; hour-glasses which receive and pour out as fast; bags which retain only dregs of the spices and let the wine escape; and sieves which retain the best only—I find some of the last sort, I doubt not but they may be hereby enlightened. And as the eyes of Eve were opened by the taste of the apple, though it be said before that she saw the beauty of the tree, so the digesting of this may, though not present fair objects, yet bring them to see the nakedness and deformity of their own reasons, founded upon a rigorous suspicion, and win them to be of that temper which Chrysostom commends: He which suspects benignity would fain be deceived, and be overcome, and is piously glad, when he finds it to be false which he did uncharitably suspect. And it may have as much vigour (as one observes of another author) as the sun in March: it may stir and dissolve humours, though not expel them. For that must be a work of a stronger power.

This is my way, and my end is to remove scandal. For certainly God often punisheth a sinner much more severely because others have taken occasion of sinning by his fact. If therefore we did correct in ourselves this easiness of being scandalised, how much easier and lighter might we make the punishment of many transgressors? For God in his judgements hath almost made us his assistants and counsellors, how far he shall punish; and our interpretation of another's sin doth often give the measure to God's justice or mercy.

If therefore, since disorderly long hair, which was pride and wantonness in Absolom and squalor and horridness in Nebuchadnezzar, was virtue and strength in Samson and sanctification in Samuel, these severe men will not allow to indifferent things the best construction they are capable of, nor pardon my inclination to do so, they shall pardon me this opinion, that their severity proceeds from a self-guiltiness, and give me leave to apply them that of Ennodius, that it is the nature of stiff wickedness to think that of others which themselves deserve, and it is all the comfort which the guilty have, not to find any innocent.

Of the Law of Nature

As lawyers use to call that impossible which is so difficult that by the rules of law it cannot be afforded but by the indulgence of the prince and exercise of his prerogative, so divines are accustomed to call that sin which for the most part is so, and which naturally occasions and accompanies sin. Of such condition is this self-homicide, which to be sin everybody hath so sucked and digested and incorporated into the body of his faith and religion that now they prescribe against any opposer, and all discourse in this point is upon the degrees of this sin and how far it exceeds all other, so that none brings the metal now to the test nor touch, but only to the balance. Therefore, yet finding ourselves under the iniquity and burden of this custom and prescription, we must obey the necessity and preposterously examine, first, why this fact should be so resolutely condemned, and why there should be this prescription in our judgement to pronounce this above all other sins irremissible; and then, having removed that which was nearest us and delivered ourselves from the tyranny of this prejudice, our judgement may be brought nearer to a straightness, and our charity awakened and extended to apprehend that this act may be free not only from those enormous degrees of sin, but from all.

They who pronounce this sinner to be so necessarily damnable are of one of these three persuasions: either they misaffirm that this act always proceeds from desperation, and so they load it with all those comminations with which from Scriptures, Fathers, histories that commonplace abounds; or else they entertain that dangerous opinion, that there is in this life an impenitibleness, and impossibility of returning to God, and that apparent to us (for else it could not justify our uncharitable censure); or else they build upon this foundation, that this act being presumed to be sin, and all sin unpardonable without repentance, this is therefore unpardonable because the very sin doth preclude all ordinary ways of repentance.

To those of the first sect, if I might be as vainly subtle as they are uncharitably severe, I should answer that all desperation is not sinful. For in the Devil it is not sin, nor doth he demerit by it, because he is not commanded to hope. Nor in a man which undertook an austere and disciplinary taming of his body by fasts or corrections were it sinful to despair that God would take from him *stimulum carnis* [a sting of the flesh]. Nor, in a priest employed to convert infidels, were it sinful to despair that God would give him the power of miracles. If therefore to quench and extinguish this *stimulum carnis* a man should kill himself, the effect and fruit of this desperation were evil and yet the root itself not necessarily so. No detestation nor dehortation against this sin of desperation (when it is a sin) can be too earnest. But yet since it may be without infidelity, it cannot be greater than that. And though Aquinas there calls it sin truly, yet he says he doth so because it occasions many sins.

And if it be, as others affirm, *poena peccati* [punishment for sin], it is then *involuntarium* [involuntary], which will hardly consist with the nature of sin. Certainly, though many devout men have justly imputed to it the cause and effect of sin, yet as in the penitential Canons greater penance is inflicted upon one who kills his wife than one who kills his mother, and the reason added, not that the fault is greater but that otherwise more would commit it, so is the sin of desperation so earnestly aggravated because, springing from sloth and pusillanimity, our nature is more slippery and inclinable to such a descent than to presumptions, which yet without doubt do more wound and violate the majesty of God than desperation doth. But howsoever that none may justly say that all which kill themselves have done it out of a despair of God's mercy (which is the only sinful despair), we shall, in a more proper place, when we come to consider the examples exhibited in Scriptures and other histories, find many who at that act have been so far from despair that they have esteemed it a great degree of God's mercy to have been admitted to such a glorifying of his name, and have proceeded therein as religiously as in a sacrifice.

One reason by which this self-homicide seems to me to escape the breach of any Law of Nature is that both express [specific] literal laws and mute law—custom—hath authorised it, not only by suffering and connivance but by appointing it. And it hath the countenance not only of many flourishing and well-policed States but also of imaginary Commonwealths which cunning authors have ideated and in which such enormous faults are not likely to be admitted.

Amongst the Athenians condemned men were their own executioners by poison, and amongst the Romans often by bloodlettings. And it is recorded of many places that all the *Sexagenarii* were by the laws of wise States precipitated from a bridge. Of which, if Pierius's conjecture be true, that this report was occasioned by a custom in Rome by which men of that age were not admitted to suffrage, and because the way to the Senate was *per pontem* [over the bridge], they which for age were not permitted to come thither were called *Depontani*, yet it is more certain that among the Ceans unprofitable old men poisoned themselves—which they did crowned with garlands, as triumphers over human misery. And the Ethiopians loved death so well that their greatest malefactors, being condemned to banishment, escaped it ordinarily by killing themselves. The civil law, where it appoints no punishment to the delinquent in this case, neither in his estate nor memory, punishes a keeper if his prisoner kill himself, out of a prejudice that if means may be afforded them, they will all do so.

And do not we see it to be the custom of all nations now to manacle and disarm condemned men, out of a sore assurance that else they would escape death by death? Sir Thomas More, a man of the most tender and delicate conscience that the world saw since St Augustine, not likely to write anything in jest mischievously interpretable, says that in Utopia the priests and magistrates did use to exhort men afflicted with incurable diseases to kill themselves, and that they were obeyed as the interpreters of God's will. But that they who killed themselves without giving an account of their reasons to them were cast out unburied.

And Plato, who is usually cited against this opinion, disputes in it, in no severer fashion, nor more peremptory, than thus:

> What shall we say of him, which kills his nearest and most dear friend, which deprives himself of life, and of the purpose of destiny, and, not urged by any sentence, or heavy misfortune, nor extreme shame, but out of a cowardliness and weakness of a fearful mind, doth unjustly kill himself? What purgatory, and what burial, by law belong to him, God himself knows. But let his friends enquire of the interpreters of the law and do as they shall direct.

You see nothing is delivered by him against it, but modestly, limitedly, and perplexedly.

Sir Thomas More

Of the Law of Reason

I believe it [the law against suicide] was first induced amongst us [the British] because we exceeded in that natural desire of dying so. For it is not a better understanding of Nature which hath reduced us from it, but the wisdom of lawmakers and observers of things fit for the institution and conservation of States.

In ancient Commonwealths the numbers of slaves were infinite. As ever both in Rome and Athens there were ten slaves for one citizen, and Pliny says that in Augustus's time Isidorus had above 4,000, and Vedius Pollio so many that he always fed his fish in ponds with their blood. And since servitude hath worn out, yet the number of wretched men exceeds the happy (for every labourer is miserable and beastlike in respect of the idle, abounding men). It was therefore thought necessary, by laws and by opinion of religion, to take from these weary and macerated [oppressed] wretches their ordinary and open escape and ease: voluntary death. And therefore it seems to be so prohibited, as (a lawyer says) hunting and usury is; and as Mahomet, to withdraw his nation from wine, brought them to a religious belief that in every grape there was a devil.

For wheresoever you find many and severe laws against an offence, it is not safe from thence to conclude an extreme enormity or heinousness in the fault but a propenseness of that people, at that time, to that fault.

So in France the laws abound against duels, to which they are headlongly apt. So are the resolutions of the Spanish casuists, and the bulls of the popes, iterated and aggravated in that nation against their bull-baiting, to which they are enormously addicted. These severe laws therefore do no more aggravate a fault than mild punishments diminish it.

Certainly in some cases we may without sin wish death, and that not only for enjoying the sight of God but even to be so delivered from the encumbrances of this life. This we may wish, and yet it is so far from being lawful to wish anything which were evil that it is sin to wish that anything which is naturally evil were not so, that so we might then wish it when it were discharged of that natural illness. Death itself therefore is not evil, nor is it evil to wish it. Is it evil to further that with more actual help which we may lawfully wish to be done?

To conclude therefore this point, that it may become lawful to wish our own death, I will only relate a history which, though it be but a matter of fact (if it be so much), yet it is of such a person as his acts govern and persuade with very many as far as rules.

In the life of St Philip Neri we read that he, being entreated (as he was, ordinarily, in like desperate cases) to come to one Paulus Maximus, a youth of fourteen, who was then ready to expire his soul by sickness, before he could perfect his Sacrifice, and the office which he had begun, before the message came to him, the young man died. When he had been dead about half an hour Neri came, and after he had uttered some loud exclamations the youth revived again, and looked up, and talked in secret with Neri a quarter of an hour. The discourse ended, Neri gave him his choice, whether he would live or die; and when the boy wished death he gave him leave to die again. Now though it were a greater miracle than any in that book, if any should believe all that are in it (for in it are attributed to Neri stranger things than the Book of Conformities imagined in St Francis) yet this much is established out of this, whether fable or history, that in their opinion who authorised this book, it was lawful in Maximus to wish his own death, since a man of so much sanctity as Neri did approve and second and accomplish that opinion of his.

The last species of homicide on this side, the last act, is an actual helping and concurrence to it. And every step and degree conducing purposely to that end is as justly by judges of consciences called homicide as Ardoinus, reckoning up all poisons—which have a natural malignity and affection to destroy man's body—forbears not a flea, though it never kill, because it endeavours it and doth all the hurt it can, and he is diligent in assigning preservatives and restoratives against it.

Since therefore this hastening of our death is the same as the entire self-homicide, let us consider how far improved custom and example and law doth either allow or command it. For that it is allowable it seems to me some proof that, before any man accuses him, a malefactor may go and declare his fault to the Judge.

Though, amongst Italian relations, that in Sansovine concerning England hath many marks and impressions of malice, yet of that custom, which he falsely says to be observed here, that men condemned to be hanged are ever accompanied to their executions by all their kindred, who then hang at their

feet to hasten their end, and that when a patient is abandoned
by the physicians his nearest kinsman strangles him with a
pillow—of this I say, that author had thus much ground, that
ordinarily at executions men—out of a charity, as they think
—do so. And women which are desperate of sick persons'
recovery use to take the pillow from under them and so give
them leave to die sooner. Have they any more the dominion
over these bodies than the person himself? Or if a man were
able to do these offices to himself, might he not do it? Or
might he not with a safe conscience put so much weights in
his pockets as should countervail their stretchings? I speak
but comparatively: might he not do it as well as they?

To my understanding such an act, either in executioner or
bystander, is no way justifiable. For it is both an injury to the
party, whom a sudden pardon might redeem, and to the
Justice, who hath appointed a painful death to deter others.
The breaking of legs in crucified men, which was done to
hasten death, was not allowed but upon petition. And the
Law might be much defrauded if such violence might be used
where the breaking of the halter delivered the prisoner from
death, as in some places it doth. Good opinions concur that
it is to do ever without doubt whatsoever is for ease or escap-
ing painful passage out of this life: in such cases a man may
more allowably do by his own act than a stranger may, for
Law of Nature inclines and excuses him. But they are by
many laws forbidden to hasten his death, for they are no
otherways interested in it than as parts of the whole body of
the State, and so it concerns them that justice be executed.
Yet we see this, and the other of withdrawing the pillows, is
ordinarily done and esteemed a pious office.

Self-preservation, which we confess to be the foundation of
general Natural Law, is no other thing than a natural affection
and appetition of good, whether true or seeming. For certainly the desire of martyrdom, though the body perish, is a
self-preservation, because thereby, out of our election, our
best part is advanced. For Heaven, which we gain so, is certainly good, life but probably and possibly. Now since this
law of self-preservation is accomplished in attaining that
which conduces to our ends, and is good to us, if I propose to
myself in this self-homicide a greater good, though I mistake
it, I perceive not where I transgress the general Law of
Nature, which is an affection of good, true or seeming; and if
that which I affect by death be truly a greater good, wherein
is the other, stricter, Law of Nature, which is rectified reason,
violated?

Another reason which prevails much with me, and delivers it [suicide] from being against the Law of Nature, is this, that in all ages, in all places, upon all occasions, men of all conditions have affected it and inclined to do it. Man labours to be discharged of his earthly sepulchre, his body. And though this may be said of all other sins, that men are propense to them, and yet, for all that frequency, they are against Nature (that is, rectified reason), yet if this sin were against particular Law of Nature (as they must hold which aggravate it by that circumstance), and that so it wrought to the destruction of our species any otherwise than intemperate lust or surfeit, or incurring penal laws and suchlike do, it could not be so general, since, being contrary to our sensitive nature, it hath not the advantage of pleasure and delight to allure us withal which other sins have.

And when I frame to myself a martyrology of all which have perished by their own means for religion, country, fame, love, ease, fear, shame, I blush to see how naked of followers all virtues are in respect of this fortitude, and that all histories afford not so many examples, either of cunning and subtle devices or of forcible and violent actions, for the safeguard of life as for destroying.

Petronius Arbiter, who served Nero, a man of pleasure, in the office of Master of his Pleasures, upon the first frown went home and cut his veins, so present and immediate a step was it to him from full pleasure to such a death.

Herennius the Sicilian could endure to beat out his own brains against a post.

Comas, who had been a captain of thieves, made his own breath the instrument of his death by stopping and recluding it.

Hannibal, because, if he should be overtaken with extreme necessity he would be beholden to none for life nor death, died with poison which he always carried in a ring.

As Demosthenes did with poison carried in a pen.

Aristarchus, when he saw that seventy-two years, nor the corrupt and malignant disease of being a severe critic, could wear him out, starved himself then.

Homer, which had written a thousand things which no man else understood, is said to have hanged himself because he understood not the Fishermen's Riddle.

Poor Terence, because he lost his 108 translated comedies, drowned himself.

And the poet Labienus, because his satirical books were burned by edict, burnt himself too.

ΒΙΑΘΑΝΑΤΟΣ.

A DECLARATION

OF THAT
PARADOXE,

OR
THESIS, that

Selfe-homicide is not ſo Naturally
Sinne, that it may never be otherwiſe.

WHEREIN

The Nature, and the extent of all thoſe Lawes,
which ſeeme to be violated by this Act,
are diligently ſurveyed.

Written by IOHN DONNE, *who afterwards received
Orders from the Church of* England, *and dyed
Deane of Saint* Pauls, London.

Jo: Saresb. de nugis Curial. Prolog.
Non omnia vera eſſe profiteor. Sed legentium uſibus inſervire.

Publiſhed by Authoritie.

LONDON,
Printed by *John Dawſon,*

'Certainly in some cases we may without sin wish death, and that not
only for enjoying the sight of God but even to be so delivered from the
encumbrances of this life,' wrote Donne in *Biathanatos*, his extraordinary treatise on suicide which was published by his son in 1646

And Zeno, before whom scarce any is preferred, because he stumbled and hurt his finger against the ground, interpreted that as a summons from the earth and hanged himself, being then almost a hundred years old.

Hippionas the poet rhymed Bubalus the painter to death with his iambics.

Yet no man, to me, seems to have made harder shift to die than Charondas who, first having made a new law that it should be death to enter the council chamber armed, not only offended that law but punished it presently by falling upon his sword.

But the general hour of such death is abundantly expressed in those swarms of the Roman gladiatory champions which in some one month cost Europe 30,000 men, and to which exercise and profusion of life, till express laws forbade it, not only men of great birth and place in the State but also women coveted to be admitted.

In Caesar's time in France, for one who died naturally there died many by this devout violence. For he says there were some which, enjoying many benefits and commodities from men of high rank, always, when the lord died, celebrated his funeral with their own. And Caesar adds that in the memory of man no one was found that ever refused it.

Which devotion I have read somewhere continues yet in all the wives in the Kingdom of Bengal in the Indies. And there not only such persons as do it in testimony of an entire dependency and of a gratitude, but the [priests] are said to have studied ways how to die, and especially then when they were in best state of health. And yet these priests, whose care was to die thus, did ever sum up and abridge all their precepts into this one, 'Let a pious death determine a good life'—such an estimation had they of this manner of dying.

How pathetically Latinus Pacatus expresses the sweetness of dying when we will. Others, saith he, after the conquest, making a braver bargain with destiny, prevented uncertain death by certain, and the slaves scaped whipping by strangling. For who ever feared after there was no hope? Or who would therefore forbear to kill himself that another might? Is another's hand easier than thine own? Or a private death fouler than a public? Or is it more pain to fall upon thy sword, and to oppress the wound with thy body, and to receive death at once, than to divide the torment, bend the knee, stretch out the neck, perchance to more than one blow?

Of the Law of God

That light which issues from the Moon doth best represent and express that which in ourselves we call the light of Nature; for as that in the Moon is permanent and ever there, and yet it is unequal, various, pale and languishing, so is our light of Nature changeable. For being at the first kindling at full, it waned presently and, by departing further and further from God, declined by general sin to almost a total eclipse, till God, coming nearer to us, first by the law and then by grace, enlightened and repaired it again conveniently to his ends, for further exercise of his mercy and justice. And then those artificial lights, which ourselves make for our use and service here, as fires, tapers and such, resemble the light of reason. For though the light of these fires and tapers be not so natural as the Moon, yet because they are more domestic and obedient to us, we distinguish particular objects better by them than by the Moon. So, by the arguments and deductions and conclusions which ourselves beget and produce, as being more serviceable and under us because they are our creatures, particular cases are made more clear and evident to us, for these we can behold and put them to any office, and examine and prove their truth or likelihood, and make them answer as long as we will ask. Whereas the light of Nature, with a solemn and supercilious majesty, will speak but once and give no reason, nor endure examination.

But because, of these two kinds of light, the first is too weak and the other false (for only colour is the object of sight, and we do not trust candlelight to discern colours), we have therefore the Sun, which is the fountain and treasure of all created light, for an emblem of that third best light of our understanding, which is the word of God. But yet, as weak, credulous men think sometimes they see two or three suns when they see none but meteors or other appearances, so are many transported with like facility or dazzling, that for some opinions which they maintain they think they have the light and authority of Scripture when, God knows, truth, which is the light of Scriptures, is diametrically under them, and removed in the farthest distance that can be. If any small place of Scripture misappear to them to be of use for justifying any opinion of theirs, then (as the word of God hath that precious nature of gold, that a little quantity thereof, by reason of a faithful tenacity and ductileness, will be brought to cover ten thousand times as much as any other metal), they extend it so far, and labour and beat it to such a thinness, as it is scarce any longer the word of God, only to give their other reasons a little tincture and colour of gold, though they have lost all the weight and estimation.

But since the Scripture itself teaches that no prophecy in the Scripture is of private interpretation, the whole Church may not be bound and concluded by the fancy of one or of a few who, being content to enslumber themselves in an opinion and lazy prejudice, dream arguments to establish and authorise that.

The Canons have prescribed certain rules of doing evil, when we are overtaken with perplexities: to choose the least. Of which St Gregory gives a natural example: that a man attempted upon a high wall, and forced to leap it, would take the lowest place of the wall. And agreeably to all these the casuists say that, in extreme necessity, I sin not if I induce a man to lend me money upon usury. And the reason is, because I incline him to a lesser sin, which is usury, when else he should be a homicide, by not relieving me. And in this fashion God himself is said to work evil in us because, when our heart is full of evil purposes, he governs and disposes us rather to this than to that evil, wherein, though all the viciousness be ours, and evil, yet the order is from God, and good. Yea, he doth positively incline one to some certain evil thus, that he doth infuse into a man some good thoughts by which he, out of his viciousness, takes occasion to think he were better do some other sin than that which he intended.

Therefore all these laws and practices concur in this, that we sometimes do such evil not only for express and positive good, but to avoid greater evil. And whatsoever any human power may dispense withal in us, we, in extreme necessity, in impossibility of resource to better counsel, in an erring conscience, and in many other cases, may dispense with ourselves. To me there appears no other interpretation safe but this, that there is no external act naturally evil, and that circumstances condition them and give them their nature, as scandal makes an indifferent thing heinous at that time which, if some person go out of the room, or wink, is not so.

Of Judas, the most sinful instrument of the most merciful work, the common, though not general, opinion is that he killed himself. But whether by hanging or no is more controverted.

For from the words in the Acts, that he threw himself down headlong, and burst asunder, and his bowels gushed out, Euthymius thinks that he was rescued whilst he hanged and carried away, and that after that he killed himself by throwing himself headlong.

And Brentius leaves that indifferent to us, to think what we will thereof. But it seems by Oecumenius that he did not only overlive this hanging but that he grew to so enormous a bigness and burden to himself that he was not able to withdraw himself out of a coach's way but had his guts crushed out so. Which he received from Papias, the disciple to St John, whose times cannot be thought ignorant or incurious of Judas's history.

And it is there said further that by others it was said that being swollen to that vastness, and corrupted with vermin, he laid himself down upon his field, and there his guts broke out. And this Theophilact follows.

And it falls out very often that some one father, of strong reputation and authority in his time, doth snatch and swallow some probable interpretation of Scripture; and then, digesting it into his homilies, and applying it in dehortations and encouragements, as the occasions and diseases of his auditory [audience] or his age require, and imagining thereupon delightful and figurative insinuations, and setting it to the music of his style (as every man which is accustomed to these meditations shall often find in himself such a spiritual wantonness and devout straying into such delicacies) that sense which was but probable grows necessary, and those who succeed had rather enjoy his wit than vex their own, as oftentimes we are loth to change or leave off a counterfeit stone, by reason of the well setting thereof.

By this means, I think, it came so generally to be believed that the fruit which Eve ate was an apple; and that Lot's wife was turned to a pillar of salt; and that Absalom was hanged by the hair of his head; and that Jephthah killed his daughter. And many other such, which grew current not from an evidence in the text but because such an acceptation was most useful and appliable. Of this number Judas's case might be.

But if it were not, that act of killing himself is not added to his faults in any place of Scriptures—no, not in those two psalms of particular accusations and bitter imprecations against him, as they are ordinarily taken to be prophetically purposed and directed.

And even of this man, whose sin, if any can exceed mercy, was such, Origen durst hope, not out of his erroneous com-

passion and sinful charity by which he thinks that even the
Devil shall be saved, but out of Judas's repentance. He says,
the Devil led him to the sin, and then induced him to that
sorrowfulness which swallowed him. But speaking of his
repentance, he says, those words, when Judas saw that he was
condemned, belong to Judas himself, for Christ was not then
condemned. And upon this conscience and consideration
began his repentance. For it may be, saith Origen, that Satan,
which had entered into him, stayed with him till Christ was
betrayed and then left him, and thereupon repentance followed. And perchance, says he, he meant to prevent, and go
before, his Master, who was to die, and so to meet him with
his naked soul that he might gain mercy by his confession
and prayers.

Petilian, against whom St Augustine writes, proceeded
further in justification of Judas's last act than any. For he said
that in suffering death when he repented, and so was a confessor, he became a martyr.

But of his actual impenitence I purposed not to speak, nor
of his repentance, but only to observe to you that this last
fact is not imputed to him, nor repentance said to be pre-
cluded thereby.

Letters

Some doubt exists as to whether the first letter given here, which appears to refer to the false start of the Azores expedition of 1597, was written by Donne, because it is not in his usual style. But he was on the expedition, he was only twenty-five, and war service can bring its own ways of expressing oneself. The recipient is unknown.

As for Donne's named correspondents:

For SIR GEORGE MORE, SIR THOMAS EGERTON, and Donne's clandestine marriage, see the Introduction. (Donne's letters to the two men use the old dates.) As his third wife, in old age, Egerton chose a Spencer of Althorp and lived miserably ever after.

SIR HENRY GOODYER was one of Donne's oldest friends and the recipient of by far the largest number of his letters. He had Catholic sympathies, a position at Court, and a chronic stack of debts. He had a penurious old age at Poles-worth in Warwickshire, partly caused by family lawsuits, and died in 1627.

JAMES HAY (LORD HAY), afterwards Viscount Don-caster and Earl of Carlisle. A lively young Scot with good looks and graceful manners, a great dandy, a terrific spender, he was a good friend to Donne, whom he introduced to Bacon and whose claims he pressed on James I. Donne left him a picture of the Virgin Mary in his will.

SIR ROBERT KER, EARL OF ANCRAM. Not to be con-fused with the other Robert Ker, usually spelt Carr, the infamous Viscount Rochester and Earl of Somerset. A mem-ber of Prince Charles's household, Ker stood godfather to Donne's daughter Margaret. Donne bequeathed him his portrait, dated about 1595, 'in the pose of a melancholy lover'.

MRS ELIZABETH RAINSFORD, Donne's mother. Thrice married, always to staunch co-religionists, yet warmly affectionate to her son, as he to her. She died at the Deanery, aged over ninety, only two months before he did. See the Introduction for her Catholic antecedents.

Sir Toby Mathew. See the Introduction. He and Donne had an edgy, wary relationship which was never quite broken off, and he made an important collection of Donne's letters.

Lady Kingsmill (née Bridget White). Was in London in the spring of 1610 but then went home to the country to marry Sir Henry Kingsmill, a neighbouring squire in Hampshire. Attracted Donne's epistolary flirtatiousness in youth and his affectionate care in age, for which reason his two quoted letters to her, though separated in date, have been placed together here. Obviously one of those bright, vivacious girls who move in the right circles and are very much the talk of their time.

Mrs Cockayne. The friend who unwisely recommended one of her protégés to Donne for a living. Not Donne's sister, though he addressed her as such, in spite of the fact that in one of his sermons he makes the point that lovers often addressed their mistresses as 'cousin', 'sister' and so on as a species of cover. Her mad husband deserted her on the birth of their last child and decamped to London to compile a Greek lexicon.

George Garrard. Another old friend, to whom Donne writes here that he would like to die in the pulpit.

Written from Plymouth, August 1597

Sir,

The first act of that play which I said I would go over the water to see is done, and yet the people hiss. How it will end I know not. It is true that Jonah was in a whale's belly three days, but he came not voluntary as I did, nor was troubled with the stink of 150 land soldiers as we; and I was there twenty days of so very bad weather that even some of the mariners have been drawn to think it were not altogether amiss to pray, and myself heard one of them say god help us. For all our pains we have seen the land of promise, Spain: whether we shall enter or no I guess not. We are now again at Plymouth, *quasi* Ply-mouth, for we do nothing but eat and scarce that. I think when we came in the burghers took us for the Spanish fleet, for they have either hid or conveyed all their money. Never was extreme beggary so extremely brave except when a company of mummers had lost their box . . . He that hath supped and hath two or three shillings is a king, for none hath a crown. Faith—lands, jerkins, knighthoods are reprobate pawns, and but for the much gay clothes (which yet are much melted) I should think we were in Utopia: all are so utterly coinless. In one bad, bare word, the want is so general that the Lord General wants—and till this day we wanted the Lord General. You will pardon me if I write nothing earnest. Salute all whom thou lovest in my name, and love me as I would deserve.

To Sir George More, 2 February 1602

Sir,

If a very respective fear of your displeasure, and a doubt that my Lord, whom I know out of your worthiness to love you much, would be so compassionate with you as to add his anger to yours, did not so much increase my sickness as that I cannot stir, I had taken the boldness to have done the office of this letter by waiting upon you myself, to have given you the truth and clearness of this matter between your daughter and me and to show to you plainly the limits of our fault by which I know your wisdom will proportion the punishment. So long since as her being at York House this had foundation, and so much then of promise and contract built upon it, as without violence to conscience might not be shaken. At her lying in town this last Parliament, I found means to see her twice or thrice. We both knew the obligations that lay upon us, and we adventured equally; and about three weeks before Christmas we married. And as, at the doing, there were not used above five persons, of which I protest to you, by my salvation, there was not one that had any dependence or relation to you, so in all the passage of it did I forbear to use any such person who by furthering of it might violate any trust or duty towards you. The reasons why I did not foreacquaint you with it (to deal with the same plainness that I have used) were these. I knew my present estate less than fit for her; I knew (yet I knew not why) that I stood not right in your opinion. I knew that to give any intimation of it had been to impossibilitate the whole matter. And then, having these honest purposes in our hearts, and those fetters in our consciences, methinks we should be pardoned if our fault be but this, that we did not, by forerevealing of it, consent to our hindrance and torment.

Sir, I acknowledge my fault to be so great as I dare scarce offer any other prayer to you in mine own behalf than this, to believe this truth, that I neither had dishonest end nor means. But for her whom I tender much more than my fortunes or life (else I would I might neither joy in this life nor enjoy the next), I humbly beg of you that she may not to her danger feel the terror of your sudden anger. I know this letter shall find you full of passion. But I know no passion can alter your reason and wisdom, to which I adventure to commend these particulars: that it is irremediably done; that if you incense my Lord you destroy her and me; that it is easy to give us happiness; and that my endeavours and industry, if it please you to prosper them, may soon make me somewhat worthier of her. If any take the advantage of your displeasure against me, and fill you with ill thoughts of me, my comfort is that you know that faith and thanks are due to them only that speak when their informations might do good, which now it cannot work towards any party.

Sir, I have truly told you this matter, and I humbly beseech you so to deal in it as the persuasions of nature, reason, wisdom and Christianity shall inform you. And to accept the vows of one whom you may now raise or scatter: which are, that as my love is directed unchangeably upon her, so all my labours shall concur to her contentment, and to show my humble obedience to yourself.
Yours in all duty and humbleness,
J. Donne
From my lodging by the Savoy, 2nd Februa: 1601
To the right wor. Sir George More, kt

The capture of Cadiz,
1596. *Below*, the Earl
of Essex, whom Donne
accompanied on the
military expedition

To Sir George More, 11 February 1602

Sir,

The inward accusations in my conscience, that I have offended you beyond any ability of redeeming it by me, and the feeling of my Lord's heavy displeasure following it, forceth me to write, though I know my fault make my letters very ungracious to you. Of nothing in this one fault that I hear said to me can I disculp myself but of the contemptuous and despiteful purpose towards you which I hear is surmised against me. How little and how short the comfort and pleasure of destroying is, I know your wisdom and religion informs you. And though perchance you intend not utter destruction, yet the way through which I fall towards it is so headlong that, being thus pushed, I shall soon be at bottom; for it pleaseth God, from whom I acknowledge the punishment to be just, to accompany my other ills with so much sickness as I have no refuge but that of mercy.

I can present nothing to your thoughts which you knew not before but my submission, my repentance, and my hearty desire to do anything satisfactory to your just displeasure. Of which I beseech you to make a charitable use and construction. From the Fleet, 11th Febr. 1601

Yours in all faithful duty and obedience,

J. Donne

To Sir Thomas Egerton, 12 February 1602

Your justice hath been merciful in making me know my offence, and it hath much profited me that I am dejected. Since then I am so entirely yours that even your disfavours have wrought good upon me. I humbly beseech you that all my good may proceed from your Lordship, and that since Sir George More, whom I leave no humble way unsought to regain, refers all to your Lordship, you would be pleased to lessen that correction which your just wisdom hath destined for me, and so to pity my sickness and other misery as shall best agree with your honourable disposition. Almighty God accompany all your Lordship's purposes, and bless you and yours with many good days.

Fleet, 12th Febr. 1601

Your Lordship's most dejected and poor servant,

J. Donne

To Sir George More, 13 February 1602

With my most unfeigned thanks [I] present to you my humble petition, that you would be pleased to hope that as that fault which was laid to me of having deceived some gentlewomen before, and that of loving a corrupt religion, are vanished and smoked away, so some uncharitable malice hath presented my debts double at least. How many of the imputations laid upon me would fall off, if I might shake and purge myself in your presence!

My conscience and such affection as in my conscience becomes an honest man emboldeneth me to make one request more, which is that by some kind and comfortable message you would be pleased to give some ease of the afflictions which I know your daughter in her mind suffers, and that (if it be not against your other purposes) I may with your leave write to her. Almighty God keep you in his favour, and restore me to his and yours.

From my chamber, whither by your favour I am come, 13th Feb. 1601

J. Donne

To Sir Thomas Egerton, 1 March 1602

How soon my history is dispatched! I was carefully and honestly bred; enjoyed an indifferent fortune. I had (and I had understanding enough to value it) the sweetness and security of a freedom and independency, without marking out to my hopes any place of profit. I had a desire to be your Lordship's servant, by the favour which your good son's love to me obtained. I was four years your Lordship's secretary, not dishonest nor greedy. The sickness of which I died is that I began in your Lordship's house this love. Where I shall be buried I know not. It is late now for me to begin that course which some years past I purposed to travel, though I could now do it, not much disadvantageously. But I have some bridle upon me now, more than then, by my marriage of this gentlewoman, in providing for whom I can and will show myself very honest, though not so fortunate.

To seek preferment here with any but your Lordship were a madness. Every great man to whom I shall address any such suit will silently dispute the case and say, Would my Lord Keeper so disgraciously have imprisoned him and flung him away if he had not done some other great fault of which we hear not? So that, to the burden of my true weaknesses I shall have this addition of a very prejudicial suspicion that I am worse than I hope your Lordship doth think me, or would that the world should think.

I have therefore no way before me but must turn back to your Lordship. I know my fault so well, and so well acknowledge it, that I protest I have not so much as inwardly grudged or startled at the punishment. I know your Lordship's disposition so well, and I know itself naturally inclines to pity. I know mine own necessity, out of which I humbly beg that your Lordship will so much entender your heart towards me as to give me leave to come into your presence. Affliction, misery and destruction are not there, and everywhere else where I am, they are.

1st March 1601
Your Lordship's most poor and most penitent servant,
J. Donne

To Sir George More, March 1602

Though I be not headlongly destroyed, I languish and rust dangerously. From seeking preferments abroad, my love and conscience restrains me. From hoping for them here, my Lord's disgracings cut me off. My imprisonments, and theirs whose love to me brought them to it, hath already cost me forty pounds. And the love of my friends, though it be not utterly grounded upon my fortunes, yet I know suffers somewhat in these long and uncertain disgraces of mine. I was bold in my last letter to beg leave of you that I might write to your daughter. Though I understand thereupon that after the Thursday you were not displeased that I should, yet I have not, and will not, without your knowledge, do it. But now I beseech you that I may, since I protest before God it is the greatest of my afflictions not to do it. God, whose pardon in such cases is never denied, gives me leave to hope that you will favourably consider my necessities. To his merciful guiding and protection I commend you, and cease to trouble you.

Mar. 1601
Yours in all humbleness and dutiful obedience,
J. Donne

To Sir Henry Goodyer, 1606

Sir,

I live so far removed that even the ill news of your great loss (which is ever swiftest and loudest) found me not till now. Your letter speaks it not plain enough, but I am so accustomed to the worst that I am sure it is so in this. I am almost glad that I knew her so little, for I would have no more additions to sorrow. If I should comfort you it were an alms acceptable in no other title than when poor give to poor, for I am more needy of it than you. And I know you well provided of Christian and learned and brave defences against all human accidents. I will make my best haste after your messenger; and if myself and the place had not been ill provided of horses, I had been the messenger, for you have taught me by granting more to deny no request.

Your honest, unprofitable friend,

                                        J. Donne

Pyrford 3 o'clock, just as yours came

To Sir Henry Goodyer, September 1608

Sir,

I write not to you out of my poor library, where to cast mine eye upon good authors kindles or refreshes sometimes meditations not unfit to communicate to near friends; nor from the highway, where I am contracted and inverted into myself; which are my two ordinary forges of letters to you. But I write from the fireside in my parlour, and in the noise of three gamesome children, and by the side of her whom, because I have transplanted into a wretched fortune, I must labour to disguise that from her by all such honest devices as giving her my company and discourse. Therefore I steal from her all the time which I give this letter, and it is therefore that I take so short a list, and gallop so fast over it.

I have not been out of my house since I received your packet. But if I melt into a melancholy whilst I write, I shall be taken in the manner. And I sit by one too tender towards these impressions; and it is so much our duty to avoid all occasions of giving them sad apprehensions.

If I have been good in hope, or can promise any little offices in the future probably, it is comfortable, for I am the worst present man in the world. Yet the instant, though it be

nothing, joins times together; and therefore this unprofitable-
ness, since I have been, and will still endeavour to be so, shall
not interrupt me now from being
Your servant and lover,

J. Donne

To Sir Henry Goodyer, September 1608

Sir,
When I must shipwreck, I would do it in a sea where mine
impotency might have some excuse; not in a sullen, weedy
lake where I could not have as much as exercise for my swim-
ming. Therefore I would fain do something, but that I cannot tell what is no wonder. For to choose is to do. But to be
no part of anybody is to be nothing. At most, the greatest
persons are but great wens and excrescences, men of wit and
delightful conversation but as moles for ornament, except
they be so incorporated into the body of the world that they
contribute something to the sustentation of the whole. This
I made account that I began early, when I understood the
study of our laws, but was diverted by the worst voluptuousness, which is an hydroptic [swollen], immoderate desire of
human learning and languages: beautiful ornaments to great
fortunes, but mine needed an occupation, and a course which
I thought I entered well into, when I submitted myself to
such a service as I thought might have employed those poor
advantages which I had. And there I stumbled too, yet I
would try again; for to this hour I am nothing, or so little that
I am scarce subject and argument good enough for one of
mine own letters.

You, Sir, are far enough from these descents, your virtue
keeps you secure and your natural disposition to mirth will
preserve you. But lose none of these holds. A slip is often as
dangerous as a bruise, and though you cannot fall to my low-
ness, yet in a much less distraction you may meet my sadness.
For he is no safer which falls from a high tower into the leads
than he which falls from thence to the ground. Make therefore to yourself some mark, and go towards it *allégrement*.
Though I be in such a planetary and erratic fortune that I can
do nothing constantly, yet you may find some constancy in
my constant advising you to it.
Your hearty true friend,

J. Donne

To Sir Henry Goodyer, probably 1608

Sir,

This letter hath more merit than one of more diligence, for I wrote it in my bed, and with much pain. I have occasion to sit late some nights in my study, which your books make a pretty library, and now I find that that room hath a wholesome, emblematic use. For having under it a vault, I make that promise me that I shall die reading, since my book and a grave are so near. But it hath another unwholesomeness, that by raw vapours rising from thence (for I can impute it to nothing else) I have contracted a sickness which I cannot name nor describe. For it hath so much of a continual cramp that it wrests the sinews, so much of a tetane [muscular spasm] that it withdraws and pulls the mouth, and so much of a gout (which they whose counsels I use say it is) that it is not like to be cured, though I am too hasty in three days to pronounce it. If it be the gout I am miserable, for that affects dangerous parts, as my neck and breast and (I think fearfully) my stomach. But it will not kill me yet. I shall be in this world like a porter in a great house, ever nearest the door but seldomest abroad. I shall have many things to make me weary, and yet not get leave to be gone. If I go, I will provide by my best means that you suffer not for me in your bonds. The estate which I should leave behind me of any estimation is my poor fame in the memory of my friends, and therefore I would be curious of it, and provide that they repent not to have loved me.

To Lord Hay, 1613

Noblest Lord,

The same conscience of mine own unworthiness which kept me so long from daring to put myself into your Lordship's sight provokes me to write now. We are ever justly more tender and jealous of those things to which we have weakest title. And therefore, finding how little pretence I have to your Lordship's favour, I am not only diligent but curious not to forfeit it.

I have been told that when your Lordship did me that extreme favour of presenting my name, his Majesty remembered me by the worst part of my history, which was my disorderly proceedings, seven years since, in my nonage

The dandy, James Hay, Earl of Carlisle, Donne's friend and correspondent

[immaturity]. As your Lordship's earnestness and alacrity in doing good, and almost unthriftiness in multiplying and heaping your favours, gave me scarce leisure to consider how great your first favour of promising was, because you overtook it presently with a greater, which was the performing of it, so I humbly beseech your Lordship to add another to these: not to be too apprehensive of any suspicion that there lies upon me any dishonourable stain, or can make my King have any prejudice against me, for that intemperate and hasty act of mine. For the Lord Chancellor and his brother-in-law, Sir George More, whose daughter I married, would both be likely, and will be ready, to declare it, for his Majesty's satisfaction or your Lordship's, that their displeasure, commenced so long since, should be thought to continue still, or interrupt any of my fortunes. This I say, lest I might have seemed to have betrayed your Lordship, and, [having] left my ill fortune by having got many victories upon myself, should dare to reach at your Lordship and think to work upon your constancy and perseverance in doing good, by making you repent your own act in favouring me.

To his mother, Mrs Elizabeth Rainsford, probably 1616

My most dear mother,
When I consider so much of your life as can fall within my memory and observation, I find it to have been a sea under a continual tempest, where one wave hath ever overtaken another. Our most wise and blessed Saviour chooseth what way it pleaseth him to conduct those which he loved to his heaven and eternal rest. The way which he hath chosen for you is strait, stormy, obscure and full of sad apparitions of death and wants and sundry discomforts; and it hath pleased him that one discomfort should succeed and touch another, that he might leave you no leisure, by any pleasure or abundance, to step out of that way, or almost to take breath in that way, by which he hath determined to bring you home, which is his glorious kingdom.

One of the most certain marks and assurances that all these are his works, and to that good end, is your inward feeling and apprehension of them, and patience in them. As long as the Spirit of God distills and dews his cheerfulness upon your heart, as long as he instructs your understanding to interpret his mercies and his judgements aright, so long your comfort must needs be as much greater than others as your afflictions are greater than theirs. The happiness which God afforded to your first young time, which was the love and care of my most dear and provident father—whose soul, I hope, hath long since enjoyed the sight of our blessed Saviour—God removed from you quickly, and hath since taken from you all the comfort that that marriage produced. All those children for whose maintenance his industry provided, and for whose education you were so carefully and so chargeably diligent, he hath now taken from you. All that worth which he left, God hath suffered to be gone from us all, so that God hath seemed to repent that he allowed any part of your life any earthly happiness, that he might keep your soul in continual exercise, and longing and assurance, of coming immediately to him. I hope therefore, my most dear mother, that your experience of the calamities of this life, your continual acquaintance with the visitations of the Holy Ghost, which gives better inward comforts than the world can outward discomforts, your wisdom to distinguish the value of this world from the next and your religious fear of offending our merciful God by repining at anything which he doth, will preserve you from any inordinate and dangerous sorrow for this loss of my most beloved sister.

For my part, which am only left now to do the office of a child, though the poorness of my fortune and the greatness of my charge hath not suffered me to express my duty towards you as became me, yet I protest to you before Almighty God and his angels and saints in heaven that I do, and ever shall, esteem myself to be as strongly bound to look to you, and provide for your relief, as for my own poor wife and children. For whatsoever I shall be able to do I acknowledge to be a debt to you, from whom I had that education which must make my fortune. This I speak not as though I feared my father Rainsford's care of you, or his means to provide for you, for he hath been with me, and, as I perceive in him a loving and industrious care to give you contentment, so I see in his business a happy and considerable forwardness. In the meantime, good mother, take heed that no sorrow nor dejection in your heart interrupt or disappoint God's purpose in you: his purpose is to remove out of your heart all such love of this world's happiness as might put him out of possession of it.

He will have you entirely. And, as God's comfort is enough, so he is inheritance enough. Join with God, and make his visitations and afflictions, as he intended them, mercies and comforts. And, for God's sake, pardon those negligences which I have heretofore used towards you, and assist me with your blessing to me and all mine, and with your prayers to our blessed Saviour, that thereby both my mind and fortune may be apt to do all my duties, especially those that belong to you.

God, whose omnipotent strength can change the nature of anything by his raising spirit of comfort, make your poverty riches, your afflictions pleasure, and all the gall and worm-wood of your life honey and manna to your taste, which he hath wrought whensoever you are willing to have it so. Which, because I cannot doubt in you, I will forbear more lines at this time, and most humbly deliver myself over to your devotions, and good opinion of me, which I desire no longer to live than I may have.

To Sir Robert Ker, *enclosing a copy of* Biathanatos, *April/May 1619*

I had need to do somewhat towards you above my promises. How weak are my performances, when even my promises are defective! ... Besides the poems, of which you took a promise, I send you another book to which there belongs this history. It was written by me many years since; and because it is upon a misinterpretable subject I have always gone so near sup-pressing it as that it is only not burnt. No hand hath passed upon it to copy it, nor many eyes to read it; only to some particular friends in both universities then, when I writ it, I did communicate it; and I remember, I had this answer, that certainly there was a false thread in it, but not easily found. Keep it, I pray, with the same jealousy. Let any that your discretion admits to the sight of it know the date of it, and that it is a book written by Jack Donne, and not by Dr Donne. Reserve it for me if I live; and if I die I only forbid it the press, and the fire. Publish it not, but yet burn it not. And between those, do what you will with it.
Your poor servant in Christ Jesus,
J. Donne

To Sir Toby Mathew, *September 1619*

Sir,
At Ratisbon I had your letter from Brussels, and in it you. For my former knowledge of your ingenuity, and mine own conscience of having demerited in nothing toward you, are

assurances to me that your professions are in earnest. I dare put myself upon the testimony of very many very good companies in England, where your person and your history have been the discourse, that I have never forsaken your honour and reputation. And you may be pleased to make this some argument of my disposition toward you, that when I have been told that you have not been so careful of me abroad, I have not been easy in believing it. And when, at some times, the authority of the reporter hath brought me to a half-belief of it, I have found other excuses in your behalf than a mere disaffection to me; and now I am safely returned to my first station again, not to believe it.

If it could be possible that any occasion of doing you a real service might be presented to me, you should see that the tree which was rooted in love, and always bore leaves ready to shadow and defend from others' malice, would bear fruit also. You know we say in the schools that grace destroys not nature. We may say too that forms of religion destroy not morality, nor civil offices. That which I add I am far from applying to you, but it is true: that we are fallen into so slack and negligent times that I have been sometimes glad to hear that some of my friends have differed from me in religion. It is some degree of an union to be united in a serious meditation of God, and to make any religion the rule of our actions. Our sweet and blessed Saviour bring us by his way to his end! And be you pleased to be assured that no man desires to renew or continue or increase a friendship with you more than . . .

J. Donne

To Sir Henry Goodyer, October 1622

October the 4th 1622, almost at midnight
Sir,
All our moralities are but our outworks, our Christianity is our citadel. A man who considers duty but the dignity of his being a man is not easily beat from his outworks, but from his Christianity never. And therefore I dare trust you, who contemplates them both.

Every distemper of the body now is complicated with the spleen, and when we were young men we scarce ever heard of the spleen. In our declinations now, every accident is accompanied with heavy clouds of melancholy, and in our youth we never admitted any. It is the spleen of the mind, and we are affected with vapours from thence. Yet truly, even this sadness that overtakes us, and this yielding to the sadness, is not so vehement a poison as those false ways in which we sought our comforts in our looser days.

You are able to make rules to yourself, and our blessed Saviour continue to you an ability to keep within those rules. And this particular occasion of your present sadness must be helped by the rule. For, for examples you will scarce find any, scarce any, that is not encumbered and distressed in his fortunes.

I had locked myself, sealed and secured myself, against all possibilities of falling into new debts, and in good faith, this year hath thrown me four hundred pounds lower than when I entered this house. I am a father as well as you, and of children (I humbly thank God) of as good dispositions; and in saying so I make account that I have taken my comparison as high as I could go, for in good faith I believe yours to be so. But as those my daughters who are capable of such considerations cannot but see my desire to accommodate them in this world, so I think they will not murmur if Heaven must be their nunnery, and they associated to the Blessed Virgin there. I know they would be content to pass their lives in a prison, rather than I should macerate myself for them, much more to suffer the mediocrity of my house and my means, though that cannot prefer them. Yours are such too, and it need not that patience, for your fortune doth not so far exercise their patience. But to leave all in God's hands, from whose hands nothing can be wrung by whining but by praying, nor by praying without the *Fiat voluntas sua* ['Thy will be done'].

Sir, you are used to my hand and, I think, have leisure to spend some time in picking out sense in rags; else I had written less, and in longer time. Here is room for an Amen. The prayer? So I am going to my bedside to make for all you and all yours, with

Your true friend and servant in Christ Jesus,
J. Donne

To Sir Robert Ker, January 1624

Sir,
Though I have left my bed, I have not left my bedside. I sit there still and, as a prisoner discharged sits at the prison door to beg fees, so I sit here to gather crumbs. I have used this leisure to put the meditations had in my sickness into some such order as may minister some holy delight. They arise to

so many sheets (perchance twenty) as that, without staying for that furniture of an Epistle that my friends importuned me to print them, I importune my friends to receive them printed. That being in hand, through this long trunk that reaches from St Paul's to St James', I whisper into your ear this question, whether there be any uncomeliness or unseasonableness in presenting matter of devotion or mortification to that prince whom I pray God nothing may ever mortify but holiness. If you allow my purposes in general, I pray cast your eye upon the title and the epistle, and rectify me in them. I submit substance and circumstance to you, and the poor author of both,

Your very humble and very thankful servant in Christ Jesus,
J. Donne

To Lady Kingsmill, Summer 1610

Madam,

I could make some guess whether souls that go to heaven retain any memory of us that stay behind if I knew whether you ever thought of us since you enjoyed your heaven, which is yourself, at home. Your going away hath made London a dead carcass. A term and a court do a little spice and embalm it, and keep it from putrefaction, but the soul went away in you. And I think the only reason why the plague is somewhat slackened is because the place is dead already, and nobody left worth the killing.

Wheresoever you are, there is London enough; and it is a diminishing of you to say so, since you are more than the rest of the world. When you have a desire to work a miracle you will return hither and raise the place from the dead, and the dead that are in it. Of which I am one, but that a hope that I have a room in your favour keeps me alive.

Your humblest, and affectionate servant J. D.
Strand, S Peter's Day at nine

To the Honourable Lady the Lady Kingsmill
upon the death of her husband, 1624

Madam,

We would wonder to see a man who, in a wood, were left to his liberty to fell what trees he would, take only the crooked and leave the straightest trees. But that man hath perchance

Sir Thomas Egerton, Donne's employer and uncle by marriage to Ann Donne, the poet's wife

a ship to build and not a house, and so hath no use of that kind of timber. Let not us, who know that in God's house there are many mansions but yet have no model, no design, of [the] building, wonder, at his taking in his materials, why he takes the young and leaves the old, or why the sickly over-live those that had better health.

We are not bound to think that souls departed have divested all affections towards them whom they left here. But we are bound to think that, for all their love, they would not be here again. Then is the will of God done in earth as it is in heaven when we neither pretermit his actions nor resist them, neither pass them over in an inconsideration, as though God had no hand in them, nor go about to take them out of his hands, as though we could direct him to do them better.

As God's Scriptures are his will, so his actions are his will: both are testaments, because they testify his mind to us. It is not lawful to add a schedule to either of his wills. As they do ill who add to his written will, his Scriptures, a schedule of apocryphal books, so do they also who, to his other will, his manifested actions, add apocryphal conditions, and a schedule of such limitations as, If God would have stayed thus long, or if God would have proceeded in this or that manner, I could have borne it. But, Madam, you who willingly sacrificed your-self to God, in your obedience to him in your own sickness, cannot be doubted to dispute with him about any part of you which he shall be pleased to require at your hands.

The difference is great in the loss of an arm or a head, of a child or a husband. But to them who are incorporated into Christ, their head, there can be no beheading. Upon you, who are a member of the spouse of Christ, the Church, there can fall no widowhood, nor orphanage upon those children to whom God is father. I have not another office by your husband's death, for I was your chaplain before in my daily prayers. But I shall enlarge that office with other collects than before, that God will continue to you that peace which you have ever had in him, and send you quiet and peaceable dispositions in all them with whom you shall have anything to do in your temporal estate and matters of this world. Amen. Your ladyship's very humble and thankful servant in Christ Jesus,

J. Donne

At my poor house at St Paul's, 26 October 1624

To Sir Robert Ker, April 1627

Sir,

A few hours after I had the honour of your letter I had another from my Lord of Bath and Wells, commanding from the King a copy of my sermon. I am in preparation of that, with diligence. Yet this morning I waited upon his Lordship and laid up in him this truth, that of the Bishop of Canterbury's sermon, to this hour I never heard syllable, nor what way, nor upon what points, he went. And for mine, it was put into that very order in which I delivered it, more than two months since.

I hoped for the King's approbation heretofore in many of my sermons, and I have had it. But yesterday I came very near looking for thanks. For, in my life, I was never, in any one piece, so studious of his service. Therefore, exceptions being taken and displeasure kindled at this, I am afraid it was rather brought thither than met there.

If you know any more fit for me (because I hold that unfit for me, to appear in my master's sight as long as this cloud hangs, and therefore this day forbear my ordinary waitings), I beseech you to intimate it to

Your very humble and very thankful servant,

J. Donne

To Sir Robert Ker, April 1627

Sir,

I was this morning at your door somewhat early, and am put into such a distaste of my last sermon as that I dare not practise any part of it; and therefore, though I said then that we are bound to speak aloud though we awaken men and make them froward, yet after two or three modest knocks at the door I went away. Yet I understood after, the King was gone abroad, and thought you might be gone with him. I came to give you an account of that which this does as well.

I have now put into my Lord of Bath and Wells's hands the sermon faithfully exscribed. I beseech you be pleased to harken farther after it. I am still upon my jealousy that the King brought thither some disaffection towards me, grounded upon some other demerit of mine, and took it not from the sermon. For I have cribrated [sifted] and recribrated and post-cribrated the sermon and must necessarily say, the King, who hath let fall his eye upon some of my poems, never saw, of mine, a hand or an eye or an affection set down with so much study and diligence and labour of syllables as in this sermon I expressed those two points which I take so much to conduce to his service: the imprinting of persuasibility and obedience in the subject, and the breaking of the bed of whisperers by casting in a bone, of making them suspect and distrust one another.

I remember I heard the old King say of a good sermon that he thought the preacher never had thought of his sermon till he spoke it: it seemed to him negligently and extemporarily spoken. And I knew that he had weighed every syllable for half a year before. Which made me conclude that the King had before some prejudice against him. So, the best of my hope is that some over-bold allusions, or expressions in the way, might divert his Majesty from vouchsafing to observe the frame and purpose of the sermon. When he sees the general scope, I hope his goodness will pardon collateral escapes.

I entreated the Bishop to ask his Majesty whether his displeasure extended so far as that I should forbear waiting, and appearing in his presence; and I had a return, that I might come. Till I had that, I would not offer to put myself under your roof. Today I come, for that purpose, to say prayers, and if in any degree my health suffer it I shall do so tomorrow. If anything fall into your observation before that (because the Bishop is likely to speak to the King of it, perchance, this night), if it amount to such an increase of displeasure as that it might be unfit for me to appear, I beseech you afford me the knowledge. Otherwise I am likely to enquire of you personally, tomorrow before nine in the morning, and to put into your presence then

Your very humble and very true and very honest servant to God and King and you,

J. Donne

I writ yesterday to my Lord Duke, by my Lord Carlile, who assured me of a gracious acceptation of my putting myself in his protection.

To Mrs Cockayne, between 1625 and 1628

My noble dear Sister,

This fever that I had now, I hoped, for divers days, to have been but an exaltation of my damps and flashings, such as exercise me sometimes four or five days and pass away without whining or complaint. But I neglected this somewhat too long, which makes me (though, after I took it into consideration, the fever itself declined quickly) much weaker than perchance otherwise I should have been. I had Dr Fox and Dr Clement with me but, I thank God, was not much trouble to them. Ordinary means set me soon upon my legs, and I have broke my close prison and walked into the garden and (but that the weather hath continued so spitefully foul) make no doubt but I might safely have done more. I eat and digest well enough. And it is no strange thing that I do not sleep well, for in my best health I am not much used to do so.

At the same time little Betty had a fever too; and for her we used Dr Wright who, by occasion, lies within two miles of us. And he was able to ease my sickness with his report of your good health, which, he told us, he had received from you. But I found it not seconded in your own letters, which I had the honour to receive by Mr Hazard.

My noble sister, I am afraid that death will play with me so long as he will forget to kill me, and suffer me to live, in a languishing and useless age, a life that is rather a forgetting that I am dead than of living. We dispute whether the dead shall pray for the living; and because my life may be short I pray with the most earnestness for you now. By the advantage of sickness I return the oftener to that holy exercise, and in it join yours with mine own soul. I would not have dignified myself or my sickness with saying so much of either but that it is in obedience to your command that I should do so. And though there lie upon me no command, yet there lies a necessity, growing out of my respect, and a nobler root than that, my love to you, to enlarge myself, as far as I have gone already, in Mr Hazard's business.

My noble sister, when you carry me up to the beginning, which it pleases you to call a promise to yourself and your noble sister, I never slackened my purpose of performing that promise. But if my promise—which was, that I should be ready to assist him in anything I could—were translated by you, or your noble sister, or him, that I would give him the next living in my gift, certainly we speak not one language, or understand not one another, and I had thought we had. This which he imagined to be vacant (for it is not yet, nor any way likely) is the first that fell to me since I made that promise. And, my noble sister, if a person of my place, from whom one scholar in each university sucks something, and must be weaned by me, and who hath otherwise a latitude of impor-

tunate friends and very many obligations, have a living once
in five or six years fall in his gift (for it is so long since I gave
any), and may not make a good choice with freedom then, it
is hard. Yet it is not my fortune to do so now, for now there
is a living fallen (though not that), I am not left to my choice.
For my Lords Carlile and Percy have chosen for me, but truly
such a man as I would have chosen. And for him they laid an
obligation upon me three years since, for the next that should
fall. Yet Mr Hazard presses you to write for that, because he
to whom my promise belongs hath another before. But doth
he or his Lord owe me anything for that? Yet Mr Hazard
importunes me to press that Chaplain of my Lord that when
he takes mine he shall resign the other to him. Which, as it is
an ignorant request (for if it be resigned, it is not in his power
to place it upon Mr Hazard), so it is an unjust request, that I
that give him fifty pounds a year should take from him forty.

But amongst Mr Hazard's manifold importunities, that
that I took worst was that he should write of domestic things,
and what I said of my son, to you, and arm you with that plea
that my son was not in Orders. But, my noble sister, though
I am far from drawing my son immaturely into Orders, or
putting into his hands any church with cure, yet there are
many prebends and other helps in the Church which a man,
without taking Orders, may be capable of, and for some such
I might change a living with cure and so begin to accommodate a son in some preparation.

But Mr Hazard is too piercing. It is good counsel (and, as
I remember, I gave it him), that if a man deny him anything,
and accompany his denial with a reason, he be not too searching whether that be the true reason or no, but rest in the
denial. For many times it may be out of my power to do a man
a courtesy which he desires, and yet I not tied to tell him the
true reason. Therefore out of his letter to you I continue my
opinion—that he meddled too far herein.

I cannot shut my letter till (whilst we are upon this consideration of reasons of denials), I tell you one answer of his
which perchance may weaken your so great assurance of his
modesty. I told him that my often sicknesses had brought me
to an inability of preaching, and that I was under a necessity
of preaching twelve or fourteen solemn sermons every year to
great auditories at Paul's, and to the Judges, and at Court,
and that therefore I must think of conferring something upon
such a man as may supply my place in these solemnities. And
surely, said I, I will offer them no man in those cases which
shall not be at least equal to myself: and, Mr Hazard, I do

not know your faculties. He gave me this answer: I will not make comparisons, but I do not doubt but I should give them satisfaction in that kind.

Now, my noble sister, whereas you repeat often that you and your sister rested upon my word and my worth, and but for my word and my worth, you would not have proceeded so far, I must necessarily make my protestation that my word and my worth is, herein, as chaste and untouched as the best maidenhead in the world. For, my noble sister, goes there no more to the giving of a scholar a church in London but that he was a young gentleman's schoolmaster? You know the ticklishness of London pulpits, and how ill it would become me to place a man in a London church that were not both a strong and a sound man. And therefore those things must come into consideration before he can have a living from me, though there was no need of reflecting upon those things when I made that general promise that I would assist his fortune in anything.

You end in a phrase of indignation and displeasure, rare in you towards me, therefore it affects me, which is that he may part from me as I received him at first, as though I were likely to hinder him. The heat that produced that word I know is past, and therefore, my most beloved sister, give me leave to say to you that he shall not part from me, but I shall keep him still in my care, and make you always my judge of all omissions.

Your faithful friend and servant

To Mrs Cockayne, 1628

I have found this rumour of my death to have made so deep impressions, and to have been so peremptorily believed, that from very remote parts I have been entreated to signify, under my hand, that I am yet alive. What gave the occasion of this rumour I can make no conjecture. And yet the hour of my death, and the day of my burial, were related in the highest place of this kingdom. I had at that time no kind of sickness, nor was otherwise than I had been ever since my fever, and am yet: that is, too weak at this time to go forth, especially to London where the sickness is near my house, and where I must necessarily open myself to more business than my present state would bear. Yet, next term, by God's grace, I will be there; which made me forbear to write because I know how faintly and lamely businesses go on by letters, in respect

of conferences. In the meantime my prayers for your happiness shall fill all the time of
Your true friend, and brother, and servant

To Mrs Cockayne, August 1628

My noblest and lovingest Sister,
Your letter, upon the two and twentieth of August, which I received this day, lays a command upon me to give you an account of my state in health. You do but ask me how I do, and if your letter had come yesterday I could not have told you that.

At my return from Kent to my gate, I found Peggy had the pox; so I withdrew to [Peckham] and spent a fortnight there. And without coming home, when I could with some justice hope that it would spread no farther amongst them (as I humbly thank God it hath not, nor much disfigured her that had it), I went into Bedfordshire. There, upon my third Sunday, I was seized with a fever, which grew so upon me as forced me to a resolution of seeking my physician at London. Thither I came in a day and a little piece; and within four miles of home I was surprised with an accident in the coach which never befell me before, nor had been much in my contemplation, and therefore affected me much.

It was a violent falling of the uvula, which, when Doctor Fox (whom I found at London, and who had not been there in ten days before) considered well, and perceived the fever complicated with a quinsy, by way of prevention of both he presently took blood. And so, with ten days' starving in a close prison—that is, my bed—I am (blessed be God) returned to a convenient temper and pulse and appetite, and learn to eat, and this day met the acceptablest guest in the acceptablest manner, your letter, walking in my chamber. All which I tell you with these peculiarities lest my sickness might be presented by rumour worse than God hath been pleased to make it. For, I humbly thank him, now I feel no present ill, nor have reason to fear worse.

To Mrs Cockayne, 1629

My noble and virtuous Sister,
When any limb or branch of a family is taken away, the virtue, the love, and (for the most part) the patrimony and fortune of

him that is gone remains with the family. The family would not think itself the less if any little quillet [narrow strip] of ground had been evicted from it. Nor must it because a clod of earth, one person of the family, is removed. In these cases there is nothing lost: one part, the soul, enjoys a present gain, and the other, the body, expects a future. We think it good husbandry to place our children's portions so as that in so many years it may multiply to so much. Shall we not be as glad to lay their bodies there where only they can be mellowed and ripened for glorification?

The perverseness of the father put you to such a necessity of hiding your sons as that this son is scarce more out of your sight, by being laid underground, than he was before. And perchance you have been longer time, at some times, from meeting and seeing one another in this world than you shall be now from meeting in the glory of the Resurrection. That may come sooner than you looked he should come from Bath. A man truly liberal, or truly charitable, will borrow money to lend. For if I be bound to assist another with my meat or with my money, I may be as much bound to assist him with my credit, and borrow to lend. We do but borrow children of God, to lend them to the world. And when I lend the world a daughter in marriage, or lend the world a son in a profession, the world does not always pay me well again: my hopes are not always answered in that daughter or that son. But of all that I lend to, the grave is my best paymaster. The grave shall restore me my child where he and I shall have but one Father, and pay me my earth when that earth shall be amber, a sweet perfume, in the nostrils of his and my Saviour. Since I am well content to send one son to the Church, the other to the wars, why should I be loth to send one part of either son to Heaven and the other to the earth?

Comfort yourself in this, my noble Sister, that for those years he lived you were answerable to God for him, for yet he was so young as a mother's power might govern him; and so long he was under your charge, and you accountable for him. Now, when he was growing into those years as needed a stronger hand, a father's care, and had not that, God hath cancelled your bonds, discharged you, and undertakes the office of a father himself. But, above all, comfort yourself in this, that it is the declared will of God. In sickness and other worldly crosses there are anxieties and perplexities: we wish one thing today, in the behalf of a distressed child or friend, and another tomorrow, because God hath not yet declared his will. But when he hath done that, in death, there is no room for any anxiety, for any perplexity, no, not for a wish, for we may not so much as pray for the dead.

I am far from quenching in you, or discharging, natural affections. But I know your easy apprehensions and over-tenderness in this kind. In so noble and numerous a family as yours is, every year must necessarily present you some such occasion of sorrow, in the loss of some near friend. And therefore I, in the office of a friend, and a brother, and priest of God, do not only look that you should take this patiently, as a declaration of God's present will, but that you take it cate-chistically, as an instruction for the future; and that God, in this, tells you that he will do so again, in some other your friends. For, to take any one cross patiently is but to forgive God for once. But to surrender oneself entirely to God is to be ready for all that he shall be pleased to do. And that his pleasure may be either to lessen your crosses, or multiply your strength, shall be the prayer of

Your brother and friend and servant and chaplain,

John Donne

To Mr George Gerrard, December 1630

Sir,

A man would almost be content to die (if there were no other benefit in death) to hear of so much sorrow, and so much good testimony from good men, as I (God be blessed for it) did upon the report of my death. Yet I perceive it went not through all, for one writ unto me that some—and he said, of my friends—conceived, that I was not so ill as I pretended, but withdrew myself to save charges and to live at ease, dis-charged of preaching. It is an unfriendly and, God knows, an ill-grounded interpretation. For in these times of necessity, and multitudes of poor, there is no possibility of saving to him that hath any tenderness in him. And, for affecting my ease, I have been always more sorry when I could not preach than any could be that they could not hear me.

It hath been my desire (and God may be pleased to grant it me) that I might die in the pulpit; if not that, yet that I might take my death in the pulpit, that is, die the sooner by occasion of my former labours. I have entreated one of my fellows to preach to my Lord Mayor at Paul's upon Christmas Day, and reserved Candlemas Day to myself for that service; about which time also will fall my Lent sermon. Unless my Lord Chamberlain believe me to be dead, and leave me out.

Devotions Upon Emergent Occasions

Written during a serious illness in 1623, published in 1624, the 'Devotions' were the first of Donne's non-controversial religious prose works to be issued in book form except for a handful of specially printed sermons. They were immediately popular, and have retained a large company of admirers ever since. See the Introduction for a fuller commentary.

Devotions

*Meditation 1: The first alteration, the first grudging
of the sickness*

Variable, and therefore miserable, condition of man! This
minute I was well, and am ill this minute. I am surprised with
a sudden change, and alteration to worse, and can impute it
to no cause nor call it by any name. We study health, and we
deliberate upon our meats and drink and air and exercises,
and we hew and we polish every stone that goes to that building, and so our health is a long and regular work. But in a
minute a cannon batters all, overthrows all, and demolishes
all: a sickness unprevented for all our diligence, unsuspected
for all our curiosity—nay, undeserved, if we consider only
disorder—summons us, seizes us, possesses us, destroys us in
an instant.

O miserable condition of man, which was not imprinted by
God whom, as he is immortal himself, had put a coal, a beam
of immortality, into us which we might have blown into a
flame but blew it out by our first sin. We beggared ourselves
by harkening after false riches, and infatuated ourselves by
harkening after false knowledge, so that now we do not only
die, but die upon the rack, die by the torment of sickness.
Nor that only, but we are pre-afflicted, super-afflicted, with
these jealousies and suspicions and apprehensions of sickness
before we can call it a sickness. We are not sure we are ill:
one hand asks the other by the pulse, and our eye asks our
urine, how we do.

O multiplied misery! We die, and cannot enjoy death because we die in this torment of sickness. We are tormented
with sickness and cannot stay till the torment come, but pre-
apprehensions and presages prophesy those torments which
induce that death before either come, and our dissolution is
conceived in these first changes, quickened in the sickness
itself, and born in death, which bears date from these first
changes. Is this the honour which man hath by being a little
world, that he hath these earthquakes in himself, sudden
shakings; these lightnings, sudden flashes; these thunders,
sudden noises; these eclipses, sudden obfuscations and dark-
enings of his senses; these blazing stars, sudden fiery exhala-
tions; these rivers of blood, sudden red waters? Is he a world
to himself only therefore, that he hath enough in himself not

only to destroy and execute himself but to presage that execution upon himself, to assist the sickness, to antedate the
sickness, to make the sickness the more irremediable by
sad apprehensions; and, as if he would make a fire the more
vehement by sprinkling water upon the coals, so to wrap a
hot fever in cold melancholy, lest the fever alone should not
destroy fast enough without this contribution, nor perfect the
work (which is destruction) except we joined an artificial sickness of our own melancholy to our natural, our unnatural,
fever.

O perplexed discomposition, O riddling distemper, O
miserable condition of man.

Meditation 2: The strength and the function of the senses and other faculties change and fail

The heavens are not the less constant because they move continually, because they move continually one and the same
way. The earth is not the more constant because it lies still
continually, because continually it changes and melts in all
parts thereof. Man, who is the noblest part of the earth, melts
so away, as if he were a statue not of earth but of snow. We
see his own envy melts him, he grows lean with that. He will
say another's beauty melts him. But he feels that a fever doth
not melt him like snow, but pour him out like lead, like iron,
like brass melted in a furnace. It doth not only melt him but
calcine him, reduce him to atoms and to ashes; not to water
but to lime. And how quickly? Sooner than thou canst receive
an answer, sooner than thou canst conceive the question.

Earth is the centre of my body, Heaven is the centre of my
soul; these two are the natural places of those two. But those
go not to these two in an equal pace. My body falls down
without pushing, my soul does not go up without pulling.
Ascension is my soul's pace and measure, but precipitation
my body's. And even angels, whose home is Heaven, and
who are winged too, yet had a ladder to go to Heaven by
steps.

The Sun who goes so many miles in a minute, the stars of
the firmament which go so very many more, go not so fast as
my body to the earth. In the same instant that I feel the first
attempt of the disease I feel the victory. In the twinkling of
an eye I can scarce see: instantly the taste is insipid and
fatuous, instantly the appetite is dull and desireless, instantly
the knees are sinking and strengthless. And in an instant

sleep, which is the picture, the copy, of death, is taken away, that the original, death itself, may succeed, and that so I might have death to the life. It was part of Adam's punishment, In the sweat of thy brows thou shalt eat thy bread. It is multiplied to me. I have earned bread in the sweat of my brows, in the labour of my calling, and I have it. And I sweat again and again from the brow to the sole of the foot, but I eat no bread, I taste no sustenance. Miserable distribution of mankind, where one half lacks meat and the other stomach.

Meditation 3: The patient takes his bed

We attribute but one privilege and advantage to man's body, above other moving creatures: that he is not as others, grovelling, but of an erect, of an upright, form, naturally built and disposed to the contemplation of Heaven. Indeed it is a thankful form, and recompense to that soul which gives it, with carrying that soul so many foot higher, towards Heaven. Other creatures look to the earth, and even that is no unfit object, no unfit contemplation, for man, for thither he must come. But because man is not to stay there, as other creatures are, man in his natural form is carried to the contemplation of that place which is his home, Heaven.

This is man's prerogative. But what state hath he in this dignity? A fever can fillip him down, a fever can depose him, a fever can bring that head which yesterday carried a crown of gold—five foot towards a crown of glory—as low as his own foot today. When God came to breathe into man the breath of life he found him flat upon the ground. When he comes to withdraw that breath from him again he prepares him to it by laying him flat upon his bed. Scarce any prison so close that affords not the prisoner two or three steps. The anchorites that barked themselves up in hollow trees and immured themselves in hollow walls, that perverse man that barrelled himself in a tub—all could stand or sit and enjoy some change of posture. A sickbed is a grave, and all that the patient says there is but a varying of his own epitaph.

Every night's bed is a type of the grave. At night we tell our servants at what hour we will rise; here we cannot tell ourselves at what day, what week, what month. Here the head lies as low as the foot, the head of the people as low as they whom those feet trod upon. And that hand that signed pardons is too weak to beg his own, if he might have it for lifting up that hand.

Strange fetters to the feet, strange manacles to the hands, when the feet and hands are bound so much the faster by how much the cords are slacker; so much the less able to do their offices by how much more the sinews and ligaments are the looser. In the grave I may speak through the stones in the voice of my friends, and in the accents of those words which their love may afford my memory. Here I am my own ghost, and rather affright my beholders than instruct them. They conceive the worst of me now, and yet fear worse; they give me for dead now, and yet wonder how I do, when they wake at midnight and ask how I do tomorrow. Miserable and (though common to all) inhuman posture, where I must practise my lying in the grave by lying still, and not practise my resurrection by rising any more.

From Meditation 5: The physician comes

As sickness is the greatest misery, so the greatest misery of sickness is solitude. When the infectiousness of the disease deters them who should assist from coming, even the physician dares scarce come. Solitude is a torment which is not threatened in Hell itself. When I am dead, and my body might infect, they have a remedy: they may bury me. But when I am but sick and might infect, they have no remedy but their absence and my solitude. It is an excuse to them that are great, and pretend, and yet are loth to come. It is an inhibition to those who would truly come, because they may be made instruments and pestiducts to the infection of others by their coming. And it is an outlawry, an excommunication, upon the patient, and separates him from all offices not only of civility but of working charity. A long sickness will weary friends at last, but a pestilential sickness averts them from the beginning.

God himself would admit a figure of society, as there is a plurality of persons in God, though there be but one God, and all his external actions testify a love of society and communion. In Heaven there are orders of angels and armies of Martyrs, and in that house many mansions. In earth families, cities, churches, colleges, all plural things. And lest either of these should not be company enough alone, there is an association of both, a Communion of Saints, which makes the militant and triumphant Church one parish; so that Christ was not out of his diocese when he was upon the earth, nor out of his temple when he was in our flesh.

God, who saw that all that he made was good, came not so near seeing a defect in any of his works as when he saw that it was not good for man to be alone. Therefore he made him a helper, and one that should help him so as to increase the number and give him her own and more society. Angels, who do not propagate nor multiply, were made at the first in an abundant number, and so were stars. But for the things of this world their blessing was: Increase.

From Prayer 5

Bless thou the learning and the labours of this man whom thou sendest to assist me; and since thou takest me by the hand and puttest me into his hands (for I come to him in thy name, who in thy name comes to me), since I clog not my hopes in him, no nor my prayers to thee, with any limited conditions, but enwrap all in those two petitions — Thy kingdom come, Thy will be done — prosper him and relieve me in thy way, in thy time, and in thy measure. Amen.

Meditation 6: The physician is afraid

I observe the physician with the same diligence as he the disease. I see he fears, and I fear with him. I overtake him, I overrun him in his fear, and I go the faster because he makes his pace slow. I fear the more because he disguises his fear, and I see it with the more sharpness because he would not have me see it. He knows that his fear shall not disorder the practice and exercise of his art, but he knows that my fear may disorder the effect and working of his practice. As the ill affections of the spleen complicate and mingle themselves with every infirmity of the body, so doth fear insinuate itself in every action — or passion — of the mind. And as the wind in the body will counterfeit any disease, and seem the stone, and seem the gout, so fear will counterfeit any disease of the mind. It shall seem love, a love of having, and it is but a fear, a jealous and suspicious fear, of losing. It shall seem valour, in despising and undervaluing danger, and it is but fear in an overvaluing of opinion and estimation, and a fear of losing that.

A man that is not afraid of a lion is afraid of a cat; not afraid of starving and yet is afraid of some joint of meat at the table, presented to feed him; not afraid of the sound of drums and trumpets and shot—and those which they seek to drown, the last cries of men—and is afraid of some particular harmonious instrument: so much afraid, as that with any of these the enemy might drive this man, otherwise valiant enough, out of the field.

I know not what fear is, nor I know not what it is that I fear now. I fear not the hastening of my death, and yet I do fear the increase of the disease. I should belie Nature if I should deny that I feared this, and if I should say that I feared death I should belie God. My weakness is from Nature, who hath but her measure; my strength is from God, who possesses and distributes infinitely. As then every cold air is not a damp, every shivering is not a stupefaction, so every fear is not a fearfulness, every declination is not a running away, every debating is not a resolving, every wish that it were not thus is not a murmuring nor a dejection, though it be thus. But as my physician's fear puts not him from his practice, neither doth mine put me from receiving from God and man, and myself, spiritual and civil and moral assistances and consolations.

From Prayer 6

O Lord, whether it be thy pleasure to dispose of this body, this garment, so as to put it to a further wearing in this world, or to lay it up in the common wardrobe, the grave, for the next, glorify thyself in thy choice now, and glorify it then with that glory, which thy Son, our Saviour Christ Jesus, hath purchased for them whom thou makest partakers of his Resurrection. Amen.

From Meditation 7: The physician desires to have others joined with him

Death is an old man's door: he appears and tells him so. And death is at a young man's back, and says nothing. Age is a sickness, and youth is an ambush; and we need so many physicians as may make up a watch and spy every inconvenience. There is scarce anything that hath not killed somebody: a hair, a feather, hath done it. Nay, that which is our best antidote against it hath done it. The best cordial hath been deadly poison. Men have died of joy, and almost forbidden their friends to weep for them when they have seen them die laughing.

The frontispiece of the 1634 edition of the *Devotions*. Donne is portrayed in his funeral shroud, as he was for his famous marble effigy by Nicholas Stone in the Deanery of St Paul's

But why do I exercise my meditation so long upon this, of having plentiful help in time of need? Is not my meditation rather to be inclined another way, to condole, and commiserate their distress, who have none? How many are sicker perchance than I, and laid on their woeful straw at home (if that corner be a home), and have no more hope of help, though they die, than of preferment, though they live, nor do no more expect to see a physician then, than to be an officer after? Of whom the first that takes knowledge is the sexton that buries them, who buries them in oblivion too? For they do but fill up the number of the dead in the bill [parish list]. But we shall never hear their names till we read them in the book of life, with our own.

How many are sicker perchance than I, and thrown into hospitals where, as a fish left upon the sand must stay the tide, they must stay the physician's hour of visiting, and then can be but visited? How many are sicker perchance than all we, and have not this hospital to cover them, not this straw to lie in, to die in, but have their gravestone under them, and breathe out their souls in the ears and in the eyes of passengers (harder than their bed, the flint of the street); that taste of no part of our physic but a sparing diet, to whom ordinary porridge would be julip [syrup] enough, the refuse of our servants bezar [antidote] enough, and the off-scouring of our kitchen tables cordial enough?

O my soul, when thou art not enough awake to bless thy God enough for his plentiful mercy in affording thee many helpers, remember how many lack them; and help them to them, or to those other things which they lack as much as them.

From Meditation 8: The King sends his own physician

No man is well that understands not, that values not, his well-being, that hath not a cheerfulness and a joy in it; and whosoever hath this joy hath a desire to communicate, to propagate, that which occasions his happiness and his joy to others. For every man loves witnesses of his happiness, and the best witnesses are experimental witnesses, they who have tasted of that in themselves which makes us happy. It consummates therefore, it perfects, the happiness of kings to confer, to transfer, honour and riches and (as they can) health upon those that need them.

From Expostulation 8

The holy King St Louis of France and our [Queen] Maud is celebrated for that, that personally they visited hospitals and assisted in the cure even of loathsome diseases. And when that religious empress, Placilla, the wife of Theodosius, was told that she diminished herself too much in those personal assistances, and might do enough in sending relief, she said, she would send in that capacity, as empress, but she would go too, in that capacity as a Christian, as a fellow member of the body of thy Son, with them.

From Meditation 9: Upon their consultation, they prescribe

In many diseases, that which is but an accident, but a symptom, of the main disease is so violent that the physician must attend the cure of that, though he pretermit [ignore] (so far as to intermit [halt]) the cure of the disease itself. Is it not so in States too? Sometimes the insolence of those that are great puts the people into commotions: the great disease and the greatest danger to the head is the insolence of the great ones. And yet they execute martial law, they come to present executions upon the people whose commotion was indeed but a symptom, but an accident, of the main disease. But this symptom, grown so violent, would allow no time for a consultation.

Is it not so in the accidents of the diseases of our mind too? Is it not evidently so in our affections, in our passions? If a choleric man be ready to strike, must I go about to purge his choler, or to break the blow? But where there is room for consultation, things are not desperate. They consult, so there is nothing rashly, inconsiderately, done. And then they prescribe, they write, so there is nothing covertly, disguisedly, unavowedly done. In bodily diseases it is not always so. Sometimes, as soon as the physician's foot is in the chamber, his knife is in the patient's arm: the disease would not allow a minute's forbearing of blood, nor prescribing of other remedies. In states and matter of government it is so too. They are sometimes surprised with such accidents as that the magistrate asks not what may be done by law, but does that which must necessarily be done in that case. But it is a degree of good in evil, a degree that carries hope and comfort in it, when we may have recourse to that which is written, and that the

proceedings may be apt and ingenuous and candid and avow-
able, for that gives satisfaction and acquiescence.

It were rather a vexation than a relief to tell a condemned
prisoner, you might have lived if you had done this, and if
you can get pardon you shall do well to take this or this
course hereafter. I am glad they know (I have hid nothing
from them), glad they consult (they hide nothing from one
another), glad they write (they hide nothing from the world),
glad that they write and prescribe physic, that there are
remedies for the present case.

From Meditation 10: They find the disease to steal
insensibly, and endeavour to meet with it so

Those are the greatest mischiefs which are least discerned;
the most insensible in their ways come to be the most sensible
in their ends. The heavens have had their dropsy, they
drowned the world; and they shall have their fever, and burn
the world. Of the dropsy, the Flood, the world had a foreknowledge 120 years before it came, and so some made provision against it and were saved. The fever shall break out in
an instant, and consume all. The dropsy did no harm to the
heavens from whence it fell; it did not put out those lights, it
did not quench those heats. But the fever, the fire, shall burn
the furnace itself, annihilate those heavens that breathe it out.
Though the Dog Star have a pestilent breath, an infectious
exhalation, yet because we know when it will rise we clothe
ourselves and we diet ourselves and we shadow ourselves to a
sufficient prevention. But comets and blazing stars, whose
effects or significations no man can interpret or frustrate, no
man foresaw. No almanac tells us when a blazing star will
break out; the matter is carried up in secret. No astrologer
tells us when the effects will be accomplished, for that's a
secret of a higher sphere than the other, and that which is most
secret is most dangerous.

It is so also here in the societies of men, in states and
commonwealths. Twenty rebellious drums make not so
dangerous a noise as a few whisperers and secret plotters in
corners. The cannon doth not so much hurt against a wall as
a mine under the wall, nor a thousand enemies that threaten
so much as a few that take an oath to say nothing.

And it is so too with the diseases of the body, and that is
my case. The pulses, the urine, the sweat all have sworn to
say nothing, to give no indication, of any dangerous sickness.

My forces are not enfeebled, I find no decay in my strength, my provisions are not cut off, I find no abhorring in mine appetite. My counsels are not corrupted or infatuated, I find no false apprehensions to work upon mine understanding. And yet they see that, invisibly—and I feel that, insensibly—the disease prevails. The disease hath established a kingdom, an empire, in me, and will have certain *arcana imperii*, secrets of state, by which it will proceed, and not be bound to declare them. But yet, against those secret conspiracies in the state the magistrate hath the rack, and against these insensible diseases physicians have their examiners; and those these employ now.

From Prayer 14

O Eternal and Most Gracious God, I humbly bless and thankfully glorify thy Holy Name, that thou hast afforded me the light of thy Spirit, against which the Prince of Darkness cannot prevail. Let thy merciful providence govern all in this sickness, that I never fall into utter darkness, and establish me in so bright a day here that the words of thy Son, spoken to his Apostles, may reflect upon me: Behold I am with you always, even to the end of the world.

Meditation 15: I sleep not day nor night

Natural men have conceived a twofold use of sleep: that it is a refreshing of the body in this life; that it is a preparing of the soul for the next; that it is a feast, and it is the grace at that feast; that it is our recreation and cheers us, and it is our catechism and instructs us. We lie down in a hope that we shall rise the stronger, and we lie down in a knowledge that we may rise no more. Sleep is an opiate which gives us rest, but such an opiate as perchance, being under it, we shall wake no more. But God intended sleep only for the refreshing of man by bodily rest, and not for a figure of death. For he intended not death itself then. But man, having induced death upon himself, God hath taken man's creature, death, into his hand, and mended it. And whereas it hath in itself a fearful form and aspect, so that man is afraid of his own creature, God presents it to him in a familiar, in an assiduous, in an agreeable and acceptable form, in sleep, that so when he awakes from sleep and says to himself, shall I be no otherwise when I am dead than I was even now when I was asleep, he may be ashamed of his waking dreams, and of his melancholic fancying out a horrid and an affrightful figure of that death which is so like sleep.

This then is the misery of my sickness, that death as it is produced from me and is mine own creature is now before mine eyes, but in that form in which God hath mollified it to us and made it acceptable in sleep, I cannot see it. How many prisoners, who have even hollowed themselves their graves upon that earth on which they have lain long under heavy fetters, yet at this hour are asleep, though they be yet working upon their own graves by their own weight? He that hath seen his friend die today, or knows he shall see it tomorrow, yet will sink into a sleep between. I cannot. And oh, if I be entering now into eternity, where there shall be no more distinction of hours, why is it all my business now to tell clocks? Why is none of the heaviness of my heart dispensed into mine eyelids, that they might fall as my heart doth? And why, since I have lost my delight in all objects, cannot I discontinue the faculty of seeing them, by closing mine eyes in sleep? But why rather, being entering into that presence where I shall wake continually and never sleep more, do I not interpret my continual waking here to be a parasceve,* and a preparation, to that?

From Prayer 15

O Eternal and Most Gracious God, who art able to make, and dost make, the sickbed of thy servants chapels of ease to them, and the dreams of thy servants prayers and meditations upon thee, let not this continual watchfulness of mine, this inability to sleep, which thou hast laid upon me, be any disquiet or discomfort to me, but rather an argument that thou wouldest not have me sleep in thy presence. So into what deviations soever I stray and wander by occasion of this sickness, O God, return thou to that minute wherein thou wast pleased with me, and consider me in that condition.

Meditation 16: From the bells of the church adjoining, I am daily remembered of my burial in the funerals of others

We have a convenient author who wrote a discourse of bells when he was prisoner in Turkey. How would he have enlarged himself if he had been my fellow-prisoner in this

* Day of preparation for the Jewish Sabbath.

sickbed, so near to that steeple which never ceases, no more than the harmony of the spheres, but is more heard.

When the Turks took Constantinople they melted the bells into ordnance [cannons]. I have heard both bells and ordnance, but never been so much affected with those as with these bells. I have lain near a steeple in which there are said to be more than thirty bells, and near another where there is one so big as that the clapper is said to weigh more than six hundred pounds, yet never so affected as here. Here the bells can scarce solemnise the funeral of any person but that I knew him, or knew he was my neighbour. We dwelt in houses near to one another before, but now he is gone into that house into which I must follow. There is a way of correcting the children of great persons, that other children are corrected in their behalf and in their names, and this works upon them who indeed had more deserved it. And when these bells tell me that now one, and now another, is buried, must not I acknowledge that they have the correction due to me, and paid the debt that I owe?

There is a story of a bell in a monastery which, when any of the house was sick to death, rang always voluntarily, and they knew the inevitableness of the danger by that. It rang once when no man was sick. But the next day one of the house fell from the steeple and died, and the bell held the reputation of a prophet still. If these bells that warn to a funeral now were appropriated to none, may not I, by the hour of the funeral, supply? How many men that stand at an execution, if they would ask, for what dies that man, should hear their own faults condemned and see themselves executed by attorney? We scarce hear of any man preferred but we think of ourselves, that we might very well have been that man. Why might not I have been that man that is carried to his grave now? Could I fit myself to stand or sit in any man's place, and not to lie in any man's grave?

I may lack much of the good parts of the meanest, but I lack nothing of the mortality of the weakest. They may have acquired better abilities than I, but I was born to as many infirmities as they. To be an incumbent by lying down in a grave, to be a doctor by teaching mortification* by example, by dying: though I may have seniors—others may be elder than I—yet I have proceeded apace in a good university and gone a great way in a little time by the furtherance of a vehement fever. And whomsoever these bells bring to the ground

* Numbing or deadening parts of the body; as it might be, in modern terms, administering an anaesthetic.

today, if he and I had been compared yesterday perchance I should have been thought likelier to come to this preferment then, than he.

God hath kept the power of death in his own hands, lest any man should bribe death. If man knew the gain of death, the ease of death, he would solicit, he would provoke death to assist him by any hand which he might use. But as when men see many of their own professions preferred, it ministers a hope that that might light upon them, so, when these hourly bells tell me of so many funerals of men like me, it presents, if not a desire that it may, yet a comfort whensoever mine shall come.

Expostulation 16

My God, my God, I do not expostulate with thee, but with them who dare do that: who dare expostulate with thee when, in the voice of thy Church, thou givest allowance to this ceremony of bells at funerals. Is it enough to refuse it because it was in use among the Gentiles? So were funerals too. Is it because some abuses may have crept in amongst Christians? Is that enough, that their ringing hath been said to drive away evil spirits? Truly, that is so far true as that the evil spirit is vehemently vexed in their ringing, because that action brings the congregation together and unites God and his people, to the destruction of that Kingdom which the evil spirit usurps.

In the first institution of thy Church in this world, in the foundation of thy Militant Church amongst the Jews, thou didst appoint the calling of the assembly in to be by trumpet; and when they were in, then thou gavest them the sound of bells in the garment of thy priest. In the Triumphant Church, thou employest both too, but in an inverted order: we enter into the Triumphant Church by the sound of bells (for we enter when we die), and then we receive our further edification, or consummation, by the sound of trumpets, at the Resurrection. The sound of thy trumpets thou didst impart to secular and civil uses too, but the sound of bells only to sacred. Lord, let us not break the Communion of Saints in that which was intended for the advancement of it. Let not that pull us asunder from one another which was intended for the assembling of us in the Militant, and associating of us to the Triumphant, Church.

But he for whose funeral these bells ring now was at home, at his journey's end, yesterday. Why ring they now? A man that is a world is all the things in the world. He is an army, and when an army marches, the vaunt [advance guard] may lodge tonight where the rear comes not till tomorrow. A man extends to his act and to his example, to that which he does and that which he teaches. So do those things that concern him, so do these bells. That which rung yesterday was to convey him out of the world in his vaunt, in his soul; that which rung today was to bring him in his rear, in his body, to the Church. And this continuing of ringing after his entering is to bring him to me in the application. Where I lie, I could hear the psalm, and did join with the congregation in it. But I could not hear the sermon, and these latter bells are a repetition sermon to me.

But, O my God, my God, do I that have this fever need other remembrances of my mortality? Is not mine own hollow voice enough to pronounce that to me? Need I look upon a death's head in a ring that have one in my face, or go for death to my neighbour's house that have him in my bosom?

We cannot, we cannot, O my God, take in too many helps for religious duties. I know I cannot have any better image of thee than thy Son, nor any better image of him than his gospel. Yet must not I, with thanks, confess to thee that some historical pictures of his have sometimes put me upon better meditations than otherwise I should have fallen upon? I know thy Church need not to have taken in from Jew or Gentile any supplies for the exaltation of thy glory or our devotion. Of absolute necessity I know she needed not. But yet we owe thee our thanks that thou hast given her leave to do so, and that as in making us Christians thou didst not destroy that which we were before, natural men, so, in the exalting of our religious devotions now we are Christians, thou hast been pleased to continue to us those assistances which did work upon the affections of natural men before. For thou lovest a good man as thou lovest a good Christian, and though grace be merely from thee, yet thou dost not plant grace but in good natures.

From Meditation 17: Now, this bell tolling softly for another says to me, Thou must die

Perchance he for whom this bell tolls may be so ill as that he knows not it tolls for him, and perchance I may think myself so much better than I am as that they who are about me and see my state may have caused it to toll for me and I know not that.

The Church is catholic, universal; so are all her actions. All that she does belongs to all. When she baptises a child, that action concerns me, for that child is thereby connected to that head which is my head too, and engrafted into that body whereof I am a member. And when she buries a man, that action concerns me: all mankind is of one author and is one volume. When one man dies, one chapter is not torn out of the book but translated into a better language, and every chapter must be so translated. God employs several translators. Some pieces are translated by age, some by sickness, some by war, some by justice. But God's hand is in every translation, and his hand shall bind up all our scattered leaves again for that library where every book shall lie open to one another.

As therefore the bell that rings to a sermon calls not upon the preacher only but upon the congregation to come, so this bell calls us all. But how much more me, who am brought so near the door by this sickness? There was a contention, as far as a lawsuit, in which both piety and dignity, religion and estimation, were mingled, which of the religious orders should ring to prayers first in the morning; and it was determined that they should ring first that rose earliest. If we understand aright the dignity of this bell that tolls for our evening prayer, we would be glad to make it ours by rising early, in that application that it should be ours as well as his whose indeed it is. The bell doth toll for him that thinks it doth. And though it intermit again, yet from that minute that that occasion wrought upon him, he is united to God.

Who casts not up his eye to the Sun when it rises? But who takes off his eye from a comet when that breaks out? Who bends not his ear to any bell which upon any occasion rings? But who can remove it from that bell which is passing a piece of himself out of this world? No man is an island entire of itself; every man is a piece of the continent, a part of the main. If a clod be washed away by the sea, Europe is the less, as well as if a promontory were, as well as if a manor of thy friend's or of thine own were. Any man's death diminishes me, because I am involved in mankind. And therefore never send to know for whom the bell tolls: it tolls for thee.

No man hath affliction enough that is not matured and ripened by it, and made fit for God by that affliction. If a man carry treasure in bullion, or in a wedge of gold, and have none coined into current monies, his treasure will not defray him as he travels. Tribulation is treasure in the nature of it, but it is not current money in the use of it except we get nearer and nearer our home, Heaven, by it. Another man may be sick too, and sick to death, and this affliction may lie in his bowels as gold in a mine and be of no use to him. But this bell, that tells me of his affliction, digs out and applies that gold to me if, by this consideration of another's danger, I take mine own into contemplation, and so secure myself by making my recourse to my God, who is our only security.

From Meditation 18: The bell rings out, and tells me, in him, that I am dead

The bell rings out. The pulse thereof is changed. The tolling was a faint and intermitting pulse upon one side; this stronger, and argues more and better life. His soul is gone out; and as a man who had a lease of a thousand years after the expiration of a short one, or an inheritance after the life of a man in a consumption, he is now entered into the possession of his better estate. His soul is gone—whither? Who saw it come in or who saw it go out? Nobody. Yet everybody is sure he had one, and hath none.

If I will ask mere philsophers what the soul is, I shall find amongst them that will tell me, it is nothing but the temperament and harmony and just and equal composition of the elements in the body which produces all those faculties which we ascribe to the soul and so in itself is nothing, no separable substance that outlives the body. They see the soul is nothing else in other creatures, and they affect an impious humility to think as low of man. But if my soul were no more than the soul of a beast I could not think so: that soul that can reflect upon itself, consider itself, is more than so.

If I will ask not mere philosophers but mixed men, philosophical divines, how the soul, being a separate substance, enters into man, I shall find some that will tell me that it is by generation, and procreation from parents, because they think it hard to charge the soul with the guiltiness of original sin if the soul were infused into a body in which it must necessarily grow foul and contract original sin whether it will or no. And I shall find some that will tell me that it is by immediate infusion from God, because they think it hard to maintain an immortality in such a soul as should be begotten and derived with the body from mortal parents.

If I will ask, not a few men but almost whole bodies, whole Churches, what becomes of the souls of the righteous at the departing thereof from the body, I shall be told by some that they attend an expiation, a purification, in a place of torment; by some, that they attend the fruition of the sight of God in a place of rest but yet but of expectation; by some that they pass to an immediate possession of the presence of God. St Augustine studied the nature of the soul as much as anything but the salvation of the soul, and he sent an express messenger to St Jerome to consult of some things concerning the soul. But he satisfies himself with this: Let the departure of my soul to salvation be evident to my faith, and I care the less how dark the entrance of my soul into my body be to my reason. It is the going out more than the coming in that concerns us.

This soul, this bell tells me, is gone out—whither? Who shall tell me that? I know not who it is, much less what he was. The condition of the man and the course of his life, which should tell me whither he is gone, I know not. I was not there in his sickness, nor at his death. I saw not his way, nor his end, nor can ask them who did, thereby to conclude, or argue, whither he is gone. But yet I have one nearer me than all these, mine own charity. I ask that, and that tells me. So I do charitably, so I do faithfully, believe that that soul is gone to everlasting rest and joy and glory.

But for the body, how poor a wretched thing is that! We cannot express it so fast as it grows worse and worse. That body, which scarce three minutes since was such a house as that that soul, which made but one step from thence to Heaven, was scarce thoroughly content to leave that for Heaven—that body hath lost the name of a dwelling-house because none dwells in it, and is making haste to lose the name of a body and dissolve to putrefaction.

Who would not be affected to see a clear and sweet river in the morning grow a kennel [channel] of muddy land water by noon and condemned to the saltness of the sea by night? And how lame a picture, how faint a representation, is that, of the precipitation of man's body to dissolution! Now all the parts built up, and knit by a lovely soul; now but a statue of clay; and now, these limbs melted off as if that clay were but snow; and now, the whole house is but a handful of sand, so much dust, and but a peck of rubbish, so much bone.

Man, before he hath his immortal soul, hath a soul of sense, and a soul of vegetation before that. This immortal soul did not forbid other souls to be in us before. But when this soul departs it carries all with it: no more vegetation; no more sense.

Such a mother-in-law is the earth, in respect of our natural mother: in her womb we grew, and when she was delivered of us we were planted in some place, in some calling, in the world. In the womb of the earth we diminish, and when she is delivered of us, our grave opened for another, we are not transplanted but transported, our dust blown away with profane dust, with every wind.

*From Meditation 19: At last the physicians,
after a long and stormy voyage, see land*

We cannot awake the July flowers in January, nor retard the flowers of the spring to autumn. We cannot bid the fruits come in May, nor the leaves to stick on in December. A woman that is weak cannot put off her ninth month to a tenth for her delivery and say she will stay till she be stronger, nor a queen cannot hasten it to a seventh that she may be ready for some other pleasure. Nature would not be spurred, nor forced to mend her pace.

Greatness loves not that kind of violence neither. There are of them that will give, that will do justice, that will pardon, but they have their own seasons for all these, and he that knows not them shall starve before that gift come, and ruin before the justice, and die before the pardon save him.

Some tree bears no fruit except much dung be laid about it, and justice comes not from some till they be richly manured. Some trees require much visiting, much watering, much labour; and some men give not their fruits but upon importunity. Some trees require incision and pruning and lopping; some men must be intimidated and syndicated with commissions before they will deliver the fruits of justice. Some trees require the early and the often access of the sun; some men open not but upon the favours and letters of Court mediation. Some trees must be housed and kept within doors; some men lock up not only their liberality but their justice and their compassion till the solicitation of a wife or a son or a friend or a servant turn the key.

Reward is the season of one man and importunity of another, fear the season of one man and favour of another, friendship the season of one man and natural affection of another; and he that knows not their seasons, nor cannot stay them, must lose the fruits. As Nature will not, so power and greatness will not be put to change their seasons. And shall we look for this indulgence in a disease, or think to shake it off before it be ripe?

From Meditation 21: God prospers their practice, and he, by them, calls Lazarus out of his tomb, me out of my bed

O what a giant is man when he fights against himself, and what a dwarf when he needs or exercises his own assistance for himself! I cannot rise out of my bed till the physician enable me; nay, I cannot tell that I am able to rise till he tell me so. I do nothing, I know nothing, of myself. How little and how impotent a piece of the world is any man alone! He can sin alone, and suffer alone, but not repent, not be absolved, without another. Another tells me I may rise, and I do so. But is every rising a preferment? Or is every present preferment a station? I am readier to fall to the earth now I am up than I was when I lay in the bed.

O perverse way, irregular motion of man! Even rising itself is the way to ruin. How many men are raised, and then do not fill the place they are raised to? No corner of any place can be empty: there can be no vacuity. If that man do not fill the place, other men will. Complaints of his insufficiency will fill it. Nay, such an abhorring is there in Nature of vacuity that if there be but an imagination of not filling, in any man, that which is but imagination neither will fill it—that is, rumour and voice—and it will be given out (upon no ground but imagination, and no man knows whose imagination) that he is corrupt in his place, or insufficient in his place, and another prepared to succeed him in his place.

A man rises sometimes and stands not, because he doth not, or is not believed to, fill his place; and sometimes he stands not, because he overfills his place. He may bring so much virtue, so much justice, so much integrity to the place as shall spoil the place, burden the place. His integrity may be a libel upon his predecessor and cast an infamy upon him, and a burden upon his successor to proceed by example, and to bring the place itself to an undervalue and the market to an uncertainty. I am up and I seem to stand and I go round; and I am a new argument of the new philosophy that the Earth moves round. Why may I not believe that the whole Earth moves in a round motion though that seem to me to stand, when as I seem to stand to my company and yet am carried in a giddy and circular motion as I stand? Man hath no centre but misery. There, and only there, he is fixed, and sure to find himself.

Everything serves to exemplify, to illustrate, man's misery, but I need go no farther than myself. For a long time I was not able to rise. At last, I must be raised by others. And now I am up, I am ready to sink lower than before.

Meditation 22: The physicians consider the root and occasion, the embers and coals and fuel of the disease, and seek to purge or correct that

How ruinous a farm hath man taken, in taking himself! How ready is the house every day to fall down, and how is all the ground overspread with weeds, all the body with diseases, where not only every turf, but every stone, bears weeds, not only every muscle of the flesh but every bone of the body hath some infirmity, every little flint upon the face of this soil hath some infectious weed, every tooth in our head such a pain as a constant man is afraid of, and yet ashamed of that fear, of that sense of the pain.

How dear and how often a rent doth man pay for this farm! He pays twice a day, in double meals, and how little time he hath to raise his rent! How many holidays call him from his labour! Every day is half-holiday, half spent in sleep. What reparations and subsidies and contributions he is put to, besides his rent! What medicines, besides his diet! And what inmates he is fain to take in, besides his own family; what infectious diseases from other men! Adam might have had Paradise for dressing and keeping it; and then his rent was not improved to such a labour as would have made his brow sweat. And yet he gave it over. How far greater a rent do we pay for this farm, this body, who pay ourselves, who pay the farm itself, and cannot live upon it!

Neither is our labour at an end when we have cut down some weed as soon as it sprung up, corrected some violent and dangerous accident of a disease which would have destroyed speedily. Nor, when we have pulled up that weed from the very root, recovered entirely and soundly from that particular disease, but the whole ground is of an ill nature, the whole soil ill disposed.

There are inclinations, there is a propensity to diseases in the body, out of which, without any other disorder, diseases will grow; and so we are put to a continual labour upon this farm, to a continual study of the whole complexion and constitution of our body. In the distempers and diseases of soils —sourness, dryness, weeping, any kind of barrenness—the remedy and the physic is, for a great part, sometimes in themselves. Sometimes the very situation relieves them. The

hanger [wood, coppice] of a hill will purge and vent his own
malignant moisture, and the burning of the upper turf of
some ground (as health from cauterising) puts a new and a
vigorous youth into that soil and there rises a kind of phoenix
out of the ashes, a fruitfulness out of that which was barren
before—and by that, which is the barrenest of all, ashes. And
where the ground cannot give itself physic, yet it receives
physic from other grounds, from other soils, which are not
the worse for having contributed that help to them—from
marl in other hills or from slimy sand in other shores.

Grounds help themselves, or hurt not other grounds from
whence they receive help. But I have taken a farm at this hard
rent, and upon those heavy covenants, that it can afford itself
no help. No part of my body, if it were cut off, would cure
another part: in some cases it might preserve a sound part,
but in no case recover an infected. And if my body may have
any physic, any medicine, from another body, one man from
the flesh of another man, it must be from a man that is dead,
and not as in other soils, which are never the worse for con-
tributing their marl, or their fat slime, to my ground.

When therefore I took this farm, undertook this body, I
undertook to drain not a marsh but a moat—where there was
not water mingled to offend but all was water. I undertook to
perfume dung where no one part but all was equally un-
savoury. I undertook to make such a thing wholesome as was
not poison by any manifest quality, intense heat or cold, but
poison in the whole substance, and in the specific form of it.
To cure the sharp accidents of diseases is a great work; to cure
the disease itself is a greater. But to cure the body, the root,
the occasion of diseases, is a work reserved for the Great
Physician, which he doth never any other way but by glorifying these bodies in the next world.

From Meditation 23: They warn me of the fearful danger of relapsing

It is not in man's body, as it is in the city, that when the bell
hath rung to cover your fire and rake up the embers, you may
lie down and sleep without fear. Though you have, by physic
and diet, raked up the embers of your disease, still there is a
fear of a relapse, and the greater danger is in that. Even in
pleasures and in pains there is a propriety, a *meum* and *tuum*,
and a man is most affected with that pleasure which is his,
his by former enjoying and experience, and most intimidated

with those pains which are his, his by a woeful sense of them in former afflictions.

A covetous person, who hath preoccupied all his senses, filled all his capacities, with the delight of gathering, wonders how any man can have any taste of any pleasure in any openness or liberality. So also in bodily pains, in a fit of the stone, the patient wonders why any man should call the gout a pain. And he that hath felt neither, but the toothache, is as much afraid of a fit of that as either of the other of either of the other. Diseases which we never felt in ourselves come but to a compassion of others that have endured them. Nay, compassion itself comes to no great degree if we have not felt in some proportion in ourselves that which we lament and condole in another.

But when we have had those torments in their exaltation ourselves we tremble at a relapse. It adds to the affliction that relapses are (and for the most part justly) imputed to ourselves, as occasioned by some disorder in us; and so we are not only passive, but active, in our own ruin. We do not only stand under a falling house but pull it down upon us, and we are not only executed (that implies guiltiness) but we are executioners (that implies dishonour) and executioners of ourselves (and that implies impiety). And amongst the many weights that aggravate a relapse this also is one, that a relapse proceeds with a more violent dispatch, and more irremediably, because it finds the country weakened and depopulated before. Upon a sickness which as yet appears not, we can scarce fix a fear, because we know not what to fear. But as fear is the busiest and irksomest affection, so is a relapse (which is still ready to come) into that which is but newly gone, the nearest object, the most immediate exercise, of that affection of fear.

From Prayer 23

O Eternal and Most Gracious God, thy Holy Apostle St Paul was shipwrecked thrice, and yet still saved. Though the rocks and the sands, the heights and the shallows, the prosperity and the adversity of this world do diversely threaten me, yet, O God, let me never make shipwreck of faith and a good conscience. And then thy long-lived, thy everlasting mercy will visit me, though that which I most earnestly pray against should fall upon me, a relapse into those sins which I have truly repented and thou hast fully pardoned.

Essays in Divinity

Published in 1651, and composed at some time while he was still considering taking Holy Orders, these *Essays* are the least personal of Donne's works, the least accessible, and the least popular. The four prayers printed at the end of the work are, however, heartfelt and moving. Three of them are here given in full.

Three Prayers

O Eternal God, who art not only first and last but in whom first and last is all one, who art not only all mercy and all justice but in whom mercy and justice is all one, who in the height of thy justice wouldest not spare thine own and only most innocent Son and yet in the depth of thy mercy wouldst not have the wretchedest liver come to destruction: behold us, O God, here gathered together in thy fear, according to thine ordinance, and in confidence of thy promise that when two or three are gathered together in thy name thou wilt be in the midst of them and grant them their petitions.

We confess, O God, that we are not worthy so much as to confess, less to be heard, least of all to be pardoned our manifold sins and transgressions against thee. We have betrayed thy temples to profaneness, our bodies to sensuality, thy fortresses to thine enemy, our souls to Satan. We have armed him with thy munition to fight against thee by surrendering our eyes, our ears, all our senses, all our faculties, to be exercised and wrought upon and tyrannised by him. Vanities and disguises have covered us, and thereby we are naked; licentiousness hath inflamed us, and thereby we are frozen; voluptuousness hath fed us, and thereby we are starved; the fancies and traditions of men have taught and instructed us, and thereby we are ignorant.

These distempers thou only, O God, who art true and perfect harmony, canst tune and rectify and set in order again. Do so then, O most merciful Father, for thy most innocent Son's sake. And since he hath spread his arms upon the cross to receive the whole world, O Lord shut out none of us, who are now fallen before the throne of thy majesty and thy mercy, from the benefit of his merits. But with as many of us as begin their conversion and newness of life this minute, this minute, O God, begin thou thy account with them and put all that is past out of thy remembrance. Accept our humble thanks for all thy mercies, and continue and enlarge them upon the whole Church.

Prayer 2

O Most Glorious and Most Gracious God, into whose presence our own consciences make us afraid to come and from
whose presence we cannot hide ourselves, hide us in the
wounds of thy Son, our Saviour Jesus Christ, and though our
sins be as red as scarlet, give them another redness which may
be acceptable in thy sight. We renounce, O Lord, all our confidence in this world, for this world passeth away and the lusts
thereof. We renounce all our confidence in our own merits,
for we have done nothing in respect of that which we might
have done, neither could we ever have done any such thing
but that still we must have remained unprofitable servants to
thee. We renounce all confidence even in our own confessions
and accusations of ourself, for our sins are above number if
we would reckon them, above weight and measure if we would
weigh and measure them, and past finding out if we would
seek them in those dark corners in which we have multiplied
them against thee. Yea, we renounce all confidence even in
our repentances.

For we have found by many lamentable experiences that
we never perform our promises to thee, never perfect our
purposes in ourselves, but relapse again and again into those
sins which, again and again, we have repented. We have no
confidence in this world, but in him who hath taken possession of the next world for us, by sitting down at thy right
hand. We have no confidence in our merits, but in him whose
merits thou hast been pleased to accept for us, and to apply
to us. We have no confidence in our own confessions and
repentances, but in that blessed Spirit who is the author of
them, and loves to perfect his own works and build up his
own foundations.

Accept them therefore, O Lord, for their sakes whose they
are: our poor endeavours, for thy glorious Son's sake, who
gives them their root, and so they are his; our poor beginnings
of sanctification, for thy blessed Spirit's sake, in whom only
our prayers are acceptable to thee; and for thy Spirit's sake
which is now in us, and must be so whensoever we do pray
acceptably to thee. Accept our humble prayers . . . etc.

Prayer 3

O Eternal and Most Merciful God, against whom, as we know and acknowledge that we have multiplied contemptuous and rebellious sins, so we know and acknowledge too that it were a mere sinful contempt and rebellion in all those to doubt of thy mercy for them, have mercy upon us. In the merits and mediation of thy Son, our Saviour Jesus Christ, be merciful unto us. Suffer not, O Lord, so great a waste as the effusion of his blood without any return to thee. Suffer not the expense of so rich a treasure as the spending of his life without any purchase to thee. But as thou didst empty and evacuate his glory here upon Earth, glorify us with that glory which his humiliation purchased for us in the Kingdom of Heaven. And as thou didst empty that Kingdom of thine, in a great part, by the banishment of those angels whose pride threw them into everlasting ruin, be pleased to repair that Kingdom, which their fall did so far depopulate, by assuming us into their places and making us rich with their confiscation.

And to that purpose, O Lord, make us capable of that succession to thine angels there. Begin in us here in this life an angelical purity, an angelical chastity, an angelical integrity to thy service, an angelical acknowledgement that we always stand in thy presence and should direct all our actions to thy glory. Rebuke us not, O Lord, in thine anger, that we have not done so till now, but enable us now to begin that great work. And imprint in us an assurance that thou receivest us now graciously: as reconciled, though enemies; and fatherly as children, though prodigal; and powerfully, as the God of our salvation, though our own consciences testify against us. Continue and enlarge thy blessings upon the whole Church.

Sermons

At the onset of the terrible plague of 1625, one of the worst
to strike London between the Black Death and the Great
Plague of 1665, Donne left the city and retreated to the home
of Lord and Lady Danvers in Chelsea. There he occupied
himself in working up from his notes and memory the texts
of eighty of his sermons, a fantastic feat both of industry and
speed. His son, John Donne Jr, also a clergyman, published
them in 1640, under the title *LXXX Sermons*, which he followed with a second instalment, *Fifty Sermons*, in 1649.
Paradoxically therefore what we admire as Donne's oratory
is less what he spoke than what he wrote, but no sensible
person has ever complained about this. The then Bishop of
Peterborough, writing to the younger John Donne, said:
'You have sent me a treasure . . . How well may your parishioners pardon your silence to them for a while, since by it you
have preached to them and their children's children, and to
all in English parishes for ever.'

The order of the extracts in the following selection is
chronological, in so far as that can be known, except for the
first, in which the preacher so to speak introduces himself by
saying something about his tastes. The division of the text
into groupings of years is mainly for ease of reading, but there
is a logic to it, I hope. In the first period, 1617–1620, Donne
is making his way, preaching for the first time at Paul's Cross,
enjoying his duties as Divinity Reader at Lincoln's Inn, bid-
ding them a high-flown farewell on leaving as Chaplain to
Lord Doncaster's embassy to the Continent, and preaching
to the Queen. The next, 1621–1624, sees his appointment to
the Deanery of St Paul's, the first of his regular Christmas
Day sermons there, and his appointment as Vicar of St
Dunstan's.

The third, 1625–1629, is the most momentous. James I
dies, and Donne preaches at Denmark House, 'some days
before the body was removed from thence, to his burial' — but

not before he has preached his first sermon before the new King, Charles I, a task he approaches with considerable trepidation. Other commemorative sermons were called for over those years: one to mark the passing of the merchant Sir William Cockayne (no relation to Donne's friend, Mrs Cockayne); one to pay tribute to Lady Danvers, formerly Magdalen Herbert, mother of George Herbert the poet, to whom Donne had owed so much.

He also preached at weddings, notably that of the Earl of Bridgewater's daughter. The juxtaposition of subject-matter and occasion in Donne's sermons would sometimes surprise us if they were preached to us today. The Earl's daughter and her bridegroom were subjected to a long and brilliant discourse about the dissolution of the human body and the scattering of its bits, while the congregation at one of his Christmas sermons went home to their dinner with phrases like 'our palate dead in a tastelessness, our stomach dead in an indigestibleness' doing duty as an hors-d'oeuvre.

Liturgically and sacramentally, Donne was 'High Church', which pleased the King and the Court, but in Biblical knowledge no Puritan could outdo him, which pleased the City Fathers. In choosing the extracts given here I have had in mind the present-day reader, of any religious affiliation or none, who may also be interested in glimpses of life at that time and in occasional details bearing on Donne's own past career.

Only one sermon is given in full, the sonorous 'Death's Duel', preached at Whitehall, 'before the King's Majesty', on 25 February 1631 (in the old calendar, 1630), being the beginning of Lent. No apology for reproducing it once again needs to be made, for if one wishes to study how Donne constructed his sermons, and how he achieved his effects, one could hardly do better than choose for that purpose his last spectacular appearance in the pulpit, and the most famous example of the preacher's art in the English language.

1617-1620

Almost every man hath his appetite and his taste disposed to some kind of meats rather than others: he knows what dish he would choose for his first and for his second course. We have often the same disposition in our spiritual diet. A man may have a particular love towards such or such a book of Scripture; and in such an affection I acknowledge that my spiritual appetite carries me still upon the Psalms of David for a first course, for the Scriptures of the Old Testament, and upon the Epistles of St Paul for a second course, for the New. And my meditations, even for these public exercises to God's Church, return oftenest to these two. For as a hearty entertainer offers to others the meat which he loves best himself, so do I oftenest present to God's people in these congregations the meditations which I feed upon at home in those two Scriptures.

If a man be asked a reason why he loves one meat better than another where all are equally good (as the books of Scripture are), he will at least find a reason in some good example, that he sees some man of good taste, and temperate withal, so do. And for my diet I have St Augustine's protestation that he loved the Books of Psalms, and St Chrysostom's that he loved St Paul's Epistles, with a particular devotion. I may have another more particular reason, because they are Scriptures written in such forms as I have been most accustomed to, St Paul's being letters and David's being poems.

For God gives us not only that which is merely necessary, but that which is convenient too. He does not only feed us, but feed us with marrow and with fatness. He gives us our instruction in cheerful forms, not in a sour and sullen and angry and unacceptable way but cheerfully in psalms, which is also a limited and a restrained form. Not in an oration, not in prose, but in psalms, which is such a form as is both curious and requires diligence in the making, and then, when it is made, can have nothing, no syllable, taken from it nor added to it. Therefore is God's will delivered to us in psalms, that we might have it the more cheerfully and that we might have it the more certainly, because where all the words are numbered and measured and weighed, the whole work is the less subject to falsification, either by subtraction or addition.

God speaks to us in a limited, in a diligent form. Let us not speak to him slackly, suddenly, unadvisedly, extemporally, occasionally, indiligently. But let all our speech to him be weighed and measured in the weights of the Sanctuary, let us be content to preach and to hear within the compass of our articles, and content to pray in those forms which the Church hath meditated for us and recommended to us.

From Donne's first sermon preached at Paul's Cross,
24 March 1617

God's hand hath been abundant towards us in raising Ministers of State so qualified and so endowed, and such Princes as have fastened their friendships, and conferred their favours, upon such persons. We celebrate seasonably, opportunely, the thankful acknowledgement of these mercies this day. For here the saddest night and the joyfullest morning that ever the daughters of this island saw made up this day. And when every one of you in the City were running up and down like ants with their eggs bigger than themselves, every man with his bags, to seek where to hide them safely, Almighty God shed down his spirit of unity and recollecting and reposedness and acquiescence upon you all.

In the death of that Queen, unmatchable, inimitable in her sex, that Queen worthy, I will not say of Nestor's years, I will not say of Methuselah's, but worthy of Adam's years if Adam had never fallen: in her death we were all under one common flood and depth of tears. But the spirit of God moved upon the face of that depth and God said, Let there be light, and there was light, and God saw that that light was good.

God took pleasure, and found a savour of rest in our peaceful cheerfulness and in our joyful and confident apprehension of blessed days in his government, whom he had prepared at first and preserved so often for us.

All love which is placed upon lower things admits satiety. But [the] love of purity always grows, always proceeds. It does not only file off the rust of our hearts in purging us of old habits, but proceeds to a daily polishing of the heart in an exact watchfulness, and brings us to that brightness that thou mayest see thy face in thy heart, and the world may see thy heart in thy face; indeed, that to both, both heart and face may be all one. Thou shalt be a looking-glass to thyself, and to others too.

St Paul's Cross. The engraving, after a painting in the Society of Antiquaries, shows a sermon preached by the Bishop of London, Dr John King, on 26 March 1620. The occasion was attended by James I and William Cockayne among other notables

The highest degree of other love is the love of woman. Which love, when it is rightly placed upon one woman, it is dignified by the Apostle with the highest comparison: Husbands love your wives, as Christ loved his Church. And God himself forbad not that this love should be great enough to change natural affection (for this, a man shall leave his father), yea, to change Nature itself: two shall be one. Accordingly, David expresses himself so in commemoration of Jonathan: Thy love to me was wonderful, passing the love of women. A love above that love *is* wonderful.

Now this love between man and woman doth so much confess a satiety as that if a woman think to hold a man long she provides herself some other capacity, some other title, than merely as she is a woman. Her wit and her conversation must continue this love and she must be a wife, a helper; else, merely as a woman, this love must necessarily have intermissions. And therefore St Jerome notes a custom of his time (perchance, prophetically enough, of our times too), that to uphold an unlawful love and make it continue, they used to call one another friend and sister and cousin, that they might apparel ill affections in good names; and those names of natural and civil love might carry on and continue a work which otherwise would sooner have withered. In parables and in mythology and in the application of fables, this affection of love, for the often change of subjects, is described to have wings, whereas the true nature of a good love is a constant union.

But our love of earthly things is not so good as to be apt to fly, for it is always grovelling upon the earth and earthly objects. As in spiritual fornications the idols are said to have ears and hear not, and eyes and see not, so in this idolatrous love of the creature, love hath wings and flies not. It flies not upward, it never ascends to the contemplation of the Creator in the creature. The poets afford us but one man that in his love flew so high as the Moon. Endymion loved the Moon. The sphere of our loves is sublunary, upon things naturally inferior to ourselves.

Lincoln's Inn, date unknown

Lying at Aix, at Aquisgrane [Aix-la-Chapelle], a well-known town in Germany, and fixing there some time for the benefit of those baths, I found myself in a house which was divided into many families, and indeed so large as it might have been a little parish, or at least a great limb of a great one. But it was of no parish. For when I asked who lay over my head, they told me a family of Anabaptists. And who over theirs? Another family of Anabaptists. And another family of Anabaptists over theirs. And the whole house was a nest of these boxes—several artificers, all Anabaptists.

I asked in what room they met for the exercise of their religion. I was told they never met. For although they were all Anabaptists, yet for some collateral differences they detested one another; and though many of them were near in blood and alliances to one another, yet the son would excommunicate the father in the room above him, and the nephew the uncle.

As St John is said to have quitted that bath into which Cerinthus the heretic came, so did I this house. I began to think, how many roofs, how many floors of separation were made between God and my prayers in that house. And such is this multiplicity of sins which we consider to be got over us, as a roof, as an arch, many arches, many roofs. All the way they separate us from God, as a roof, as an arch. And then, an arch will bear any weight. An habitual sin got over our head as an arch will stand under any sickness, any dishonour, any judgement of God, and never sink towards any humiliation.

From a sermon preached to Queen Anne at Denmark House,
14 December 1617

As the Prophets and the other secretaries of the Holy Ghost, in penning the books of Scripture, do for the most part retain and express in their writings some impressions and some air of their former professions—those that had been bred in courts and cities, those that had been shepherds and herdsmen, those that had been fishers, and so of the rest—ever inserting into their writings some phrases, some metaphors, some allusions, taken from that profession which they had exercised before, so that soul that hath been transported upon any particular worldly pleasure, when it is entirely turned upon God and the contemplation of his all-sufficiency and abundance, doth find in God fit subject and just occasion to exercise the same affection piously and religiously which had before so sinfully transported and possessed it.

A covetous person who is now truly converted to God, he will exercise a spiritual covetousness still, he will desire to have him all. He will have good security, the seal and assurance of the Holy Ghost, and he will have his security often renewed by new testimonies, and increases of those graces in him. He will have witnesses enough, he will have the testimony of all the world, by his good life and conversation. He will gain every way at God's hand, he will have wages of God, for he will be his servant. He will have a portion from God, for he will be his son. He will have a reversion, he will be sure that his name is in the book of life. He will have pawns, the seals of the Sacraments. Nay, he will have a present possession : all that God hath promised, all that Christ hath purchased, all that the Holy Ghost hath the stewardship and dispensation of, he will have all in present, by the appropriation and investiture of an actual and applying faith. A covetous person converted will be spiritually covetous still.

So will a voluptuous man, who is turned to God, find plenty and deliciousness enough in him to feed his soul as with marrow and with fatness, as David expresses it. And so an angry and passionate man will find zeal enough in the house of God to eat him up.

All affections which are common to all men, and those too which, in particular, particular men have been addicted unto, shall not only be justly employed upon God but also securely employed, because we cannot exceed nor go too far in employing them upon him. According to this rule St Paul, who had been so vehement a persecutor, had ever his thoughts exercised upon that; and thereupon after his conversion he fulfills the rest of the sufferings of Christ in his flesh. He suffers most. He makes most mention of his sufferings of any of the Apostles.

And according to this rule too Solomon, whose disposition was amorous, and excessive in the love of women, when he turned to God he departed not utterly from his old phrase and language, but having put a new and a spiritual tincture and form and habit into all his thoughts and words, he conveys all his loving approaches and applications to God, and all God's gracious answers to his amorous soul, into songs and epithalamions, and meditations upon contracts and marriages between God and his Church and between God and his soul, as we see so evidently in all his other writings.

All the sunshine, all the glory of this life, though all these be testimonies of God's love to us, yet all these bring but a winter's day, a short day and a cold day and a dark day. For except we love too, God doth not love with an everlasting love. God will not suffer his love to be idle, and since it profits him nothing if it profits us nothing neither, he will withdraw it.

The sun hath no benefit by his own light, nor the fire by his own heat, nor a perfume by the sweetness thereof, but only they who make their use, and enjoy this heat and fragrance.

Whitehall, 19 April 1618

Miserable man! A toad is a bag of poison and a spider is a blister of poison, and yet a toad and a spider cannot poison themselves. Man hath a dram of poison, original sin, in an invisible corner we know not where, and he cannot choose but poison himself, and all his actions, with that.

Lincoln's Inn, Spring or Summer 1618

When we are come to a sense of God's purpose by his corrections, it is a seasonable time to fly to his mercy, and to pray that he would remove them from us, and to present our reasons to spare us. Give us this day our daily bread, for thou hast given us stones and scorpions, tribulations and afflictions. Give us our cordials now, and our restoratives, for thy physic hath evacuated all the peccant humour and all our natural strength. Shine out in the light of thy countenance now, for this long cold night hath benumbed us. Since the dross is now evaporated, now withdraw thy fire. Since thy hand hath anew cast us, now imprint in us anew thine image. Since we have not disputed against thy corrections all this while, O Lord, open thou our lips now and accept our remembering of thee. Accept our petition, and the reason of our petition, for thine arrows stick fast in us, and thy hand presseth us sore.

These arrows which are lamented here are all those miseries which sin hath cast upon us: labour, and the child of that, sickness, and the offspring of that, death; and the security of conscience, and the terror of conscience, the searing of the conscience and the over-tenderness of the conscience. God's quiver and the Devil's quiver and our own quiver and our neighbour's quiver afford and furnish arrows to gall and wound us. These arrows proceeding from sin, and sin proceeding from temptations, and inducing tribulations, it shall advance your spiritual edification most to fix your consideration upon those fiery darts as they are temptations, and as they are tribulations. Origen says he would wish no more, for the recovery of any soul, but that she were able to see those scars which these fiery darts have left in her, the deformity which every sin imprints upon the soul, and the attenuating and wearing out and consumption of the soul by a continual succession of more and more wounds upon the same place. So then these arrows are those temptations and those tribulations which are accompanied with these qualities of arrows shot at us: that they are shot from others, not in our power; and swift and sudden, soon upon us; and not discernible in their coming but by an exact diligence.

One danger in our arrows, as they are temptations, is that they come unexpectedly. They come we know not from whence, from others. That's danger. But in our temptations there is a greater danger than that. For a man cannot shoot an arrow at himself, but we can direct temptations upon ourselves. If we were in a wilderness we could sin, and where we are we tempt temptations and wake the Devil when, for anything that appears, he would sleep. A certain man drew a bow at a venture, says that story. He had no determinate mark, no express aim upon any one man. He drew his bow at a venture and he hit, and he slew King Ahab. A woman of temptation drew a bow at a venture, as that story speaks: she paints, she curls, she sings, she gazes and is gazed upon. There's an arrow shot at random: she aimed at no particular mark, and thou puttest thyself within shot and meetest the arrow. Thou soughtest the temptation, the temptation sought not thee. A man is able to oppress others, he boasts himself because he is able to do mischief; and he shoots his arrow at random, he lets it be known that he can prefer them that second his purposes; and thou puttest thyself within shot and meetest the arrow and makest thyself his instrument. Thou soughtest the temptation, the temptation sought not thee. When we expose ourselves to temptations, temptations hit us that were not expressly directed nor meant to us.

And even then, when we begin to fly from temptations, the arrow overtakes us. After we have parlayed with a temptation, debated whether we should embrace it or no and entertained some discourse with it, though some tenderness, some remorse, make us turn our back upon it and depart a little from it, yet the arrow overtakes us. Some reclinations, some retrospects, we have. A little of Lot's wife is in us, a little sociableness and conversation, a little point of honour, not to be false to former promises, a little false gratitude and thankfulness in respect of former obligations, a little of the compassion and charity of Hell that another should not be miserable for want of us, a little of this—which is but the good nature of the

Devil—arrests us, stops us, fixes us—till the arrow, the temptation, shoot us in the back, even when we had a purpose of departing from that sin, and kill us over again.

Thus it is when we meet a temptation and put ourselves in the arrow's way. And thus it is when we fly not fast enough, nor far enough, from a temptation. But when we do all that, and provide as safely as we can to get, and do get, quickly out of distance, yet the wicked bend their bows that they may privily shoot at the upright in heart. It is a work of darkness, detraction. And they can shoot in the dark. They can wound and not be known, they can whisper thunder and pass an arrow through another man's ear into mine heart.

Every temptation, every tribulation, is not deadly, but their multiplicity disorders us, discomposes us, unsettles us, and so hazards us. Not only every periodical variation of our years, youth and age, but every day hath a diverse arrow, every hour of the day a diverse temptation. An old man wonders then how an arrow from an eye could wound him when he was young, and how love could make him do those things which he did then. And an arrow from the tongue of inferior people, that which we make shift to call honour, wounds him deeper now, and ambition makes him do as strange things now as love did then. A fair day shoots arrows of visits and comedies and conversation, and so we go abroad. And a foul day shoots arrows of gaming or chambering and wantonness, and so we stay at home.

And then, these arrows stick in us. Consider it but in one kind, diseases, sickness. They stick in us so as that we are not sure that any old diseases mentioned in physicians' books are worn out. But that every year produces new, of which they have no mention, we are sure.

We can scarce express the number, scarce sound the names, of the diseases of man's body. Six thousand year hath scarce taught us what they are, how they affect us, how they shall be cured in us. Nothing, this side the Resurrection, can teach us. They stick to us so as that they pass by inheritance, and last more generations in families than the inheritance itself does; and when no land, no manor, when no title, no honour, descends upon the heir, the stone of the gout descends upon him. And as though our bodies had not naturally diseases and infirmities enough, we contract more, inflict more (and that out of necessity too) in mortifications and macerations and disciplines of this rebellious flesh.

I must have this body with me to Heaven, or else salvation

itself is not perfect. And yet I cannot have this body thither except as St Paul did his: I beat down this body, attenuate this body by mortification. Wretched man that I am, who shall deliver me from this body of death? I have not body enough for my body, and I have too much body for my soul: not body enough, not blood enough, not strength enough to sustain myself in health, and yet body enough to destroy my soul and frustrate the grace of God in that miserable, perplexed, riddling condition of man.

Lincoln's Inn, Spring or Summer 1618

The Book of Psalms is a mysterious book. And if we had not a lock, every man would thrust in, and if we had not a key we could not get in ourselves. Our lock is the analogy of the Christian faith: that we admit no other sense, of any place in the psalms, than may consist with the articles of the Christian faith. For so, no heretic, no schismatic, shall get in by any countenance of any place in the psalms. And then our key is that intimation which we receive in the title of the psalm, what duty that psalm is principally directed upon. And so we get into the understanding of the psalm,* and profiting by the psalm. Our key in this psalm, given us in the title thereof, is that it is a psalm of remembrance.

Plato placed all learning in the memory. We may place all religion in the memory too. All knowledge that seems new today, says Plato, is but a remembering of that which your soul knew before. All instruction which we can give you today is but the remembering you of the mercies of God which have been new every morning. Nay, he that hears no sermons, he that reads no scriptures, hath the Bible without book. He hath a Genesis in his memory: he cannot forget his creation. He hath an Exodus in his memory: he cannot forget that God hath delivered him from some kind of Egypt, from some oppression. He hath a Leviticus in his memory: he cannot forget that God hath proposed to him some law, some rules, to be observed. He hath all in his memory, even to the Revelation: God hath revealed to him, even at midnight alone, what shall be his portion in the next world. And if he dare but remember that night's communication between God and him, he is well-near learned enough.

There may be enough in remembering ourselves. But

---

* The text was Psalms 38.3: 'There is no soundness in my flesh because of thine anger; neither is there any rest in my bones because of my sin.'

sometimes, that's hardest of all. Many times we are farthest off from ourselves, most forgetful of ourselves. It was a narrow enlargement, it was an addition that diminished the sense, when our former translators added that word 'themselves': 'All the world shall remember themselves'. There is no such particularity as 'themselves' in that text, but it is only, as our later translators have left it, 'All the world shall remember', and no more. Let them remember what they will, what they can, let them but remember thoroughly, and then, as it follows there, They shall turn unto the Lord, and all the kindreds of the nations shall worship him. Therefore David makes that the key into this psalm: a psalm for remembrance.

Lincoln's Inn, 1618

It was long in the Roman State before they came to a distinction of hours. All their reckoning for some hundreds of years was, this was done after the rising and this after the setting of the sun, but the distinction of hours in the degrees of the ascending or descending of the sun they had not.

We reckon all things so too. We reckon from the rising of the sun when any great fortune fell upon us, when we came to years, when the father dies and leaves the estate, when the mother dies and leaves the jointure, when the predecessor dies and leaves the office. And we reckon from the setting of the sun when any great calamity falls upon us, when a decree passed against us and swept away such a manor, when a shipwreck impoverished us, when a fire, a rot, a murrain [pestilence], a fever, overthrew our bodies or our estates.

The rising and setting of the sun, height of prosperity, depth of adversity, we observe. But we observe not the degrees of the ascending of the sun, how God hath led us every step and preserved us in many particular dangers in our rising, nor the degrees of the descending of this sun we observe not. We observe not that God would show us in the loss of our children the sinful wantonness in which they were begotten and conceived, in the loss of health the sinful voluptuousness in which the body was pampered, in the loss of goods the sinful extortion in which they were gathered. We consider sometimes in general Job's *nudus egressus*, that we came naked out of our mothers' womb, that we rose of nothing; and in general Job's *nudus revertar*, that we shall return naked again, that we shall carry away no more than we brought. But we consider not in particular that it is the Lord that gave and the

Lord that takes away, and thereupon bless the name of the Lord for it, in all his steps and degrees of our rising and falling.

God hath not only given thee a natural day, from period to period, to consider thy birth and thy death—this thou wast born to, and this thou diest worth—but he hath given thee an artificial day, and a day which he hath distinguished into hours by continual benefits, and a day which thou hast distinguished into hours by continual sins. And he would have thee remember those hours, when and how and by what degrees, by what means, he raised thee and humbled thee again, and at what time and place with what actions thou hast provoked his anger. And then thou wilt find that it was in the cool of the evening, it was late, before God came to correct Adam. But he hath filled us with mercy in the morning, that we might be glad and rejoice all the day.

If any sinner can conceit that wish, that God did not see him, he should lose more by it than he should get. Though he would be glad not to be seen by him in his sinful pleasures, yet he would be sorry not to be seen by him in his miseries and afflictions—and the miseries, the afflictions, of this life are more than the pleasures in the most habitual sinner. A man that would be glad that God saw not his extortions, his oppressions, his grinding of the poor by colour of an office, would yet be sorry that God saw not those privy whisperings, those machinations and plots and practices above in high places to traduce him, to defame him, to supplant him and wring his office from him—perchance for things he never did, though he hath done as ill. And then we make ourselves supervisors, overseers of God, if we will appoint, so far as in our wishes, what he should see and what not. In corners where nothing sees us, God sees us; and in Hell, where we shall see nothing, he shall see us too. He calleth those things which be not, as though they were, says the Apostle. He looketh upon all things after they be brought to pass, says the wise man. And he knew them ere ever they were made.

You would think him a weak lawyer that could not foresee what would be the issue of a case which depended wholly upon the law, without relation to the opinion of the judge or the affection of the jury; and a weak astrologer that could not foresee eclipses and positions of the heavens; and a weak council that could not foresee the good or ill of such a war, or such a peace, or such a marriage. And shall the sight and knowledge of God depend upon our actions? Omniscience is an attribute of his, as well as omnipotence. God can be no more ignorant of a thing than impotent in it. And whatsoever is his attribute was always so. Was not God omnipotent, had he not all power, till I was made, upon whom he exerciseth part of that power which he did not before I was made? Was he not omniscient, did he not know all things, before those things were produced into action and execution? God ever knew all things that were, that are, and that shall be, and that may be, and that may not be because he will not have them be, for if he would, they should be. He knows them otherwise than they are, for he knows future things as present, and he knows contingent things as certain and necessary.

It is said of Christ, he who knew no sin was made sin for us. Experimentally, actually, personally, he knew no sin. But in his eternal knowledge he ever knew all our particular sins and he knew the general root of all, the sin of Adam, before that sin was, or before that man was. But was this knowledge or foreknowledge the cause of it? God forbid! And therefore let us be afraid of coming so near this detestable and abominable opinion as to express ourselves in misinterpretable terms, and phrases too bold and too different from the modest and sober use of the ancient doctors and fathers, that there is in God an effectual and an actual, and a positive and a consulted and a deliberate reprobation of certain men, before their sins, yea before their creation, was considered, or that there is in man a necessary damnation which he was made for and created to.

God's knowledge of sin prints not a necessity of sin. An astrologer's knowledge of an eclipse causes not that eclipse. My knowledge that he that will fall from a steeple will break his bones did not thrust him down nor precipitate him to that ruin. But God might have preserved him from sin. And so, cannot an astrologer work upon an eclipse, nor I upon a desperate man that will cast himself down? It is true, God might have preserved him from sin by making him better—and so he might by making him worse too. He might have preserved him by making him an angel in a confirmed estate, and he might have preserved him by making him a beast without a reasonable soul, for then he could not have sinned and he had been the better for it. But God's will was to make him a man, and as a man he finds the reason of his sin to be the perverseness of his own will.

Who perverts that? Did God? *Abominandum, detestandum.* But God might have prevented this perverseness, he might have made him so strong as that he could not have perverted himself. But then God had not made him man. God did abundantly enough in making him good, and able to continue so. And he does abundantly enough in giving us those general declarations of his desire that we should all return to that goodness, that he would have no man to perish but that all men should come to repentance. He sees all things, even sins, and foresees them. But yet his foresight is no cause of them.

Drown that body of sin which thou hast built up in thee, drown that world of sin which thou hast created (for we have a creation as well as God). Man is God's creature and the sinner is man's creature. Spare thy world no more than God spared his, who drowned it with the Flood. Drown thine too with repentant tears. But when that work is religiously done, be as merciful to thy soul as he was to mankind. Drown it no more, suffer it not to lie under the water of distrustful diffidence; for so thou mayest fall too low to be able to tug up against the tide again, so thou mayest be swallowed in Cain's whirlpool, to think thy sins greater than can be forgiven. God sees every tear, our first tear, and is affected with that. And when God hath provided that thy sins shall rise no more to thy condemnation at the last day, if thou raise them up here to the vexation of thy conscience, thou art a litigious man to thine own destruction. The beginning of our sinful concupiscences and the beginning of our repentance are seen by God, and God of his mercy stops those desires at the beginning; either he keeps away the Devil or the woman. He takes away either my lust to that sin or the occasion and opportunity for the sin. In his mercy he stops me at the beginning of my desire, and in his mercy he perfects the beginnings of my repentance.

From a sermon preached to the Lords, Easter Day 1619

We are all conceived in close prison. In our mothers' wombs we are close prisoners all. When we are born, we are born but to the liberty of the house; prisoners still, though within larger walls, and then all our life is but a going out to the place of execution, to death. Now was there ever any man seen to sleep in the cart between Newgate and Tyburn? Between the prison and the place of execution does any man sleep? And we sleep all the way. From the womb to the grave we are never thoroughly awake, but pass on with such dreams and imaginations as these: I may live as well as another, and why should I die, rather than another? But awake and tell me:

Who is that other that thou talkest of? What man is he that liveth and shall not see death?

Those other degrees of punishment which God inflicted upon Adam and Eve, and in them upon us, were as absolutely and illimitedly pronounced as this of death, and yet we see they are many ways extended or contracted. To man it was said, In the sweat of thy brows thou shalt eat thy bread—and how many men never sweat till they sweat with eating? To the woman it was said, Thy desire shall be to thy husband, and he shall rule over thee—and how many women have no desire to their husbands, how many overrule them? Hunger and thirst and weariness and sickness are denounced upon all. And yet, if you ask me, What is that man that hungers and thirsts not, that labours not, that sickens not? I can tell you of many that never felt any of these. But contract the question to that one of death. What man is he that shall not taste death? And I know none.

Whether we consider the summer solstice, when the day is sixteen hours and the night but eight, or the winter solstice, when the night is sixteen hours and the day but eight, still all is but twenty-four hours and still the evening and the morning make but a day. The Patriarchs in the Old Testament had their summer day, long lives. We are in the winter, short-lived. But which of them, or us, come not to our night in death?

If we consider violent deaths, casual deaths, it is almost a scornful thing to see with what wantonness and sportfulness death plays with us. We have seen a man cannon-proof in the time of war and slain with his own pistol in the time of peace. We have seen a man recovered after his drowning and live to hang himself. But for that one kind of death which is general (though nothing be in truth more against nature than dissolution and corruption, which is death), we are come to call that death natural death than which, indeed, nothing is more unnatural. The generality makes it natural. Moses says that man's age is seventy, and eighty is labour and pain. And yet himself was more than eighty, and in a good state and habitude, when he said so. No length, no strength, enables us to answer this *Quis homo?*, What is man?

It is every man's case, then: every man dies. And though it may perchance be a mere Hebraism to say that every man shall see death, perchance it amounts to no more but to that phrase, to taste death. Yet thus much may be implied in it too, that as every man must die, so every man may see that he must die. As it cannot be avoided, so it may be understood.

A beast dies, but he does not see death. St Basil says that he saw an ox weep for the death of his yoke-fellow, but St Basil might mistake the occasion of that ox's tears. Many men die too, and yet do not see death. The approaches of death amaze them and stupefy them. They feel no colluctation [wrestling] with powers and principalities upon their deathbed. That is true. They feel no terrors in their consciences, no apprehensions of judgement upon their deathbed. That is true. And this we call going away like a lamb. But the Lamb of God had a sorrowful sense of death. His soul was heavy unto death, and he had an apprehension that his Father had forsaken him.

Death and life are in the power of the tongue, says Solomon. If my tongue, suggested by my heart, and by my heart rooted in faith, can say, I will not die, I will not die. If I can say, and my conscience do not tell me that I belie mine own state, if I can say that the blood of my Saviour runs in my veins, that the breath of his Spirit quickens all my purposes, that all my deaths have their Resurrection, all my sins their remorses, all my rebellions their reconciliations, I will harken no more after this question as it is intended of a natural death. I know I must die that death. What care I? Nor of the death of sin, why despair I? But I will find out another death, a death of rapture and of ecstasy, that death which St Paul died more than once, the death which St Gregory speaks of. The contemplation of God and Heaven is a kind of burial and sepulchre and rest of the soul. And in this death of rapture and ecstasy, in this death of the contemplation of my interest in my Saviour, I shall find myself, and all my sins, interred and entombed in his wounds, and, like a lily in paradise, out of red earth, I shall see my soul rise out of his blade, in a candour and an innocence contracted there, acceptable in the sight of his Father.

From 'A Sermon of Valediction at my going into Germany',
Lincoln's Inn, 18 April 1619

Job remembers with much sorrow how he was in the days of his youth, when God's providence was upon his tabernacle; and it is a late but a sad consideration to remember with what tenderness of conscience, what scruples, what remorses, we entered into sins in our youth, how much we were afraid of all degrees and circumstances of sin for a little while, and how indifferent things they are grown to us and how obdurate we are grown in them now. This was Job's sorrow, and this was

Tobias's comfort: When I was but young all my tribes fell away, but I alone went after to Jerusalem. Though he lacked the counsel and the example of his elders, yet he served God. For it is good for a man that he bear his yoke in his youth. For even when God had delivered over his people purposely to be afflicted, yet himself complains in their behalf that the persecutor laid the very heaviest yoke upon the ancient.

It is a lamentable thing to fall under a necessity of suffering in our age. Wouldest thou consecrate a chalice to God that is broken? No man would present a lame horse, a disordered clock, a torn book, to the King. Thy body is thy beast, and wilt thou present that to God when it is lamed and tired with excess of wantonness? When thy clock (the whole course of thy time) is disordered with passions and perturbations? When thy book (the history of thy life) is torn, a thousand sins of thine own torn out of thy memory? Wilt thou then present thyself thus defaced and mangled to Almighty God? Chastity is not chastity in an old man, but a disability to be unchaste; and therefore thou dost not give God that which thou pretendest to give, for thou hast no chastity to give him. An old man comes to the infirmities of childhood again, but he comes not to the strength of youth again.

Do this then in thy best strength, and when thy natural faculties are best able to concur with grace. But do it in the days when thou hast thy heart's desire. For if thou have worn out this word in one sense, that it be too late now to remember him in the days of youth (that's spent forgetfully), yet as long as thou art able to make a new choice, to choose a new sin, that when thy heats of youth are not overcome but burnt out, then thy middle age chooses ambition and thy old age chooses covetousness. As long as thou art able to make thy choice, thou art able to make a better than this. God testifies that power that he hath given thee: I call heaven and earth to record this day that I have set before you life and death. Choose life. If this choice like you not, if it seem evil unto you to serve the Lord, saith Joshua, then choose ye this day whom ye will serve.

Here's the election day. Bring that which ye would have into comparison with that which ye should have, that is, all that this world keeps from you with that which God offers to you. And what will ye choose to prefer before him? For honour and favour and health and riches, perchance you cannot have them though you choose them. But can you have more of them than they have had to whom those very things have been occasions of ruin? The market is open till the bell

ring. Till thy last bell ring the Church is open, grace is to be
had there. But trust not upon that rule, that men buy cheapest
at the end of the market, that Heaven may be had for a breath
at last, when they that hear it cannot tell whether it be a sigh
or a gasp, a religious breathing and anhelation [aspiration]
after the next life, or natural breathing out and exhalation of
this. But find a spiritual good husbandry in that other rule,
that the prime of the market is to be had at first. For howsoever in thine age there may be by God's strong working a day
of youth, in making thee then a new creature, yet when age
hath made a man impotent to sin, it is not a day of choice.
But remember God now when thou hast a choice, that is, a
power to advance thyself, or to oppress others by evil means.
Now, in those thy happy and sunshine days, remember him.

From the first section of a sermon preached at The Hague,
19 December 1619

These two [Andrew and Peter] then our Saviour found as he
walked by the Sea of Galilee. No solitude, no tempest, no
bleakness, no inconvenience averts Christ and his Spirit from
his sweet and gracious and comfortable visitations. But yet,
this that is called here the Sea of Galilee was not properly a
sea, but according to the phrase of the Hebrews who call all
great meetings of waters by that one name, a sea, this, which
was indeed a lake of fresh water, is called a sea.

From the root of Mount Libanus spring two rivers, Jor
and Dan; and those two, meeting together, joining their
waters, join their names too, and make that famous river
Jordan: a name so composed as perchance our river is,
Thamesis, of Thame and Isis. And this river Jordan, falling
into this flat, makes this lake of sixteen miles long and some
six in breadth. Which lake, being famous for fish, though of
ordinary kinds yet of an extraordinary taste and relish, and
then of extraordinary kinds too, not found in other waters,
and famous because divers famous cities did engirt it and
become as a garland to it—Capernaum and Chorazim and
Bethsaida and Tiberias and Magdalo, all celebrated in the
Scriptures—was yet much more famous for the often recourse
which our Saviour, who was of that country, made to it.

For this was the sea where he amazed Peter with that great
draught of fishes that brought him to say, Depart from me,
O Lord, for I am a sinful man. This was the sea where himself walked upon the waters, and where he rebuked the

tempest, and where he manifested his almighty power many times. And by this lake, this sea, dwelt Andrew and Peter, and, using the commodity of the place, lived upon fishing in this lake. And in that act our Saviour found them, and called them to his service.

Leave thy superfluous desire of having the riches of this world. Though thou mayest flatter thyself that thou desirest to have, only that thou mightest leave it, that thou mightest employ it charitably, yet it might prove a net and stick too close about thee to part with it.

He that hath least hath enough to weigh him down from Heaven by an inordinate love of that little which he hath or an inordinate and murmuring desire of more. And he that hath most hath not too much to give for Heaven. Heaven is always so much worth as thou art worth. A poor man may have Heaven for a penny, that hath no greater store. And God looks that he to whom he hath given thousands should lay out thousands upon the purchase of Heaven.

The market changes as the plenty of money changes. Heaven costs a rich man more than a poor, because he hath more to give. But in this rich and poor are both equal, that both must leave themselves without nets, that is, without those things which, in their own consciences, they know retard the following of Christ. Whatsoever hinders my present following, that I cannot follow today, whatsoever may hinder my constant following, that I cannot follow tomorrow and all my life, is a net, and I am bound to leave that.

*From the Second Sermon revised from the sermon preached at
The Hague, 19 December 1619*

So early, so primary a sin is pride, as that out of every mercy and blessing which God affords us (and his mercies are new every morning) we gather pride. We are not the more thankful for them and yet we are the prouder of them. Nay, we gather pride not only out of those things which mend and improve us (God's blessings and mercies), but out of those actions of our own that destroy and ruin us we gather pride.

Sins overthrow us, demolish us, destroy and ruin us, and yet we are proud of our sins. How many men have we heard boast of their sins, and (as St Augustine confesses of himself) belie themselves, and boast of more sins than ever they committed! Out of everything, out of nothing, sin grows. We are

come to see even children strive for place and precedence, and
mothers are ready to go to the Heralds to know how cradles
shall be ranked, which cradle shall have the highest place.
Nay, even in the womb there was contention for precedence:
Jacob took hold of his brother Esau's heel and would have
been born before him.

And as our pride begins in our cradle, it continues in our
graves and monuments. It was a good while in the primitive
Church before they were buried in the church: the best contented themselves with the churchyards. After, a holy ambition (may we call it so), a holy pride, brought them to the
church threshhold, to the church door, because some great
martyrs were buried in the porches and devout men desired
to lie near them, as one prophet did to lie near another. But
now, persons whom the Devil kept from church all their lives,
separatists, libertines, that never came to any church; and
persons whom the Devil brought to church all their lives—
for such as come merely out of the obligation of the law and
to redeem that vexation, or out of custom or company or
curiosity or a perverse and sinister affection to the particular
preacher, though they come to God's house come upon the
Devil's invitation—such as one devil, that is, worldly respect,
brought to church in their lives, another devil, that is, pride
and vainglory, brings to church after their deaths, in an affectation of high places and sumptuous monuments in the church.
And such as have given nothing at all to any pious uses, or
have determined their alms and their dole which they have
given in that one day of their funeral, and no farther, have
given large annuities, perpetuities, for new painting their
tombs, and for new flags and scutcheons every certain number
of years.

O the earliness! O the lateness! How early a spring and no
autumn! How fast a growth and no declination of this branch
of this sin, pride! This love of place and precedence, it rocks
us in our cradles, it lies down with us in our graves. There are
diseases proper to certain things, rots to sheep, murrain to
cattle. There are diseases proper to certain places, as the sweat
was to us. There are diseases proper to certain times, as the
plague is in divers parts of the Eastern countries, where they
know assuredly when it will begin and end. But for this infectious disease of precedence and love of place, it is run over
all places, as well cloisters as courts, and over all men, as well
spiritual as temporal, and over all times, as well the Apostles'
as ours.

The world is a sea in many respects and assimilations. It is a sea, as it is subject to storms and tempests: every man (and every man is a world) feels that. And then, it is never the shallower for the calmness. The sea is as deep, there is as much water in the sea, in a calm as in a storm. We may be drowned in a calm and flattering fortune, in prosperity, as irrecoverably as in a wrought sea, in adversity.

So the world is a sea. It is a sea as it is bottomless to any line which we can sound it with, and endless to any discovery that we can make of it. The purposes of the world, the ways of the world, exceed our consideration. But yet we are sure the sea hath a bottom, and sure that it hath limits that it cannot overpass. The power of the greatest in the world, the life of the happiest in the world, cannot exceed those bounds which God hath placed for them.

So the world is a sea. It is a sea as it hath ebbs and floods, and no man knows the true reason of those floods and those ebbs. All men have changes and vicissitudes in their bodies (they fall sick), and in their estates (they grow poor), and in their minds (they become sad); at which changes—sickness, poverty, sadness—themselves wonder, and the cause is wrapped up in the purpose and judgement of God only, and hid even from them that have them.

And so the world is a sea. It is a sea, as the sea affords water enough for all the world to drink, but such water as will not quench the thirst. The world affords conveniences enough to satisfy nature, but these increase our thirst with drinking, and our desire grows and enlarges itself with our abundance; and though we sail in a full sea, yet we lack water.

So the world is a sea. It is a sea, if we consider the inhabitants. In the sea, the greater fish devour the less; and so do the men of this world too. And as fish, when they mud themselves, have no hands to make themselves clean but the current of the waters must work that, so have the men of this world no means to cleanse themselves from those sins which they have contracted in the world of themselves till a new flood, waters of repentance, drawn up and sanctified by the Holy Ghost, work that blessed effect in them.

All these ways the world is a sea. But especially it is a sea in this respect, that the sea is no place of habitation but a passage to our habitations. So the Apostle expresses the world: Here we have no continuing city, but we seek one to come. We seek it not here, but we seek it whilst we are here, else we shall never find it. Those are the two great works which we are to do in this world: first, to know that this world is not our home; and then to provide us another home whilst we are in this world.

Therefore the Prophet says: Arise and depart, for this is not your rest. Worldly men that have no farther prospect promise themselves some rest in this world: Soul, thou hast much goods laid up for many years; take thine ease, eat, drink and be merry, says the rich man. But this is not your rest—indeed, no rest; at least not yours. You must depart, depart by death, before ye come to that rest. But then you must arise before you depart. For except ye have a resurrection to grace here, before you depart, you shall have no resurrection to glory in the life to come, when you are departed.

Now in this sea every ship that sails must necessarily have some part of the ship under water. Every man that lives in this world must necessarily have some of his life, some of his thoughts, some of his labours, spent upon this world. But that part of the ship by which he sails is above water. Those meditations, and those endeavours, which must bring us to Heaven are removed from this world and fixed entirely upon God.

Whitehall, 2 April 1620

Tell a natural, voluptuous man of two sorts of torments in Hell, one of privation (he shall not see God) and the other of real torments (he shall be actually tormented). The loss of the sight of God will not so much affect him, for he never saw him in his life—not in the marking of his grace, not in the glass of his creatures—and he thinks it will not much trouble him there to lack his sight, whom he never saw here. But when he comes to think of real torments he sees some examples of them here in this life upon himself, and if he have but the toothache he will think that, if that were to last eternally, it were an unsufferable thing. And therefore Solomon affects us with that sensible addition: Love not this world.

St Jerome made it not a proverb, but he found it one, and so he cites it: A rich man is dishonest himself, or at least he succeeds a dishonest predecessor. We have a better proverb against that proverb: the reward of humility and the fear of God is riches and glory and life. If we were able to digest and concoct these temporal things into good nourishment, God's natural way is and would be to convey to us the testimony of his spiritual graces in outward and temporal benefits. He had rather we were rich, because we might advance his glory the more.

At least they are equal and any great measure of either, either of riches or of poverty, are equal in their danger too. Poverty as well as riches may put us from our Christian constancy, and therefore they are both prayed against. How riches are to be esteemed when they are compared with poverty is another question, but how compared with Heaven is no question.

Riches may do harm to their owners. It is no easy matter for a rich man to find out the true owners of all his riches. Thou art not owner of all that the right owner cannot recover of thee, that all that is his by law should be his. Certainly no rich man hath dealt much in this world but he hath something of which himself knows not the right owner. When he receives usury for his money, that interest is not his money. But when he receives usury again for that, there neither the interest nor principal was his own money. He takes usury for that money of which himself was not the owner, because it was ill-gotten.

If thou do truly know the owner, restore it to him. If, after a diligent examination of thyself, thou do not know the particular owner, yet thou knowest it is none of thine [but canst not] give it him whose it was at first, both before thou hadst it and before he from whom thou gottest it corruptly had it, give it to God in giving it to his poor and afflicted members. Give it him and give it willingly and give it now, for that that thou givest at thy death thou dost but leave by thy last will; thou dost not give. He only gives that might keep; thou givest unwillingly. Howsoever they have it by thy will, yet it is against thy will that they have it. Thou givest then, but art sorry that they to whom thou givest came so soon to it.

And then, we become slaves to our last sickness often: oftentimes apoplexies stupefy us and we are dull, and fevers enrage us and we are mad. We are in a slavery to the disease and, says the law, slaves have no power to make a will. Make thy will, and make it to be thy will, give it the effect and execute thy will whilst thou art a free man, in state of health. Restore that which is not thine, for even that of which thou art true owner may be reserved to thy harm; much more that which is none of thine.

Every man may find in himself that he hath done some sins which he would not have done if he had not been so rich, for there goes some cost to the most sins. His wantonness in wealth makes him do some: his wealth hath given him a confidence that that fault would not be looked into, or that it would be bought out if it were. Some sins we have done because we are rich, but many more because we would be rich, and this is a spiritual harm the riches do their owners. And for temporal harm, if it were hard to find in our own times examples of men which have incurred great displeasure, undergone heavy calamities, perished in unrecoverable shipwreck, all which they had escaped if they had not been eminently and enormously rich, we might in ancient history, both profane and holy, find such precedents enough. The rich merchant at sea is afraid that every fisherman is a pirate, and the fisherman fears not him. And if we should survey the body of our penal laws, whensoever the abuse of them makes them snares and springs to entangle men, we should see that they were principally directed upon rich men. Neither can rich men comfort themselves in it that, though they be subject to more storms than other men, yet they have better ground tackling, they are better able to ride it out than other men. For it goes more to the heart of that rich merchant which we spoke of to cast his goods overboard than it does to the fisherman to lose his boat, and perchance his life.

It is true the poor man's brow sweats without. The rich man's heart bleeds within. And the poor man can sooner wipe his face than the rich man his heart. The rich man is worse troubled to get a stomach than the poor man to satisfy his, and his loathing to meat is more wearisome than the other's desire of it. Sum up the diseases that voluptuousness by the ministry of riches imprints in the body, the battery that malice, by the provocation of riches, lays to the fortune, the sins that confidence in our riches heaps upon our souls—and we shall see that, though riches be reserved to their owners, yet it is to their harm.

In small diseases (saith St Basil) we go to the physician's house. In greater diseases we send for the physician to our house. But in violent diseases, in the stupefaction of an apoplexy, in the damp of a lethargy, in the furnace of a pleurisy, we have no sense, no desire, of a physician at all. When this inordinate love of riches begins in us we have some tenderness of conscience and we consult with God's Ministers. After, we admit the reprehensions of God's Ministers when they speak to our consciences. But at last the habit of our sin hath seared us up and we never find that it is we that the preacher means. We find that he means others, but not us. Our wit and our malice is awake, but our conscience is asleep. We can make a sermon a libel against others, and cannot find a sermon in a sermon to ourselves. It is a sickness, and an evil sickness.

The wise man seeth the plague and shunneth it: therein consists the wisdom. But for the fool, when he sees a thief, he runneth with him. When he sees others thrive by ill getting and ill keeping, he runs with them, he takes the same course as they do. Beloved, it is not intended that true and heavenly wisdom may not consist with riches. The poor man and the rich are in Heaven together; and to show us how the rich should use the poor, Lazarus is in Abraham's bosom. The rich should succour and relieve and defend the poor in their bosoms. But when our Saviour declares a wisdom belonging to riches (as in the parable of the Unjust Steward), he places not this wisdom in the getting nor in the holding of riches, but only in the using of them: make you friends of your riches that they may receive you into everlasting habitations.

Heaven and earth are as a musical instrument: if you touch a string below, the motion goes to the top. Any good done to Christ's poor members upon earth affects him in Heaven. This is the wisdom of their use. But the wisdom of their getting and keeping is to see that it is an evil sickness to get too laboriously, or to reserve too gripingly, things which tend naturally to the owner's evil. And the greatest iniquity of all is towards ourselves, to take those riches to our heart which Christ calls the thorns that choke the good seeds and the Apostle calls temptations and snares and foolish and noisome lusts which drown men in perdition and in destruction and which the wise man hath seen, and hath showed us here, to be reserved to the owners for their evil.

Heaven is a feast and Heaven is a treasure. If ye prepare not for his feast by being worthy guests at his table, if you embrace not his treasure by being such merchants as give all for his pearl, another feast and another treasure are expressed, and heightened in two such words as never any tongue of any author but the Holy Ghost himself spoke: you shall be drunk with wormwood, you shall taste nothing but bitter affliction, and that shall make you reel, for you shall find in your affliction no rest for your souls.

But use the creatures of God as creatures and not as God, with a confidence in them; and you shall find in a good conscience all the hid treasures of wisdom and knowledge. You shall know how to be rich in this world by an honest getting of riches, and how to be rich in the next world by a Christianly use of those riches here.

Lincoln's Inn, probably during the Easter Term, 1620

Corruption in the skin, says Job, in the outward beauty: these be the records of vellum, these be the parchments, the indictments and the evidences that shall condemn many of us at the last day. Our own skins. We have the book of God, the law, written in our own hearts. We have the image of God imprinted in our own souls. We have the character and seal of God stamped in us in our baptism. And all this is bound up in this vellum, in this parchment, in this skin of ours; and we neglect book and image and character and seal and all, for the covering.

It is not a clear case, if we consider the original words properly, that Jezebel did paint, and yet all translators and expositors have taken a just occasion, out of the ambiguity of those words, to cry down that abomination of painting. It is not a clear case, if we consider the propriety of the words, that Absalom was hanged by the hair of his head, and yet the Fathers and others have made use of that indifferency and verisimilitude to explode that abomination of cherishing and curling hair to the inveigling and ensnaring and entangling of others. Thou art guilty of a murder, says St Jerome, though nobody die. Thou hast poisoned a cup if any would drink, thou hast prepared a temptation if any would swallow it.

Tertullian thought he had done enough, when he had writ his book against the excess of women in clothes. But he was fain to add another with more vehemence that went beyond their clothes to their skin. And he concludes, there's vainglory in their excess of clothes, but there's prostitution in drawing the eye to the skin. Pliny says that when thin silk stuffs were first invented at Rome, it was but an invention that women might go naked in clothes, for their skins might be seen through those clothes, those thin stuffs. Our women are not so careful, but they expose their nakedness professedly, and paint it, to cast birdlime for the passenger's eye.

Beloved, good diet makes the best complexion, and a good conscience is a continual feast. A cheerful heart makes the best blood and peace with God is the true cheerfulness of heart. Thy Saviour neglected his skin so much as that at last he scarce had any; all was torn with the whips and scourges. And thy skin shall come to that absolute corruption as that, though a hundred years after thou art buried one may find thy bones and say, this was a tall man, this was a strong man, yet we shall soon be past saying, upon any relic of thy skin, this was a fair man. Corruption seizes the skin, all outward beauty quickly; and so it does the body, the whole frame and constitution, which is another consideration: after my skin, my body.

When of the whole body there is neither eye nor ear nor any member left, where is the body? And what should an eye do there where there is nothing to be seen but loathsomeness; or a nose there, where there is nothing to be smelt but putrefaction? Or an ear, where in the grave they do not praise God? Doth not that body that boasted but yesterday of that privilege above all creatures, that it only could go upright, lie today as flat upon the earth as the body of a horse or of a dog? And doth it not tomorrow lose his other privilege of looking up to heaven? Is it not farther removed from the eye of heaven, the sun, than any dog or horse by being covered with the earth, which they are not? Painters have presented to us, with some horror, the skeleton, the frame of the bones of a man's body. But the state of a body in the dissolution of the grave no pencil can present to us. Between that excremental jelly that thy body is made of at first, and that jelly which thy body dissolves to at last, there is not so noisome, so putrid a thing in nature. This skin (this outward beauty), this body (this whole constitution), must be destroyed, says Job.

Thy skin and thy body shall be ground away, trod away upon the ground. Ask where that iron is that is ground off of a knife or axe. Ask that marble that is worn off of the threshhold in the church porch by continual treading. And with that iron, and with that marble, thou mayest find thy father's skin and body. The knife, the marble, the skin, the body are ground away, trod away. They are destroyed. Who knows the revolutions of dust? Dust upon the king's highway and dust upon the king's grave are both, or neither, dust royal, and may change places. Who knows the revolutions of dust? Skin and body, beauty and substance, must be destroyed, and destroyed by worms. After my skin, worms shall destroy this body.

Destroyed by worms: it makes the destruction the more contemptible. Thou that wouldst not admit the beams of the sun upon thy skin and yet hast admitted the pollutions of sin. Thou that wouldst not admit the breath of the air upon thy skin and yet hast admitted the spirit of lust and unchaste solicitations to breathe upon thee in execrable oaths and blasphemies to vicious purposes. Thou, whose body hath, as far as it can, putrefied and corrupted even the body of thy Saviour, in an unworthy receiving thereof in this skin, in this

'We are all conceived in a close prison'. Donne's words would have struck a chord among his Christian audience, in an age when confinement in the Tower or Newgate Prison, *below*, were harsh punishments to be faced for public transgressions in this world, not to mention the torments of an everlasting Hell in the next

body, must be the food of worms, the prey of destroying
worms. After a low birth thou mayest pass an honourable
life; after a sentence of an ignominious death thou mayst have
an honourable end. But in the grave canst thou make these
worms silk worms? They were bold and early worms that ate
up Herod before he died. They are bold and everlasting
worms which, after thy skin and body is destroyed, shall remain as long as God remains, in an eternal gnawing of thy
conscience—long, long after the destroying of skin and body
by bodily worms.

Whitehall, 30 April 1620

For the first temporal blessing of peace we may consider the
loveliness, the amiableness of that, if we look upon the horror
and ghastliness of war, either in effigy, in that picture of war
which is drawn in every leaf of our own chronicles, in the
blood of so many princes and noble families, or if we look upon
war itself at that distance where it cannot hurt us, as God had
formerly kindled it amongst our neighbours and as he hath
transferred it now to remoter nations, whilst we enjoy yet a
Goshen in the midst of all those Egypts.

In all cities, disorderly and facinorous [monstrously
wicked] men covet to draw themselves into the skirts and
suburbs of those cities, that so they may be the nearer the
spoil which they make upon passengers. In all kingdoms that
border upon other kingdoms, and in islands which have no
other border but the sea, particular men, who by dwelling in
those skirts and borders may make their profit of spoil, delight in hostility and have an adverseness and detestation of
peace. But it is not so within. They who till the earth and breed
up cattle, and employ their industry upon God's creatures
according to God's ordinance, feel the benefit and apprehend
the sweetness and pray for the continuance of peace.

St Basil, in a homily which he made in a time of dearth and
drought, says that the air was the worse for being so good and
the fouler for being so fair, and inverts the words of our
Saviour [and] says, Here are workmen enough but no harvest
to gather. In that homily he notes a barrenness in that which
used to be fruitful and a fruitfulness in that which used to be
barren. He prophesied of our times, when not only so many
families have left the country for the city in their persons, but
have brought their lands into the city. They have brought all
their evidences into scriveners' shops and changed all their
renewing of leases every seven years into renewing of bonds

every six months. They have taken a way to inflict a barrenness upon land and to extort a fruitfulness from gold by usury.
Monsters may be got by unnatural mixtures, but there is no
race, no propagation of monsters. Money may be raised by
this kind of use, but it is the sweat of other men and it will not
stick to thine heir. Nay, commonly it brings not that outward
blessing of plenty with it. For, for the most part, we see no
men live more penuriously, more sordidly, than these men do.

Lincoln's Inn, probably late November or early December 1620

First, then, the voice of condoling and lamentation: God
laments the necessity that he is reduced to, and those judgements which the sins of men have made inevitable. In reading
an Act of Parliament, or of any law that inflicts the heaviest
punishment that can be imagined upon a delinquent and
transgressor of that law, a man is not often much affected,
because he needs not, when he does but read that law, consider that any particular man is fallen under the penalty and
bitterness thereof. But if, upon evidence and verdict, he be
put to give judgement upon a particular man that stands
before him at the Bar, according to that law, that that man
that stands there that day must that day be no man; that that
breath breathed in by God to glorify him must be suffocated
and strangled with a halter, or evaporated with an axe, he
must be hanged or beheaded; that those limbs which make
up a cabinet for that precious jewel, the image of God, to be
kept in, must be cut into quarters or torn with horses; that
that body which is a consecrated temple of the Holy Ghost
must be chained to a stake and burnt to ashes—he that is not
affected in giving such a judgement upon such a man hath no
part in the bowels of Christ Jesus that melt in compassion
when our sins draw and extort his judgements upon us in the
mouth of those prophets, those men whom God sends.

1621-1624

To the Countess of Bedford, then at Harrington House, 7 January 1621

Look upon the water and we are as that, and as that spilt upon the ground. Look to the earth and we are not like that, but we are earth itself. At our tables we feed upon the dead, and in the temples we tread upon the dead. And when we meet in a church God hath made many echoes, many testimonies, of our death, in the walls and in the windows; and he only knows whether he will not make another testimony of our mortality, of the youngest amongst us, before we part, and make the very place of our burial our deathbed.

Lincoln's Inn, probably Trinity Term 1621

When there is a long time to the Assizes there may be some hope of taking off, or of smothering, evidence, or working upon the Judge, or preparing for a pardon; or, if it were a great booty, a great possession which we had gotten, even that might buy out our peace. But this world is no such thing, neither for the extent that we have in it (it is but little that the greatest hath), nor for the time that we have in it. In both respects it is but a sojourning,* it is but a pilgrimage, says Jacob, and but the days of my pilgrimage, every one of them quickly at an end and all of them quickly reckoned. Here we have no continuing city: first, no city, no such large being, and then no continuing at all. It is but a sojourning. We have but a parish, we are but parishioners in this world, and they that labour to purchase whole shires usurp more than their portion. And yet what is a great shire in a little map? Here we are but passengers, wayfaring men. This life is but the highway, and thou canst not build thy hopes here. Nay, to be buried in the highway is no good mark, and therefore bury not thyself, thy labours, thy affections, upon this world. Fear him whom thou callest Father and who is shortly to be thy judge, for here thou art no more than a sojourner. But yet remember withal that thou *art* so much; thou *art* a sojourner. This life is not a parenthesis, a parenthesis that belongs

* The text was I Peter 1.17: 'And if ye call on the Father, who without respect of persons judgeth according to every man's work, pass the time of your sojourning here in fear.'

not to the sense, a parenthesis that might be left out as well as put in. More depends upon this life than so. Upon every minute of this life depend millions of years in the next, and I shall be glorified eternally, or eternally lost, for my good or ill use of God's grace offered to me this hour. Therefore, where the Apostle says of this life, We are absent from the Lord, yet he says, We are at home in the body. This world is so much our home as that he that is not at home now, he that hath not his conversation in Heaven here, shall never get home. For this, where we are now, is the suburb of the Great City, the porch of the Triumphant Church and the grange or country house of the same landlord, belonging to his heavenly palace, in the heavenly Jerusalem. Be it but a sojourning, yet thou must pay God something for thy sojourning, pay God his rent of praise and prayer; and be it but a sojourning, yet thou art bound to it for a time. Though thou sigh with David, Woe is me that I sojourn so long here, though the miseries of thy life make thy life seem long, yet thou must stay out that time which he, who took thee in, appointed; and by no practice, no, not so much as by a deliberate wish or unconditioned prayer, seek to be delivered of it.

Because thy time here is such a sojourning as is quickly at an end, and yet such a sojourning as is never at an end (for our endless state depends upon this), fear him who shall so certainly and so soon be a just judge of it.

From a sermon preached at St Paul's, Christmas Day 1621

In all philosophy there is not so dark a thing as light. As the sun, which is the beginning of natural light, is the most evident thing to be seen, and yet the hardest to be looked upon, so is natural light to our reason and understanding. Nothing clearer, for it is clearness itself; nothing darker, it is enwrapped in so many scruples. Nothing nearer, for it is round about us; nothing more remote, for we know neither entrance nor limits of it. Nothing more easy, for a child discerns it; nothing more hard, for no man understands it. If we wink, we cannot choose but see it; if we stare, we know it never the better.

They had a precious composition for lamps amongst the ancients, reserved especially for tombs, which kept light for many hundreds of years. We have had in our age experience, in some casual openings of ancient vaults, of finding such lights as were kindled, as appeared by their inscriptions, fifteen or sixteen hundred years before. But as soon as that light comes to our light, it vanishes. So this eternal and this supernatural light, Christ and faith, enlightens, warms, purges, and does all the profitable offices of fire and light if we keep it in the right sphere, in the proper place (that is, if we consist in points necessary to salvation and revealed in the Scripture). But when we bring this light to the common light of reason, to our inferences and consequences, it may be in danger to vanish itself, and perchance extinguish our reason too.

Divers men walk by the seaside, and the same beams of the sun give light to them all. One gathereth by the benefit of that light pebbles or speckled shells for curious vanity, and another gathers precious pearl, or medicinal amber, by the same light. So the common light of reason illumines us all. But one employs this light upon the searching of impertinent vanities, another, by a better use of the same light, finds out the mysteries of religion and, when he hath found them, loves them, not for the light's sake but for the natural and true worth of the thing itself.

Some men, by the benefit of this light of reason, have found out things profitable and useful to the whole world: as, in particular, printing, by which the learning of the whole world is communicable to one another, and our minds and our inventions, our wits and compositions, may trade and have commerce together, and we may participate of one another's understandings as well as of our clothes and wines and oils and other merchandise. So, by the benefit of this light of reason, they have found out artillery, by which wars come to quicker ends than heretofore and the great expense of blood is avoided. For the numbers of men slain now, since the invention of artillery, are much less than before, when the sword was the executioner.

Others, by the benefit of this light, have searched and found the secret corners of gain and profit, wheresoever they lie. They have found wherein the weakness of another man consisteth and made their profit of that, by circumventing him in a bargain. They have found his riotous and wasteful inclination and they have fed and fomented that disorder, and kept open that leak, to their advantage and the other's ruin. They have found where was the easiest and most accessible way to solicit the chastity of a woman, whether discourse, music or presents, and according to that discovery they have pursued hers and their own eternal destruction. By the benefit of this light men see through the darkest and most impervious places that are—that is, courts of princes and the greatest officers in courts—and can submit themselves to second and to advance the humours of men in great place, and so make their profit of the weakness which they have discovered in these great men.

All the ways both of wisdom and of craft lie open to this light, this light of natural reason. But when they have gone all these ways by the benefit of this light, they have got no further than to have walked by a tempestuous sea and to have gathered pebbles and speckled cockle shells. Their light seems to be great out of the same reason that a torch in a misty night seemeth greater than in a clear, because it hath kindled and inflamed much thick and gross air round about it. So the light and wisdom of worldly men seemeth great, because he hath kindled an admiration or an applause in airy flatterers, not because it is so indeed.

But if thou canst take this light of reason that is in thee, this poor snuff that is almost out in thee, thy faint and dim knowledge of God that riseth out of this light of nature, if thou canst, in those embers, those cold ashes, find out one small coal, and wilt take the pains to kneel down and blow that coal with thy devout prayers, and light thee a little candle (a desire to read that Book which they call the Scriptures and the Gospel and the Word of God). If with that little candle thou canst creep humbly into low and poor places, if thou canst find thy Saviour in a manger, and in his swathing clouts, in his humiliation, and bless God for that beginning. If thou canst find him flying into Egypt, and find in thyself a disposition to accompany him in a persecution, in a banishment—if not a bodily banishment, a local banishment, yet a real, a spiritual banishment, a banishment from those sins, and that sinful conversation, which thou hast loved more than thy parents or country or thine own body, which perchance thou hast consumed and destroyed with that sin. If thou canst find him contenting and containing himself at home in his father's house and not breaking out—no, not about the work of our salvation—till the due time was come when it was to be done; and if, according to that example, thou canst contain thyself in that station and vocation in which God hath planted thee, and not, through a hasty and precipitate zeal, break out to an imaginary and intempestive [untimely] and unseasonable reformation, either in civil or ecclesiastical business which belong not to thee. If, with this little poor light, these first degrees of knowledge and faith, thou canst follow him into the garden and gather up some of the drops of his precious blood and sweat which he shed for thy soul. If thou canst follow him to Jerusalem, and pick up some of those tears which he shed upon that city, and upon thy soul. If thou canst follow him to the place of his scourging, and to his crucifying, and provide thee some of that balm which must cure thy soul. If, after all this, thou canst turn this little light inward, and canst thereby discern where thy diseases and thy wounds and thy corruptions are, and canst apply those tears and blood and balm to them, thou shalt never envy the lustre and glory of the great lights of worldly men—which are great by the infirmity of others or by their own opinion, great because others think them great, or because they think themselves so —but thou shalt find that, howsoever they magnify their lights, their wit, their learning, their industry, their fortune, their favour, yet thou shalt see that thou, by thy small light, hast gathered pearl and amber, and they, by their great lights, nothing but shells and pebbles.

They have determined the light of nature upon the book of nature, this world, and thou hast carried the light of nature higher. Thy natural reason, and even human arguments, have brought thee to read the Scriptures, and to that love God hath set to the seal of faith. Their light shall set at noon: even in their height some heavy cross shall cast a damp upon their soul, and cut off all their succours and divest them of all comforts. And thy light shall grow up, from a fair hope to a modest assurance and infallibility that that light shall never go out, nor the works of darkness nor the prince of darkness ever prevail upon thee.

But as thy light of reason is exalted by faith here, so thy light of faith shall be exalted into the light of glory and fruition, in the Kingdom of Heaven. Before the sun was made, there was a light which did that office of distinguishing night and day. But when the sun was created, that did all the offices of the former light and more. Reason is that first and primogenial light, and goes no farther in a natural man. But in a man regenerate by faith, that light does all that reason did and more—and all his moral and civil and domestic and indifferent actions (though they be never done without reason), yet their principal scope and mark is the glory of God. And though they seem but moral or civil or domestic, yet they have a deeper tincture, a heavenly nature, a relation to God in them.

Lincoln's Inn, probably Trinity Term 1621

Enlarge your thoughts a little upon Judas's case. Judas was of those who had tasted of the word of God, and the powers of the world to come. He had lived in the conversation, in the pedagogy, in the discipline of Christ, and sold him at a low price, as every man that is so unprovident as to offer a thing for sale shall do. And he stayed not till they came to him with, What will you take for your Master?, but he went to them with, What will you give me for Christ? Yet Christ admits him, admits him to supper, and after all this calls him friend. For after all this Christ had done two, perchance three, offices of a friend to Judas. He washed his feet, and perchance he gave him the Sacrament with the rest. And by assigning the sop for a particular mark he let him see that he knew he was a traitor, which might have been enough to have reclaimed him. It did not, but he proceeded in his treason, and in the most mischievous and treacherous performing of it, to betray him with a kiss.

He kisses in a biting kiss, and conveys treason in a testimony of love. It is an apophthegm of Luther's, A persecutor is ill, but he that persuades me to anything which might submit me to the persecutor's rage is worse; but he that hath persuaded me and then betrays me is worst of all. When all that happens, when a man's enemies are the men of his own house, when amongst ourselves men arise and draw away the disciples, remember that Judas defamed this kiss before: he kissed his Master and so betrayed him.

I am but a man myself, says St Augustine, and I look but for men to live amongst. I cannot hope to have my house clearer than Noah's Ark, and there, in eight, there was one ill; nor in Jacob's house, and there the son went up to the father's bed; nor than David's, and there the brother forced the sister; nor than Christ's, and there Judas betrayed his Master, and with a kiss. Which alone does so aggravate the fact as that for the atrocity and heinousness thereof three of the Evangelists remember that circumstance, that he betrayed him with a kiss; and as though it might seem impossible, incredible, to man that it could be so, St John omits that circumstance, that it was done with a kiss.

In Joab's treachery, in Judas's treason, is the kiss defamed, and in the carnal and licentious abuse of it it is every day depraved. They mistake the matter much that think all adultery is below the girdle. A man darts out an adultery with his eye, in a wanton look, and he wraps up adultery with his fingers, in a wanton letter; and he breathes in an adultery with his lips, in a wanton kiss. But though this act of love be so defamed both ways—by treachery, by licentiousness—yet God chooses this metaphor, he bids us 'Kiss the Son'.*

It is a true and a useful rule that ill men have been types of Christ and ill actions figures of good. Much more may things not ill in themselves, though deflected and distorted to ill, be restored to good again. And therefore doth God, in more than this one place, expect our love in a kiss. For if we be truly in love with him it will be a holy and an acceptable metaphor unto us; else it will have a carnal and a fastidious [loathsome] taste. He that comes to read Solomon's love song, and loves not him upon whom that song is directed, will rather endanger than profit himself by that reading. A heart frozen and congealed with the love of this world is not capable, not sensible, of the fires of the Holy Ghost. As Greek itself is barbarous to him that understands not Greek, so is the language of love, and the kiss which the Holy Ghost speaks of here, to him that always grovelleth and holds his face upon the earth.

From the sermon preached at the marriage of Mistress Margaret Washington at the Church of St Clement Danes, 30 May 1621

The second use of marriage was for children, and therefore St Augustine puts the case, to contract before that they will have no children makes it no marriage but an adultery. To deny themselves to one another is as much against marriage as to give themselves to another; to hinder it by physic or any other practice, nay, to hinder it so far as by a deliberate wish or prayer against children, consists not well with this second use of marriage. And yet, in this second use we do not so much consider generation as regeneration, not so much procreation as education, nor propagation as transplantation, of children. For this world might be filled full enough of children though there were no marriage. But Heaven could not be filled, nor the places of the fallen angels supplied, without that care of children's religious education which from parents in lawful marriage they are likeliest to receive. How infinite and how miserable a circle of sin do we make if, as we sinned in our parents' loins before we were born, so we sin in our children's actions when we are dead, by having given them either example or liberty of sinning.

We have a fearful commination from God upon a good

---

* The text was Psalms 2.12: 'Kiss the Son, lest he be angry, and you perish from the way, when his wrath is kindled but a little. Blessed are all they that put their trust in him.'

man, upon Eli, for his not restraining the licentiousness of his sons: I will do a thing in Israel, says God there, at which every man's ears that hears it shall tingle. And it was executed: Eli fell down and broke his neck. We have also a promise of consolation to women for children: She shall be saved in childbearing, says the Apostle. But as Chrysostom and others of the ancients observe and interpret that place, it is not if she but if they — if the children — continue in faith, in charity, in holiness and sobriety. The salvation of the parents hath so much relation to the children's goodness as that if they be ill by the parents' example or indulgence, the parents are as guilty as the children. Art thou afraid thy child should be stung by a snake, and wilt thou let him play with the old Serpent, in opening himself to all temptations? Art thou afraid to let him walk in an ill air, and art thou content to let him stand in that pestilent air that is made of nothing but oaths, and execrations of blasphemous mouths, round about him? It is St Chystostom's complaint, we pay dear for our children's damnation by paying at first for all their childish vanities, and then for their sinful insolencies at any rate; and we might have them saved, and ourselves to the bargain — which were a frugal way, and a debt well hedged in — for much less than our, and their, damnation stands us in.

If you have a desire, says that blessed Father, to leave them certainly rich, do some such thing for God's service as you may leave God in their debt. He cannot break: his estate is inexhaustible. He will not break promise nor break day. He will show mercy unto thousands in them that love him and keep his commandments. And here also may another shower of his benedictions fall upon them whom he hath prepared and presented here: Let the wife be as a fruitful vine, and their children like olive plants. To thy glory, let the parents express the love of parents and the children, to thy glory, the obedience of children, till they both lose that secular name of parents and children and meet all alike, in one new name, all Saints in thy Kingdom and fellow-servants there.

Whitehall on the First Friday in Lent, 8 March 1622

We die every day, and we die all the day long. And because we are not absolutely dead we call that an eternity, an eternity of dying. And is there comfort in that state? Why, that is the state of Hell itself: eternal dying, and not dead.

[Death] comes equally to us all, and makes us all equal

when it comes. The ashes of an oak in the chimney are no epitaph of that oak, to tell me how high or how large that was. It tells me not what flocks it sheltered while it stood, nor what men it hurt when it fell. The dust of great persons' graves is speechless too: it says nothing, it distinguishes nothing. As soon the dust of a wretch whom thou wouldest not, as of a prince whom thou couldest not look upon, will trouble thine eyes if the wind blow it thither. And when a whirlwind hath blown the dust of the churchyard into the church, and the man sweeps out the dust of the church into the churchyard, who will undertake to sift those dusts again and to pronounce, This is the patrician, this is the noble flower, and this the yeomanly, this the plebeian bran?

Death is the last, and in that respect the worst, enemy. In an enemy that appears at first, when we are or may be provided against him, there is some of that which we call honour, but in the enemy that reserves himself unto the last, and attends our weak estate, there is more danger. Keep it where I intend it, in that which is my sphere, the conscience. If mine enemy meet me betimes in my youth, in an object of temptation (so Joseph's enemy met him in Potiphar's wife), yet if I do not adhere to this enemy, dwell upon a delightful meditation of that sin, if I do not feel and foment that sin, assist and encourage that sin, by high diet, wanton discourse, other provocation, I shall have reason on my side and I shall have grace on my side, and I shall have the history of a thousand that have perished by that sin on my side. Even spittles [hospitals for the poor] will give me soldiers to fight for me by their miserable example against that sin. Nay, perchance sometimes the virtue of that woman whom I solicit will assist me. But when I lie under the hands of that enemy that hath reserved himself to the last, to my last bed—then, when I shall be able to stir no limb in any other measure than a fever or a palsy shall shake them, when everlasting darkness shall have an inchoation in the present dimness of mine eyes, and the everlasting gnashing in the present chattering of my teeth, and the everlasting worm in the present gnawing of the agonies of my body and anguishes of my mind, when the last enemy shall watch my remediless body and my disconsolate soul there, there, where not the physician in his way, perchance not the priest in his, shall be able to give any assistance, and when he hath sported himself with my misery upon that stage, my deathbed, [and] shall shift the scene and throw me from that bed into the grave, and there triumph over me— God knows how many generations, till the Redeemer, my

Redeemer, the Redeemer of all me, body as well as soul, come again. As death is the enemy which watches me at my last weakness, and shall hold me when I shall be no more, till that angel come who shall say, and swear, that time shall be no more—in that consideration, in that apprehension, he is the powerfullest, the fearfullest, enemy. And yet even there this enemy shall be destroyed.

From a sermon preached at the Spittle, Easter Monday 1622

I may be bold to say, that this city hath the ablest preaching clergy of any city in Christendom. Must I be fain to say, that the clergy of this city hath the poorest entertainment of any city that can come into comparison with it? It is so. And that to which they have pretences and claims to be farther due to them is detained, not because that which they have is enough, but because that which they claim is too much. The circumstance of the quantity and proportion keeps off the consideration of the very right, so that this clergy is therefore poor because they should be rich, therefore kept without any part because so great a part seems to belong to them.

Grieve not the spirit of God, grieve not the spiritual man, the man of God neither. He that preaches from a sad heart, under the sense of a great charge and small means, cannot preach cheerfully to you. Provide, says the Apostle, that they who watch over your souls may do it with joy and not with grief—for, says he, that's unprofitable for you. You receive not so much profit by them as you might do if they might attend your service entirely, when [whereas] they are distracted with chargeable suits abroad, or macerated [crushed] with penurious fortunes at home.

Consider how much other professionals—of arms, of merchandise, of agriculture, of law itself—are decayed of late. And thence (though not only thence) it is that so many more in our times than ever before, of honourable and worshipful families, apply themselves to our profession, to the Ministry. Let therefore this light shine in your hearts. Bless God for this blessed increase, and shine in your tongues. Glorify God in a good interpretation of the actions of his Ministers, and shine in your hands. Cherish and comfort them so that they may not be put to bread and water that give you bread and wine, nor mourn in smoky corners who bring you the sunshine of the glorious Gospel, the Gospel of consolation, into the congregation.

Lincoln's Inn, Ascension Day 1622

If God punish our negligence of his former favours so far as to rain snares even at our tables, that almost at every table that we come to we shall meet some that would ensnare us, is not this caveat necessary in these times: Take heed that thou be not snared? Since they have laid their snares, they will take some, and thou mayest be one. And therefore take heed of their snares.

There is a snare laid for thy son, a persuasion to send him to foreign universities. They will say, not to change his religion—for religion, let him do as he shall see cause—but there he shall be better taught and better bred than at home. There is a snare laid for thy servants. What need they come to church, they have nothing to lose. Who will indict them? Who will persecute them? And yet in due time such servants may do the cause as much good as the masters. There is a snare laid for thy wife. Her religion, say they, doth not hinder her husband's preferment. Why should she refuse to apply herself to them? We have used to speak proverbially of a curtain sermon, as of a shrewd thing. But a curtain Mass, a curtain Requiem, a snare in thy bed, a snake in thy bosom, is somewhat worse. I know not what name we may give to such a woman's husband, but I am sure such a wife hath committed adultery—spiritual adultery—and that with her husband's knowledge, call him what you will.

There is a snare for thy servant, for thy son, for thy wife, and for thy fame too; and how far soever thou wert from it, they will have the world believe thou diedst a Papist. If thy declination be towards profit, if thy bias turn that way, there is a snare in the likeness of a chain, of a jewel, a pension. If it be society and conversation, there may be a snare in meeting more good company at Masses than at thy parish church. If it be levity, and affectation of new things, there may be a snare of things so new in that religion as that this Kingdom never saw them yet, not then when this Kingdom was of that religion.

The Apostle doth not say that we ourselves and our own concupiscences shall not separate us from God. So, though excommunications have not, invasions have not, powder plots have not, yet God knows what those snares may work upon us. *In laqueo suo comprehendantur*, says David. Now *laqueus* is a snare, as their malice intends it for us; and *laqueus* is a halter, as our laws intend it for them. And *in laqueo suo*, as it's theirs, let them be taken. Our good and great God, in his power and mercy, hath destroyed idolatry, but in his wisdom he hath left exercise for our diligence in some danger, and that danger is a snare. And therefore, take heed thou be not snared.

St Paul's, Midsummer Day 1622

How far then is that wretched and sinful man from giving any testimony or glory to Christ in his life, who never comes to the knowledge and consideration why he was sent into this life, who is so far from doing his errand that he knows not what his errand was, nor whether he received any errand or no. Thou passest through this world like a flash, like a lightning, whose beginning or end nobody knows, like an *ignis fatuus* in the air which does not only not give light for any use, but not so much as portend or signify anything. And thou passest out of the world as thy hand passes out of a basin of water, which may be somewhat the fouler for thy washing in it but retains no other impression of thy having been there. And so does the world for thy life in it.

Poor bankrupt, that hast sinned out thy soul so profusely, so lavishly that thou darest not cast up thine accounts, thou darest not ask thyself whether thou have any soul left! How far art thou from giving any testimony to Christ that thou darest not testify to thyself, nor hear thy conscience take knowledge of thy transgressions, but haddest rather sleep out thy days, or drink out thy days, than leave one minute for compunction to lay hold on.

God cannot be mocked, saith the Apostle, nor God cannot be blinded. He seeth all the way, and at thy last gasp he will make thee see too, through the multiplying glass, the spectacle, of desperation. O bestow as much labour as thou hast done to find corners for sin, to find out those sins in those corners where thou hast hid them. As princes give pardons by their own hands but send judges to execute justice, come to [God] for mercy in the acknowledgement of thy sins and stay not till justice come to thee, when he makes inquisition for blood.

Go home with this spark of God's spirit in you, and there look upon your rentals, and know your oppressions and extortions; look upon your shop books and know your deceits and falsifications; look upon your wardrobes and know your excesses; look upon your children's faces and know your fornications. Till then, till you come to this scrutiny, this survey, this sifting of the conscience, if we should cry Peace, peace, yet there were no peace.

Paul's Cross, 15 September 1622. From a sermon preached on the orders of James I and printed 'by commandment'

If we should tell some men that Calvin's Institutions were a catechism, would they not love catechising the better for that name? And would they not love it the better if they gave me leave to tell them that of which I had the experience? An artificer of this city brought his child to me, to admire (as truly there was much reason) the capacity, the memory, especially of the child. It was but a girl, and not above nine years of age: her parents said less, some years less. We could scarce propose any verse of any book or chapter of the Bible but that that child would go forward without book. I began to catechise this child. And truly she understood nothing of the Trinity, nothing of any of those fundamental points which must save us. And the wonder was doubled, how she knew so much, how so little.

Candlemas 1623

That soul that is accustomed to direct herself to God upon every occasion, that, as a flower at sun-rising, conceives a sense of God in every beam of his and spreads and dilates itself towards him in a thankfulness in every small blessing that he sheds upon her; that soul that, as a flower at the sun's declining, contracts and gathers in and shuts up herself as though she had received a blow whensoever she hears her Saviour wounded by an oath or blasphemy or execration; that soul who, whatsoever string be struck in her, bass or treble, her high or her low estate, is ever tuned toward God—that soul prays sometimes when it does not know that it prays. I hear that man name God and ask him, What said you? And perchance he cannot tell. But I remember that he casts forth some of those darts of a devout soul (as St Augustine calls them) which, though they have not particular deliberations and be not formal prayers, yet they are the pregnant evidences and blessed fruits of a religious custom. Much more is it true which St Bernard says there of them, God hears that voice of the heart which the heart itself hears not—that is, at first considers not.

Those occasional and transitory prayers, and those fixed and stationary prayers for which, many times, we bind ourselves to private prayer at such a time, are payments of this debt in such pieces, and in such sums, as God, no doubt, accepts at our hands. Begin therefore to pay these debts to thyself betimes. For, as we told you at the beginning, some of you are too tender at noon, some at evening. Even at your noon and warmest sunshine of prosperity you owe yourselves a true information how you came by that prosperity, who gave it to you, and why he gave it. Let not the olive boast of her own fatness, nor the fig tree of her own sweetness, nor the vine of her own fruitfulness, for we were all but brambles. Let no man say, I could not miss a fortune, for I have studied all my youth. How many men have studied more nights than he hath done hours, and studied themselves blind and mad in the mathematics, and yet wither in beggary in a corner? Let him never add, But I studied in a useful and gainful profession. How many have done so too, and yet never compassed the favour of a Judge? And how many that have had all that have struck upon a rock, even at full sea, and perished there?

As for spiritual happiness, it is not in him that would run, nor in him that doth, but only in God that prospers his course. So, for the things of this world, it is in vain to rise early and to lie down late, and to eat the bread of sorrow. For except the Lord build the house, they labour in vain; except the Lord keep the city, the watchman waketh but in vain. Come not therefore to say, I studied more than my fellows and therefore am richer than my fellows. But say, God that gave me my contemplations at first gave me my practice after, and hath given me his blessing now.

How many men have worn their brains upon other studies and spent their time and themselves therein? How many men have studied more in thine own profession and yet, for diffidence in themselves, or some disfavour from others, have not had thy practice? How many men have been equal to thee in study, in practice, and in getting too, and yet upon a wanton confidence that that world would always last, or upon the burden of many children and an expensive breeding of them, or for other reasons which God hath found in his ways, are left upon the sand at last, in a low fortune? Whilst the sun shines upon thee in all these, pay thyself the debt of knowing whence and why all this came, for else thou canst not know how much or how little is thine, nor thou canst not come to restore that which is none of thine but unjustly wrung from others. Pay therefore this debt of surveying thine estate and then pay thyself thine own too, by a cheerful enjoying and using that which is truly thine, and do not deny nor defraud thyself of those things which are thine, and so become a wretched debtor to thy back or to thy belly, as though the world had not enough or God knew not what were enough for thee.

Pay this debt to thyself of looking into thy debts, of surveying, of severing, of serving thyself with that which is truly thine, at thy noon, in the best of thy fortune, and in the strength of thy understanding, that when thou comest to pay thy other, thy last debt, to thyself, which is to open a door out of this world by the dissolution of body and soul, thou have not all thy money to tell over when the sun is ready to set, all the account to make of every bag of money and of every quillet [narrow strip] of land—whose it is, and whether it be his who looks for it from thee, or his from whom it was taken by thee; whether it belong to thine heir that weeps joyful tears behind the curtain, or belong to him that weeps true and bloody tears in the hole in a prison. There will come a time when that land that thou leavest shall not be his land, when it shall be nobody's land, when it shall be no land, for the earth must perish. There will be a time when there shall be no manors, no acres in the world, and yet there shall lie manors and acres upon thy soul, when land shall be no more, when time shall be no more, and thou pass away, not into the land of the living but of eternal death.

Then the accuser will be ready to interline the schedules of thy debts, thy sins, and insert false debts by abusing an over-tenderness which may be in thy conscience then, in thy last sickness, in thy deathbed. Then he will be ready to add a cypher more to thy debts, and make hundreds thousands, and abuse the faintness which may be in thy conscience then, in thy last sickness, in thy deathbed. Then he will be ready to abuse even thy confidence in God, and bring thee to think that, as a pirate ventures boldly home, though all that he hath be stolen, if he be rich enough to bribe for a pardon, so, howsoever those families perish whom thou hast ruined, and those whole parishes whom thou hast depopulated, thy soul may go confidently home too if thou bribe God then with an hospital, or a Fellowship in a college, or a legacy to any pious use in appearance and in the eye of the world.

From a sermon preached at Whitehall, the First Friday in Lent
1623

Here, in this world, we who stay lack those who are gone out of it. We know they shall never come to us; and when we shall go to them, whether we shall know them or no, we dispute. They who think that it conduces to the perfection of happiness in Heaven that we should know one another think piously if they think we shall. For as, for the maintenance of public peace, States and Churches may think diversely in points of religion that are not fundamental, and yet both be true and orthodox Churches, so, for the exaltation of private devotion in points that are not fundamental, diverse men may think diversely and both be equally good Christians. Whether we shall know them there is problematical and equal; that we shall not till then is dogmatical and certain. Therefore we weep.*

I know there are philosophers that will not let us weep, nor lament the death of any; and I know that in the Scriptures there are rules, and that there are instructions conveyed in that example, that David left mourning as soon as the child was dead. And I know that there are authors of a middle nature, above the philosophers and below the Scriptures, the apocryphal books; and I know it is said there, Comfort thyself, for thou shalt do him no good that is dead, thou shalt make thyself worse and worse, in the worst degree. But yet all this is but of inordinate lamentation. For in the same place the same wise man says, My son, let thy tears fall down over the dead; weep bitterly and make great moan, as he is worthy. When our Saviour Christ had uttered his *Consummatum est*, all was finished and their rage could do him no more harm. When he had uttered his *In manus tuas*, he had delivered, and God had received, his soul. Yet how did the whole frame of nature mourn in eclipses and tremble in earthquakes and dissolve and shed in pieces in the opening of the Temple, because he was dead!

Truly, to see the hand of a great and mighty monarch, that hand that hath governed the civil sword, the sword of justice, at home, and drawn and sheathed the foreign sword of war abroad; to see that hand lie dead and not be able to nip or fillip away one of his own worms; to see the brain of a great and religious counsellor (and God bless all from making, all from calling, any great that is not religious), to see that brain

* The text was John 11.35: 'Jesus wept.'

that produced means to becalm gusts at council tables, storms
in parliaments, tempests in popular commotions, to see that
brain produce nothing but swarms of worms and no proclama-
tion to disperse them; to see a reverend prelate that hath resisted heretics and schismatics all his life fall like one of them
by death, and perchance be called one of them when he is
dead; to recollect all, to see great men made no men, to be
sure that they shall never come to us, not to be sure that we
shall know them when we come to them; to see the lieutenants
and images of God, kings, and sinews of the State, religious
counsellors, the spirit of the Church, zealous prelates; and
then to see vulgar, ignorant, wicked and facinorous men
thrown all by one hand of death into one cart, into one common tideboat, one hospital, one almshouse, one prison, the
grave, in whose dust no man can say, This is the king, this is
the slave, this is the bishop, there is the heretic, this is the
counsellor, this is the fool—even this miserable equality of so
unequal persons, by so foul a hand, is the subject of this
lamentation.

Good friends, useful friends, though they may commit
some errors, and though for some misbehaviours they may
stink in our nostrils, must not be derelicted, abandoned to
themselves. Many a son, many a good heir, finds an ill air
from his father: his father's life stinks in the nostrils of all the
world and he hears everywhere exclamations upon his father's
usury and extortion and oppression. Yet it becomes him by a
better life, and by all other means, to rectify and redeem his
father's fame. *Quatriduanus est* [he hath been four days dead]
is no plea for my negligence in my family—to say, my son or
my servant hath proceeded so far in ill courses that now it is
no purpose to go about to reform him.

Truly it is no very charitable disposition if I give all at my
death to others [yet] keep all all my life to myself. For how
many families have we seen shaked, ruined, by this distemper,
that though the father mean to alienate nothing of the inheritance from the son at his death, yet because he affords him not
a competent maintenance in his life, he submits his son to an
encumbering of his fame with ignominious shiftings, and an
encumbering of the estates with irrecoverable debts. I may
mean to feast a man plentifully at Christmas, and that man
may starve before in Lent. Great persons may think it is in
their power to give life to persons and actions by their benefits
when they will, and before that will be up and ready both may
become incapable of their benefits. Jesus would not give this
family [of Lazarus], whom he pretended to love, occasion of

jealousy, of suspicion, that he neglected them. And therefore, though he came not presently to that great work which he intended at last, yet he left them not comfortless by the way: Jesus wept.

Every man is but a sponge, and but a sponge filled with tears. And whether you lay your right hand or your left upon a full sponge, it will weep. Whether God lay his left hand, temporal calamities, or his right hand, temporal prosperity, even that temporal prosperity comes always accompanied with so much envy in others, as that that man who abounds most, that sponge, shall weep.

I am far from concluding all to be impenitent that do not actually weep and shed tears. I know there are constitutions, complexions, that do not afford them. And yet the worst epithet which the best poet could fix upon Pluto himself was to call him *illachrymabilis*, a person that could not weep. But to weep for other things and not to weep for sin, or, if not to tears, yet not to come to that tenderness, to that melting, to that thawing, that resolving of the bowels which good souls feel: this is a sponge that is a sponge dried up into a pumice stone. The lightness, the hollowness of a sponge is there still, but (as the pumice is) dried in the Etna of lust, of ambition, of other flames in this world.

To mourn passionately for the love of this world which is decrepit and upon the deathbed, or immoderately for the death of any that is passed out of this world, is not the right use of tears. That hath good use which Chrysologus notes, that when Christ was told of Lazarus's death, he said he was glad. When he came to raise him to life, then he wept. For though his Disciples gained by it (they were confirmed by a miracle), though the family gained by it (they had their Lazarus again), yet Lazarus himself lost by it, by being re-imprisoned, recommitted, resubmitted to the manifold incommodities of this world.

The Fathers have infinitely delighted themselves in this descant, the blessed effect of holy tears. He amongst them that remembers [reminds] us that in the old law all sacrifices were washed, he means that our best sacrifice, even prayer itself, receives an improvement, a dignity, by being washed in tears. He that remembers us that if any room of our house be on fire we run for water, means that in all temptations we should have recourse to tears. He that tells us that money being put in a basin is seen at a farther distance if there be water in the basin than if it be empty, means also that our most precious devotions receive an addition, a multiplication, by holy tears. A hard heart is a foul heart [says St Bernard].

Would you shut up the Devil in his own channel, his channel of brimstone, and make that worse? St Jerome tells the way: Thy tears torment him more than the fires of Hell. Will you needs have holy water? Truly, true tears are the holiest water. And for Purgatory, it is liberally confessed by a Jesuit, One tear will do thee as much good as all the flames of Purgatory.

All our sins are written in God's book, says St Chrysostom. If there I can fill my sponge with tears, and so wipe out all my sins out of that book, it is a blessed use of the sponge.

To weep for sin is not a damp of melancholy, to sigh for sin is not a vapour of the spleen. But as Monica's confessor said still unto her, in the behalf of her son St Augustine, the son of these tears cannot perish.

Weep these tears truly and God shall perform to thee, first, that promise which he makes in Isaiah, The Lord shall wipe all tears from thy face, all that are fallen by any occasion of calamity here in the Militant Church; and he shall perform that promise which he makes in the Revelation. The Lord shall wipe all tears from thine eyes: that is, dry up the fountain of tears, remove all occasion of tears hereafter, in the Triumphant Church.

St Paul's, in the evening, Easter Day 1623

But what needs all this heat, all this animosity, all this vehemence, about the Resurrection? May not man be happy enough in Heaven though his body never come thither? Upon what ground will ye ground the Resurrection? Upon the omnipotence of God? The omnipotence of God hath always been the sanctuary of heretics—that is, always their refuge—in all their incredible doctrines: God is able to do it, can do it. You confess, the Resurrection is a miracle, and miracles are not to be multiplied nor imagined without necessity, and what necessity of bodies in Heaven?

Beloved, we make the ground and foundation of the Resurrection to be not merely the omnipotency of God, for God will not do all that he can do. But the ground is the almighty will of God revealed by him to us. We know, out of the omnipotence of God, it may be, and we know out of the Scriptures it must be. That works upon our faith, this upon our reason, that it is man that must be saved, man that must be damned. And to constitute a man there must be a body as well as a soul. Nay, the immortality of the soul will not so well lie in proof without a resuming of the body.

Naturally the soul and body are united. When they are separated by death it is contrary to nature, and consequently the soul is the less perfect for this separation. And it is not likely that the perfect natural state of the soul, which is to be united to the body, should last but three or four score years, and in most much less, and the unperfect state—that in the separation—should last eternally, for ever. So that either the body must be believed to live again, or the soul believed to die.

From a sermon preached upon the Penitential Psalms, April/June 1623

He that goes about his worldly business, and goes about it in God's name, in the fear and favour of God, remains in God's presence still. When the angels of God are sent to visit his children in the midst of Sodom, or where they lie and languish in sordid and nasty corners, and in the loathsomeness of corrupt and infectious diseases, or where they faint in miserable dungeons, this commission, Go to that Sodom, to that Spittle, to that dungeon, puts not those angels out of the presence of God. No descent into Hell, of what kind soever you conceive that descent into Hell to have been, put the Son of God out of Heaven by descending into Hell. No leave, no commandment that God gives us to do the works of our calling here excludes us from him. But as the Saints of God shall follow the Lamb wheresoever he goes in Heaven, so the Lamb of God shall follow his Saints wheresoever they go upon earth, if they walk sincerely.

From a sermon preached at St Paul's, in the evening, Easter Day 1624

We wonder, and justly, at the effusion, at the pouring out of blood, in the sacrifices of the old law; that that little country, scarce bigger than some three of our shires, should spend more cattle in some few days' sacrifice at some solemnities, and every year in the sacrifices of the whole year, than perchance this Kingdom could give to any use. Seas of blood and yet but brooks, tons of blood and yet but basins, compared with the sacrifices, the sacrifices of the blood of men in the persecution of the Primitive Church. For every ox of the Jew

The title-page of Donne's *LXXX Sermons*, published by his son in 1640. The inscription above the author's portrait reads: 'Bee Wise as Serpents but inosent as Dovs'

the Christian spent a man, and for every sheep and lamb a mother and her child; and for every herd of cattle sometimes a town of inhabitants, a legion of soldiers, all martyred at once. So that they did not stand to fill their martyrologies with names but with numbers, they had not room to say, such a day such a Bishop, such a day such a General, but the day of five hundred, the day of five thousand. Martyrs, and the martyrdom of a city or the martyrdom of an army—this was not a Red Sea such as the Jews passed, a sinus [bay], a creek, an arm, an inlet, a gut of a sea, but a red ocean that over-flowed and surrounded all parts. And from the depth of this sea God raised them, and such was their resurrection: such as that they, which suffered, lay and bled with more ease than the executioner stood and sweated, and embraced the fire more fervently than he blew it; and many times had this triumph in their death, that even the executioner himself was, in the act of execution, converted to Christ and executed with them. Such was their resurrection.

From the second sermon preached by the Author after he came to St Dunstan's, 25 April 1624

There is a fear which grows out of a second nature, custom, and so is half natural to those men that have it. The custom of the place we live in, or of the times we live in, or of the company we live in. Topical customs of such a place, chronical customs of such an age, personal customs of such a company. The time or the place or the persons in power have advanced and drawn into fashion and reputation some vices, and such men as depend upon them are afraid not to concur with them in their vices. For amongst persons and in times and places that are vicious, an honest man is a rebel: he goes against that State and that government which is the kingdom of sin. Amongst drunkards, a sober man is a spy upon them. Amongst blasphemers, a prayer is a libel against them. And amongst dissolute and luxurious persons a chaste man is a Bridewell, his person, his presence is a house of correction.

In vicious times and companies a good man is unacceptable and cannot prosper. And because, as amongst merchants, men trade half upon stock and half upon credit, so in all other courses, because men rise according to the opinion and estimation in them upon whom they depend, they are afraid to cross the vices of the time so far as by being virtuous in their own particular. They are afraid it will be called a singularity, and a schismatical and seditious disposition, and taken for a reproach and a rebuke laid upon their betters, if they be not content to be as ill as those their betters are.

Now the fear of the Lord brings the *Quo Warranto* against all these privileged sins and privileged places and persons, and overthrows all these customs and prescriptions. The fear of the Lord is not a topical, not a chronical, not a personal, but a catholic, a canonical, a circular, a universal fear. It goes through all, and over all. And when this half-natural fear, this fear grown out of custom, suggests to me that if I be thus tender-conscienced, if I startle at an oath, if I be sick at a health, if I cannot conform myself to the vices of my betters I shall lose my master, my patron, my benefactor, this fear of the Lord enters, and presents the infallible loss of a far greater master and patron and benefactor if I comply with the other. And therefore, as you were called hither to learn how to regulate the natural fear, that that fear do not deject you into a diffidence of God's mercy, so come hither to learn the fear of God against this half-natural fear. That is, be guided by the Word of God how far you are to serve the turns of those persons upon whom ye depend, and when to leave their commandments unperformed.

From a sermon preached at St Dunstan's, Trinity Sunday 1624

As we consider what we have received in Baptism, so, if we be not only (as St Augustine speaks) white-limbed Christians, Christians on the outside, we must consider what we are to do upon all this. We are baptised, says St Cyprian, not in a Father without a Son, nor in either or both without a Holy Ghost, but in the fullness of the Trinity. And this mystery of the Trinity is, says St Jerome, the rule of our faith: this only regulates our faith, that we believe aright of the Trinity. It is, says St Basil, as though there were but this one article: it is, says he, the foundation, the sum, it is all the Christian religion to believe aright of the Trinity. By this we are distinguished from the Jews, who accept no plurality of persons; and by this we are distinguished from the Gentiles, who make as many several persons as there are several powers and attributes belonging to God. Our religion, our holy philosophy, our learning, as it is rooted in Christ, so it is not limited, not determined, in Christ alone. We are not baptised in his name alone, but our study must be the whole Trinity, for he that believes not in the Holy Ghost as well as in Christ is no

Christian. And as that is true which St Augustine says, as
there is not so steep a place to clamber up, nor so slippery a
place to fall upon, as the doctrine of the Trinity, so is that also
true which he adds: There is not so fulfilling, so accomplish-
ing, so abundant an article as that of the Trinity, for it is all
Christianity.

*From a sermon preached to the Earl of Exeter and his Company
in his Chapel at St John's, 13 June 1624*

Our first step then, in this first part, is the sociableness, the
communicableness, of God. He loves holy meetings, he loves
the Communion of Saints, the household of the faithful. His
delight, says Solomon, is to be with the sons of men, and that
the sons of men should be with him. Religion is not a melancholy. The Spirit of God is not a damp, the Church is not a
grave. It is a fold, it is an ark, it is a net, it is a city, it is a kingdom, not only a house but a house that hath many mansions
in it. Still it is a plural thing, consisting of many. And very
good grammarians amongst the Hebrews have thought and
said that that name by which God notifies himself to the
world, in the very beginning of Genesis, which is *Elohim*, as
it is a plural word there, so it hath no singular. They say we
cannot name God but plurally, so sociable, so communicable,
so extensive, so derivative of himself is God and so manifold
are the beams and the emanations that flow out from him.

    There is but one God. But yet was that one God ever alone?
There were more generations (infinitely infinite) before the
world was made than there have been minutes since it was
made. All that while, there were no creatures. But yet was
God alone any one minute of all this? Was there not always a
Father and a Son and a Holy Ghost? And had not they always
an acquiescence in one another, an exercise of affection (as we
may so say), a love, a delight and a complacency towards one
another? So, as the Father could not be without the Son and
the Holy Ghost, so as neither Son nor Holy Ghost could be
without the Father nor without one another, God was from
all eternity collected into one God yet from all eternity he derived himself into Three Persons. God could not be so alone
but that there have been Three Persons as long as there hath
been one God.

    Had God company enough of himself? Was he satisfied in
the Three Persons? We see he proceeded further. He came
to a creation. And as soon as he had made light (which was

his first creature), he took a pleasure in it. He said it was good. He was glad of it—glad of the sea, glad of the earth, glad of the sun and moon and stars. And he said of every one, It is good. But when he had made all, peopled the whole world, brought all creatures together, then he was very glad, and then he said not only that it was good but that it was very good. God was so far from being alone as that he found not the fullness of being well till all was made, till all creatures met together in an host, as Moses calls it. Then the good was extended into very good.

Did God satisfy himself with this visible and discernible world with all on earth and all between that and him? Were those four monarchies, the four elements, and all the subjects of those four monarchies (if all the four elements have creatures) company enough for God? Was that heptarchy, the seven kingdoms of the seven planets, conversation enough for him? Let every star in the firmament be (so some take them to be) a several world, was all this enough? We see, God drew persons nearer to him than sun or moon or stars or anything which is visible and discernible to us. He created angels. How many? How great? Arithmetic lacks numbers to express them, proportion lacks dimensions to figure them. So far was God from being alone.

And yet God had not shed himself far enough. He had the Leviathan, the whale in the sea, and Behemoth and the elephant upon the land; and all these great heavenly bodies in the way, and angels in their infinite numbers and manifold offices in Heaven. But because angels could not propagate nor make more angels, he enlarged his love in making man, that so he might enjoy all natures at once, and have the nature of angels and the nature of earthly creatures in one person. God would not be without man, nor he would not come single, not alone, to the making of man. But it is let us—us—make man. God, in his whole council, in his whole college, in his whole society, in the whole Trinity, makes man, in whom the whole nature of all the world should meet.

St Paul's, in the evening, Christmas Day 1624

The air is not so full of motes, of atoms, as the Church is of mercies. And as we can suck in no part of air but we take in those motes, those atoms, so here in the congregation we cannot suck in a word from the preacher, we cannot speak, we cannot sigh a prayer to God, but that that whole breath and air is made of mercy. But we call not upon you to consider God's ordinary mercy, that which he exhibits to all in the ministry of his Church, nor his miraculous mercy, his extraordinary deliverances of States and Churches. But we call upon particular consciences to call to mind God's occasional mercies to them, such mercies as a regenerate man will call mercies, though a natural man would call them accidents, or occurrences, or contingencies.

A man wakes at midnight full of unclean thoughts and he hears a passing bell. This is an occasional mercy, if he call that his own knell, and consider how unfit he was to be called out of the world then, how unready to receive that voice, 'Fool, this night they shall fetch away thy soul.' The adulterer, whose eye waits for the twilight, goes forth and casts his eyes upon forbidden houses, and would enter, and sees a 'Lord have mercy upon us' upon the door. This is an occasional mercy, if it brings him to know that they who lie sick of the plague within pass through a furnace, but, by God's grace, to Heaven; and he without carries his own furnace to Hell, his lustful loins to everlasting perdition. If I should declare what God hath done (done occasionally) for my soul, where he instructed me for fear of falling, where he raised me when I was fallen, perchance you would rather fix your thoughts upon my illness, and wonder at that, than at God's goodness, and glorify him in that; rather wonder at my sins than at his mercies, rather consider how ill a man I was than how good a God he is.

God made sun and moon to distinguish seasons, and day and night, and we cannot have the fruits of the earth but in their seasons. But God hath made no decree to distinguish the seasons of his mercies. In Paradise the fruits were ripe the first minute, and in Heaven it is always autumn, his mercies are ever in their maturity. We ask our daily bread, and God never says, you should have come yesterday; he never says, you must again tomorrow. But today, if you will hear his voice, today he will hear you. He brought light out of darkness, not out of a lesser light; he can bring thy summer out of winter, though thou have no spring. Though in the ways of fortune, or understanding, or conscience, thou hast been benighted till now, wintered and frozen, clouded and eclipsed, damped and benumbed, smothered and stupefied till now — now God comes to thee, not as in the dawning of the day, not as in the bud of the spring, but as the sun at noon, to illustrate all shadows. All occasions invite his mercies, and all times are his seasons.

Whom God loves, he loves to the end; and not only to their own end, to their death, but to his end; and his end is that he might love them still. His hailstones and his thunderbolts and his showers of blood (emblems and instruments of his judgements) fall down in a direct line and affect and strike some one person or place. His sun and moon and stars (emblems and instruments of his blessings) move circularly and communicate themselves to all. As the sun does not set to any nation, but withdraw itself and return again, God, in the exercise of his mercy, does not set to thy soul, though he benight it with an affliction.

Thou canst not have so good a title to a subsequent blessing as a former blessing: where thou art an ancient tenant, thou wilt look to be preferred before a stranger; and that is thy title to God's future mercies, if thou have been formerly accustomed to them. The sun is not weary with six thousand years' shining; God cannot be weary of doing good. And therefore never say, God hath given me these and these temporal things, and I have scattered them wastefully, surely he will give me no more; these and these spiritual graces, and I have neglected them, abused them, surely he will give me no more. For, for things created, we have instruments to measure them. We know the compass of a meridian and the depth of a diameter of the earth; and we know this even of the uppermost sphere in the heavens. But when we come to the throne of God himself, the orb of the Saints, and the angels that see his face, and the virtues and powers that flow from thence, we have no balance to weigh them, no instruments to measure them, no hearts to conceive them.

So, for temporal things, we know the most that man can have, for we know all the world. But for God's mercy and his spiritual graces, whatsoever he hath done for thy soul, or for any other, in applying himself to it, he can exceed that. Only he can raise a tower whose top shall reach to Heaven. God is a circle himself, and he will make thee one. Go not thou about to square either circle, to bring that which is equal in itself to angles and corners, into dark and suspicions of God or of thyself: that God can give, or that thou canst receive, no more mercy than thou hast had already.

1625-1631

St Paul's, 29 January 1625

I ask not Mary Magdalen, whether lightness were not a
burden (for sin is certainly, sensibly, a burden), but I ask
Susanna whether even chaste beauty were not a burden to
her. And I ask Joseph whether personal comeliness were not
a burden to him. I ask not Dives, who perished in the next
world, the question, but I ask them who are made examples
of Solomon's rule, of that sore evil (as he calls it), riches kept
to the owners thereof for their hurt, whether riches be not a
burden.

All our life is a continual burden, yet we must not groan; a
continual squeezing, yet we must not pant. And as in the
tenderness of our childhood we suffer, and yet are whipped if
we cry, so we are complained of if we complain and made
delinquents if we call the times ill. And that which adds
weight to weight, and multiplies the sadness of this consideration, is this, that still the best men have had most laid upon
them.

As soon as I hear God say that he hath found an upright
man that fears God and eschews evil, in the next lines I find a
commission to Satan to bring in Sabeans and Chaldeans upon
his cattle and servants, and fire and tempest upon his children,
and loathsome disease upon himself. As soon as I hear God
say that he hath found a man according to his own heart, I see
his sons ravish his daughters and then murder one another,
and then rebel against the father and put him into straits for
his life. As soon as I hear God testify of Christ at his Baptism,
This is my beloved Son, in whom I am well pleased, I find
that Son of his led up by the Spirit to be tempted of the Devil.
And after I hear God ratify the same testimony again at his
Transfiguration (This is my beloved Son, in whom I am well
pleased), I find that beloved Son of his deserted, abandoned,
and given over to Scribes and Pharisees and publicans and
Herodians, and priests and soldiers and people and Judges
and witnesses and executioners, and he that was called the
beloved Son of God and made partaker of the glory of Heaven
in this world, in his Transfiguration, is made now the sewer
of all the corruption, of all the sins of this world, as no Son of
God but a mere man, as no man but a contemptible worm—
as though the greatest weakness in this world were man, and

the greatest fault in man were to be good. Man is more miserable than other creatures, and good men more miserable than any other men.

I would always raise your hearts, and dilate your hearts, to a holy joy, to a joy in the Holy Ghost. There may be a just fear that men do not grieve enough for their sins. But there may be a just jealousy, and suspicion too, that they may fall into inordinate grief and diffidence of God's mercy. And God hath reserved us to such times as, being the later times, give us even the dregs and lees of misery to drink. For God hath accompanied and complicated almost all our bodily diseases of these times with an extraordinary sadness, a predominant melancholy, a faintness of heart, a cheerlessness, a joylessness of spirit. And therefore I return often to this endeavour of raising your hearts, dilating your hearts with a holy joy, joy in the Holy Ghost. For under the shadow of his wings you may, you should, rejoice.

Howling is the noise of Hell, singing the voice of Heaven; sadness the damp of Hell, rejoicing the serenity of Heaven. And he that hath not this joy here lacks one of the best pieces of his evidence for the joys of Heaven, and hath neglected or refused that earnest by which God uses to bind his bargain, that true joy in this world shall flow into the joy of Heaven as a river flows into the sea. This joy shall not be put out in death and a new joy kindled in me in Heaven. But as my soul, as soon as it is out of my body, is in Heaven, and does not stay for the possession of Heaven nor for the fruition of the sight of God, till it be ascended through air and fire and moon and sun and planets and firmament to that place which we conceive to be Heaven, but without the thousandth part of a minute's stop, [so] soon as it issues is in a glorious light, which is Heaven. For all the way to Heaven is Heaven; and as those angels which came from Heaven hither bring Heaven with them and are in Heaven here, so that soul that goes to Heaven meets Heaven here; and as those angels do not divest Heaven by coming, so these souls invest Heaven in their going.

As my soul shall not go towards Heaven, but go by Heaven to Heaven, to the Heaven of Heavens, so the true joy of a good soul in this world is the very joy of Heaven. And we go thither, not that, being without joy, we might have joy infused into us, but that, as Christ says, Our joy might be full, perfected, sealed with an everlastingness. For as he promises that no man shall take our joy from us, so neither shall death itself take it away, nor so much as interrupt it or discontinue it. But as in the face of death, when he lays hold upon me, and in the face of the Devil, when he attempts me, I shall see the face of God, so in the agonies of death, in the anguish of that dissolution, in the sorrows of that valediction, in the irreversibleness of that transmigration, I shall have a joy which shall no more evaporate than my soul shall evaporate: a joy that shall pass up, and put on a more glorious garment above, and be joy superinvested in glory. Amen.

From a sermon preached at St Paul's, the Sunday after the Conversion of St Paul, 30 January 1625

The Lord and only the Lord knows how to wound us out of love. More than that, how to wound us into love. More than all that, to wound us into love not only with him that wounds us but into love with the wound itself, with the very affliction that he inflicts upon us. The Lord knows how to strike us so that we shall lay hold upon that hand that strikes us and kiss that hand that wounds us. No man kills his enemy therefore that his enemy might have a better life in Heaven: that is not his end in killing him. It is God's end. Therefore he brings us to death, that by that gate he might lead us into life everlasting.

How low soever God be pleased to cast you, though it be to the earth, yet he does not so much cast you down in doing that as bring you home. Death is not a banishing of you out of this world, but it is a visitation of your kindred that lie in the earth; neither are any nearer of kin to you than the earth itself, and the worms of the earth.

You heap earth upon your souls and encumber them with more and more flesh by a superfluous and luxuriant diet. You add earth to earth in new purchases and measures not by acres but by manors, nor by manors but by shires. And there is a little quillet [narrow strip], a little close, worth all these: a quiet grave. And therefore, when thou readest that God makes thy bed in thy sickness, rejoice in this, not only that he makes that bed where thou dost lie, but that bed where thou shalt lie; that that God that made the whole earth is now making thy bed in the earth, a quiet grave where thou shalt sleep in peace till the angel's trumpet wake thee, at the Resurrection, to that Judgement where thy peace shall be made before thou comest, and writ and sealed in the blood of the Lamb.

From a sermon preached to the King's Majesty at Whitehall,
24 February 1625

How poor a clod of earth is a manor! How poor an inch, a shire! How poor a span, a kingdom! And how poor a pace, the whole world! And yet how prodigally we sell Paradise, Heaven, souls, consciences, immortality, eternity, for a few grains of this dust! What had Eve for Heaven? So little as that the Holy Ghost will not let us know what she had, nor what kind of fruit. Yet something Eve had. What had Adam for Heaven but a satisfaction that he had pleased an ill wife as St Jerome states his fault, that he ate that fruit lest he should cast her, whom he loved so much, into an inordinate dejection? But if he satisfied her, and his own uxoriousness, any satisfaction is not nothing.

But what had I for Heaven? Adam sinned and I suffer. I forfeited before I had any possession or could claim any interest. I had a punishment before I had a being, and God was displeased with me before I was I. I was built up scarce fifty years ago in my mother's womb, and I was cast down almost six thousand years ago in Adam's loins. I was born in the last age of the world, and died in the first.

How, and how justly, do we cry out against a man that hath sold a town or sold an army! And Adam sold the world. He sold Abraham and Isaac and Jacob and all the Patriarchs and all the Prophets. He sold Peter and Paul and both their regiments, both the glorious hemispheres of the world, the Jews and the Gentiles. He sold Evangelists and Apostles and Disciples, and the Disciple whom the Lord loved, and the beloved Mother of the Lord herself, say what they will to the contrary. And if Christ had not provided for himself by a miraculous generation, Adam had sold him. If Christ had been conceived in original sin he must have died for himself —nay, he could not have died for himself, but must have needed another Saviour.

Both St Jerome and St Ambrose, both which seem, in other places, to go another way, that only they are sold under sin which have abandoned and prostituted themselves to particular sins, do yet return to this sense, that because the embers, the spawn, the leaven of original sin remains, by Adam's sale, in the best, the best are sold under sin.

So the Jews were and so were we—sold by Adam to original sin very cheap. But in the second sale, as we are sold to actual and habitual sins by ourselves, cheaper. For so says this Prophet, You have sold yourselves for nothing. Ourselves, that is, all ourselves: our bodies to intemperance and riot and licentiousness, and our souls to a greediness of sin. And all this for nothing. For sin itself, for which we sell ourselves, is but a privation, and privations are nothing. What fruit had you of those things of which you are now ashamed, says the Apostle. Here is barrenness and shame. Barrenness is a privation of fruit, shame is a privation of that confidence which a good conscience administers; and when the Apostle tells them, they sold themselves for barrenness and shame, it was for privation, for nothing.

The adulterer waits for the twilight, says Job. The twilight comes, and serves his turn, and sin tonight looks like a purchase, like a treasure. But ask this sinner tomorrow, and he hath sold himself for nothing: for debility in his limbs, for darkness in his understanding, for emptiness in his purse, for absence of grace in his soul. And debility and darkness and emptiness and absence are privations, and privations are nothing.

All the name of substance or treasure that sin takes is that in the Apostle, You have treasured up the wrath of God against the day of wrath. And this is a fearful privation, of the grace of God here and of the face of God hereafter: a privation so much worse than nothing as that they upon whom it falls would fain be nothing, and cannot.

From the first sermon preached to King Charles at St James',
3 April 1625

The third house that falls into our present survey is our dwelling-house, or family. And of this house the foundation is peace. For peace compacts all the pieces of a family together: husband and wife in love and in obedience; father and son in care and in obedience; master and servant in discipline and in obedience. Still obedience is one ingredient in all peace: there is no peace where there is no obedience.

Now every smoke does not argue the house to be on fire. Every domestic offence taken or given does not destroy this foundation, this peace, within doors. There may be a thunder from above, and there may be an earthquake from below, and yet the foundation of the house safe. From above there may be a defect in the superior, in the husband, the father, the master; and from below in the wife, the son, the servant. There may be a jealousy in the husband, a morosity in the father, an imperiousness in the master; and there may be an inobsequiousness and an indiligence in the wife, there may be levity and inconsideration in the son, and there may be unreadiness, unseasonableness in a servant. And yet foundations stand, and peace maintained, though not by an exquisite performing of all duties yet by a mutual support of one another's infirmities. This destroys no foundation.

Yet if there be such a fire kindled within doors that the husband's jealousy come to a substraction of necessary means at home, or to defamation abroad, or the wife's levity induce just imputation at home, or scandal abroad; if the father's wastefulness amount to a disinheriting, because he leaves nothing to be inherited, or the son's incorrigibleness occasion a just disinheriting though there be enough; if the master make slaves of servants, and macerate [oppress] them; or the servants make prize of the master and prey upon him: in these cases, and such as these, there is a wrinching, a shrinking, a sinking, an undermining, a destroying of foundations, the foundation of this third house which is the family, peace.

Call not light faults by heavy names. Call not all sociableness and conversation disloyalty in thy wife, nor all levity or pleasurableness incorrigibleness in thy son, nor all negligence or forgetfulness perfidiousness in thy servant; nor let every light disorder within doors shut thee out of doors, or make thee a stranger in thine own house. In a smoky room it may be enough to open a window, without leaving the place. In domestic unkindness and discontents it may be wholesomer to give them a concoction at home, in a discreet patience, or to give them a vent at home, in a moderate rebuke, than to think to ease them, or put them off, with false diversions abroad. As States subsist in part by keeping their weaknesses from being known, so is it the quiet of families to have their chancery and their parliament within doors, and to compose and determine all emergent differences there. For so also, foundations being kept undestroyed, the righteous shall do as they should do, enjoy a religious unity, and a civil unity, the same soul towards God, the same heart towards one another, in a holy and in a happy peace. And peace is the foundation of this third house, the family.

Study to be quiet, says the Apostle. Indeed it is the proper business of the mind and body too, of thoughts and actions too, to be quiet. And yet, alas, how many break their sleep in the night about things that disquiet them in the day too, and trouble themselves in the day about things that disquiet them all night too! We disquiet ourselves too much in being over-tender, over-sensible, of imaginary injuries. Let many injuries pass over, says the moral man, for he that knows not of an injury, or takes no knowledge of it, for the most part hath no injury. They that are too inquisitive what other men say of them, they disquiet themselves, for that which others would but whisper, they publish.

Do not antedate misery, do not prophesy ruin, do not concur with mischief, nor contribute to mischief so far as to over-fear it before, nor to misinterpret their ways whose ends you cannot know. And do not call the cracking of a pane of glass a destroying of foundations. Dispute not laws, but obey them when they are made. Call not every entrance of such a Judge as thou thinkest insufficient a corrupt entrance, nor every judgement which he enters, and thou understandest not, or likest not, a corrupt judgement. As in natural things it is a weakness to think that everything that I know not how it is done, is done by witchcraft, so it is also in civil things, if I know not why it is done, to think it is done for money. Let the law be sacred to thee, and the dispensers of the law reverend. Keep the law, and the law shall keep thee.

Misinterpret not God's former corrections upon thee, how long, how sharp soever. Call not his physic poison, nor his fish scorpions, nor his bread stone. Accuse not God for that he hath done, nor suspect not God for that he may do, as though God had made thee only because he lacked a man to damn. In all scruples of conscience say with St Peter, Lord, whither shall I go? Thou hast the words of eternal life. And God will not leave thee in the dark. In all oppression from potent adversaries say with David, Against thee, O Lord, only have I sinned. And God will not make the malice of another man his executioner upon thee. Say with David, Thou hast been a strong tower to me; I will abide in thy tabernacle; I will never go out. I know thou hast a Church, I know I am in it, and I will never depart from it. And so, foundations being never destroyed, the righteous shall do as the righteous have always done, enjoy the evidence, and the verdict, and the judgement, and the possession of a good conscience. First govern thyself well. And as Christ said, he shall say again, Thou hast been faithful in a little. Take more.

St Paul's, in the evening, Easter Day 1625

Transgressors that put God's organ out of tune, that discompose and tear the body of man with violence, are those inhuman persecutors who with racks and tortures and prisons and fires and exquisite inquisitions throw down the bodies of the true God's true servants to the idolatrous worship of their imaginary gods, that torture men into Hell and carry them through the inquisition into damnation. St Augustine moves a question, and institutes a disputation, and carries it somewhat problematically, whether torture be to be admitted at all, or no. That presents a fair probability which he says against it. We presume, says he, that an innocent man should be able to hold his tongue in torture. That is no part of our purpose in torture, says he, that he that is innocent should accuse himself, by confession, in torture. And if an innocent man be able to do so, why should we not think that a guilty man, who shall save his life by holding his tongue in torture, should be able to do so?

And then, where is the use of torture? It is a slippery trial and uncertain (says Ulpian) to convince by torture. For many times (says St Augustine again) he that is yet but questioned, whether he be guilty or no, before that be known, is, without all question, miserably tortured. And whereas, many times, the passion of the Judge, and the covetousness of the Judge, and the ambition of the Judge, are calamities heavy enough upon a man that is accused, in this case of torture (says that Father) for the most part even the ignorance of the Judge is the greatest calamity of him that is accused. If the Judge knew that he were innocent, he should suffer nothing. If he knew he were guilty, he should not suffer torture. But because the Judge is ignorant and knows nothing, therefore the prisoner must be racked and tortured and mangled.

Denmark House, some few days before the body of King James was removed from thence, to his burial, 26 April 1625

Here, at your coming hither now, you have two glasses wherein you may see yourselves from head to foot: one is the text, your Head, Christ Jesus, represented unto you in the name and person of Solomon: 'Behold King Solomon crowned', etc. And another under your feet, in the dissolution of this great monarch, our royal master, now laid lower by death than any of us, his subjects and servants.

First then behold yourselves in that first glass. Behold King Solomon: Solomon the son of David—but not the son of Bathsheba but of a better mother, the most blessed Virgin Mary. For Solomon in this text is not a proper name but an

The nave of Old St Paul's Cathedral. Though the exterior had been altered by the time Hollar made this engraving, the interior of the cathedral remained much as Donne would have known it

appellative, a significative word. Solomon is the peacemaker, and our peace is made in and by Christ Jesus—and he is that Solomon whom we are called upon to see here.

There is not a better evidence nor a more binding earnest of everlasting joy in the next world than to find joy of heart in the tribulations of this. Fix thyself therefore upon this first glass, this Solomon, thy Saviour—Behold King Solomon crowned—and by conforming thyself to his holy sadness and humiliation thou shalt also become like him in his joy and glory.

But then the hand of God hath not set up, but laid down, another glass wherein thou mayest see thyself: a glass that reflects thyself and nothing but thyself. Christ, who was the other glass, is like thee in everything, but not absolutely, for sin is excepted. But in this glass presented now (the body of our royal but dead master and sovereign) we cannot, we do not, except sin. Not only the greatest man is subject to natural infirmities (Christ himself was so) but the holiest man is subject to original and actual sin, as thou art, and so a fit glass for thee to see thyself in.

Jet shows a man his face as well as crystal. Nay, a crystal glass will not show a man his face except it be steeled, except it be darkened, on the back side. Christ, as he was a pure crystal glass, as he was God, had not been a glass for us to have seen ourselves in except he had been steeled, darkened with our human nature. Neither was he ever so thoroughly darkened as that he could present us wholly to ourselves because he had no sin, without seeing of which we do not see ourselves. Those therefore that are like thee in all things—subject to human infirmities, subject to sins—and yet are translated, and translated by death, to everlasting joy and glory are nearest and clearest glasses for thee to see thyself in. And such is this glass, which God hath proposed to thee, in this house.

And therefore never go forth to see, but go in and see, a Solomon crowned with his mother's crown. And when you shall find that hand that has signed to one of you a patent for title, to another for pension, to another for dispensation, dead; that hand that settled possessions by his seal, in the Keeper, and rectified honours by the sword, in his Marshal, and distributed relief to the poor, in his Almoner, and health to the diseased by his immediate touch, dead; that hand that balanced his own three Kingdoms so equally, as that none of them complained of one another nor of him, and carried the keys of all the Christian world, and locked up and let out armies in their due season, dead—how poor, how faint, how pale, how momentary, how transitory, how empty, how frivolous, how dead things must you necessarily think titles and possessions and favours and all, when you see that hand, which was the hand of destiny, of Christian destiny, of the Almighty God, lie dead!

It was not so hard a hand when we touched it last, nor so cold a hand when we kissed it last. That hand which was wont to wipe all tears from all our eyes doth now but press and squeeze us as so many sponges, filled one with one, another with another cause of tears. Tears that can have no other bank to bound them but the declared and manifested will of God. For till our tears flow to that height that they might be called a murmuring against the declared will of God, it is against our allegiance, it is disloyalty, to give our tears any stop, any termination, any measure.

At midnight remember them who resolve into dust, and make them thy glasses to see thyself in. Look now especially upon him whom God hath presented to thee now, and with as much cheerfulness as ever thou heardest him say, Remember my favours, or, Remember my commandments, hear him say now with the wise man, Remember my judgement, for thine also shall be so: Yesterday for me and today for thee. He doth not say tomorrow, but today, for thee.

Behold him therefore crowned with the crown that his mother gives him, his mother, the earth. In ancient times, when they used to reward soldiers with particular kinds of crowns, there was a great dignity in a crown of grass. That denoted a conquest, or a defence, of that land. He that hath but a turf of grass in a churchyard hath a crown from his mother, and even in that burial taketh seisure [possession] of the Resurrection, as by a turf of grass men give seisure of land.

He leaveth that heart, which was accustomed to the half-joys of the earth, in the earth, and he hath enlarged his heart to a greater capacity of joy and glory, and God hath filled it according to that new capacity. But when you have gone in and mourned upon him, and you have gone forth and laid his sacred body in consecrated dust, and come then to another going forth in many several ways—some to the service of their new master and some to the enjoying of their fortunes conferred by their old; some to the raising of new hopes, some to the burying of the old, and all; some to new and busy endeavours in Court, some to contented retirings in the country—let none of us go so far from him, or from one another, in any of our ways, but that all we that have served him may meet once a day, the first time we see the sun, in the ears of Almighty God, with humble and hearty prayer, that he will be pleased to hasten that day in which it shall be an addition even to the joy of that place, as perfect as it is and as infinite as it is, to see that face again, and to see those eyes open there which we have seen closed here. Amen.

St Paul's, 8 May 1625

Incontinency, and all vices that arise immediately out of the corruption of nature and are not induced by other circumstances, have as much inclination from poverty as from riches. May we not say more? I doubt we may. He must be a very sanctified man whom extreme poverty and other afflictions do not decline towards a jealousy and a suspicion and a distrusting of God. And then, the sins that bend towards desperation are so much more dangerous than those that bend towards presumption, [in] that he that presumes hath still mercy in his contemplation. He does not think that he needs no mercy but that mercy is easily had: he believes there is mercy, he doubts not of that. But the despairing man imagines a cruelty, an unmercifulness, in God and destroys the very nature of God himself.

Ordinary poverty (that is, a difficulty, with all their labours and industry, to sustain their family and the necessary duties of their place) is a shrewd and a slippery temptation. But for that street beggary which is become a calling (for parents bring up their children to it, nay, they do almost take prentices to it; some expert beggars teach others what they shall say, how they shall look, how they shall lie, how they shall cry)— for these, whom our laws call incorrigible, I must say of them (in a just accommodation of Our Saviour's words, It is not meet to take the children's bread and to cast it to dogs): it is not meet that this vermin should devour any of that which belongs to them who are truly poor. Neither is there any measure, any proportion of riches, that exposes man naturally to so much sin as this kind of beggary doth.

It would require a longer disquisition than I can afford to it now, whether riches or poverty (considered in lesser proportions, ordinary riches, ordinary poverty) open us to more and worse sins. But consider them in the highest and in the lowest—abundant riches, beggarly poverty—and it will scarce admit doubt but that the incorrigible vagabond is farther from all ways of goodness than the corruptest rich man is. And therefore labour we all earnestly in the ways of some lawful calling, that we may have our portion of this world by good means.

All degrees of poverty are dangerous and slippery, even to a murmuring against God, or an invading of the possessions and goods of other men. But especially the lowest, the desperate degree of beggary, and then especially when we cannot say it is inflicted by the hand of God but contracted by our own laziness or our own wastefulness.

St Paul's, Christmas Day 1625

It is an observation of St Cyril that none of the Saints of God, nor such as were noted to be exemplarily religious and sanctified men, did ever celebrate with any festival solemnity their own birthday. Pharaoh celebrated his own nativity, but who would make Pharaoh his example? And besides, he polluted that festival with the blood of one of his servants. Herod celebrated his nativity, but who would think it an honour to be like Herod? And besides, he polluted that festival with the blood of John Baptist. But the just contemplation of the miseries and calamities of this life, into which our birthday is the door and the entrance, is so far from giving any just occasion of a festival as it hath often transported the best disposed Saints and servants of God to a distemper, to a malediction and cursing of their birthday.

How much misery is presaged to us, when we come so generally weeping into the world that perchance in the whole body of history we read but of one child, Zoroaster, that laughed at his birth. What miserable revolutions and changes, what downfalls, what breaknecks and precipitations may we justly think ourselves ordained to if we consider that, in our coming into this world out of our mothers' womb, we do not make account that a child comes [not] right except it come with the head forward, and thereby prefigure that headlong falling into calamities which it must suffer after. Though therefore the days of the Martyrs, which are, for our example, celebrated in the Christian Church, be ordinarily called the birthday of the Martyrs, yet that is not intended of their birth in this world but of their birth in the next, when, by death, their souls were new delivered of their prisons here, and they newly born into the Kingdom of Heaven that day. Upon that reason the day of their death was called their birthday and celebrated in the Church by that name.

Only to Christ Jesus the fullness of time was at his birth, not because he also had not a painful life to pass through, but because the work of our redemption was an entire work, and all that Christ said or did or suffered concurred to our salvation, as well his Mother's swathing him in little clouts as Joseph's shrouding him in a funeral sheet; as well his cold lying in the manger as his cold dying upon the cross; as well the *puer natus* as the *consummatum est*, as well his birth as his death is said to have been the fullness of time.

Christ had one privilege in his birth which never any prince had or shall have: that is, that he chose what mother he would have, and might have been born of what woman he would have chosen. And in this large and universal choice, though he chose a woman full of grace to be his mother, yet, that he might give spiritual comfort to all sorts of women—first to those who should be unjustly suspected and insimulated [charged] of sin and incontinency when indeed they were innocent—he was content to come of a mother who should be subject to that suspicion, and whom her husband should think to be with child before he married her and therefore purpose to put her away.

And then, to fill those women who had been guilty of that sin with relief in their consciences against the wrath of God, and with reparation of their reputation and good name in the world, it was his unsearchable will and pleasure that in all that genealogy and pedigree which he and his Spirit hath inspired the Evangelists to record of his ancestors, there is not one woman named of whom Christ is descended who is not dangerously noted in the Scriptures to have had some aspersion of incontinence upon her—as both St Jerome and St Ambrose and St Chrysostom observe of Tamar, of Bathsheba, and of Ruth also.

So then Christ Jesus, who came only for the relief of sinners, is content to be known to have come not only of poor parents but of a sinful race. And though he exempted his blessed Mother, more than any, from sin, yet he is now content to be born again of sinful mothers. In that soul that accuses itself most of sin, in that soul that calls now to mind—with remorse and not with delight—the several times and places and ways wherein she hath offended God, in that soul that acknowledges itself to have been a sink of uncleanness, a tabernacle, a synagogue of Satan, in that soul that hath been as it were possessed with Mary Magdalen's seven devils, yea with him whose name was legion, with all devils: in that sinful soul would Christ Jesus fain be born this day, and make that soul his mother, that he might be a regeneration to that soul.

We cannot afford Christ such a birth in us as he had to be born of a virgin. For every one of us wellnigh hath married himself to some particular sin, some beloved sin, that he can hardly divorce himself from. Nay, no man keeps his faith to that one sin that he hath married himself to, but mingles himself with other sins also. Though covetousness, whom he loves as the wife of his bosom, have made him rich, yet he will commit adultery with another sin, with ambition; and he will part, even with those riches, for honour. Though ambition be his wife, his married sin, yet he will commit adultery with another sin, with licentiousness, and he will endanger his honour to fulfill his lust. Ambition may be his wife, but lust is his concubine. We abandon all spiritual chastity, all virginity, we marry our particular sins, and then we divide our loves with other sins too. Thou hast multiplied thy fornications and yet art not satisfied, is a complaint that reaches us all in spiritual fornications and goes very far in carnal. And yet, for all this, we are capable of this conception: Christ may be born in us for all this. As God said unto the Prophet, Take thee a wife of fornications, and children of fornications. So is Christ Jesus content to take our souls, though too often mothers of fornications.

As long as we are united and incorporated in his beloved spouse, the Church, conform ourselves to her, grow up in her, harken to his word in her, feed upon his Sacraments in her, acknowledge a seal of reconciliation by the absolution of the Minister in her, so long (how unclean soever we have been, if we abhor and forsake our uncleanness now) we participate of the chastity of that spouse of his, the Church, and in her are made capable of this conception of Christ Jesus. And so it is as true this hour of us as it was when the Apostle spoke these words, This is the fullness of time, when God sent his Son.

St Dunstan's, 'The first sermon after our dispersion by the sickness',* 15 January 1626

God intended life and immortality for man, and man by sin induced death upon himself at first. When man had done so, and by that now man was condemned, man must die. Yet God gave him, though not an absolute pardon, yet a long

* The text was Exodus 12.30: 'For there was not a house where there was not one dead.'

reprieve; though not a new immortality, yet a life of seven and eight hundred years upon earth. And then, misery by sin growing upon man, and this long life which was enlarged in his favour being become a burden unto him, God abridged and contracted his seven hundred to seventy, and his eight hundred to eighty years. The years of his life came to be three score years and ten, and if misery do suffer him to exceed those, even the exceeding itself is misery.

Death then is from ourselves, it is our own. But the executioner is from God, it is his. He gives life. No man can quicken his own soul, but any man can forfeit his own soul. And yet, when he hath done so, he may not be his own executioner. For as God giveth life, so he killeth. Not as the cause of death, for death is not his creature, but because he employs what person he will, and executes by what instrument it pleases him to choose, age or sickness, or justice or malice, or (in our apprehension) fortune.

God will accomplish his work if he have begun it, his oath and word if he have said or sworn it, his purpose and determination if he have intended it. Nothing shall frustrate or evacuate his purpose. He will achieve his ends, though there be never a soul that doth not sigh, never a heart that doth not ache, never a vein that doth not bleed, never a house in which there is not one dead.

There are dispositions which will not be rectified without the hammer, and are not malleable neither, not fit to be rectified by the hammer, till a hot fire of vehement affliction have mollified them. Thespesius they say was a man desperately vicious, irrecoverably wicked. His friends asked the Oracle whether ever he would mend. The Oracle answered, he would when he was dead. He died of a sudden fall—at least to the eyes and in the understanding of the world he died. But he recovered and came to life again, and then reported such fearful visions which he had seen in the other world, upon the souls of some of his companions and of his own father, as that, out of the apprehension of those terrors in his ecstasy, in his second life he justified the Oracle, and after he had been dead lived well. Many such stories are in the legends. But I take this at the fountain where they take most of theirs, that is, out of Plutarch, for Plutarch and Virgil are two principal evangelists of the legendaries. The moral of them all is, that God will imprint a knowledge of his majesty, and a terror of his judgements, though the heart be iron.

But as in a river that is swelled, though the water do bring down sand and stones and logs, yet the water is there still; and the purpose of Nature is to vent that water, not to pour down that sand or those stones. So, though God be put to mingle his judgements with his mercies, yet his mercy is there still and his purpose is ever in those judgements to manifest his mercy. Where the channel is stopped by those sands and stones and logs, the water will find another channel; where the heart is hardened by God's corrections, and thereby made incapable of his mercy, yet the water will find a channel, the mercy of God will flow out and show itself to others though not to him. His mercy will take effect somewhere.

Even in this city no doubt but that the hand of God fell upon thousands in this deadly infection, who were no more affected with it than to cry out, We can but die, and we must die, let us eat and drink and take our pleasure and make our profits, for tomorrow we shall die—and so were cut off by the hand of God, some even in their robberies in half-empty houses, and in their drunkenness in voluptuous and riotous houses, and in their lusts and wantonness in licentious houses, and so took in infection and death, like Judas's sop, death dipped and soaked in sin. Men whose lust carried them into the jaws of infection in lewd houses, and seeking one sore perished with another; men whose rapine and covetousness broke into houses and, seeking the wardrobes of others, found their own winding sheet in the infection of that house where they stole their own death; men who sought no other way to divert sadness but strong drink in riotous houses, and there drank up David's cup of of malediction, the cup of condemned men, of death, in the infection of that place. For these men that died in their sins, that sinned in their dying, that sought and hunted after death so sinfully—we have little comfort of such men. In the phrase of this text, They were dead. For they are dead still. As Moses said of the Egyptians I am afraid we may say of these men: We shall see them no more for ever.

[But in] the house where we stand now, the house of God and of his Saints, God affords us a fair beam of this consolation. Put off all confidence, all standing, all relying upon worldly assurances, and consider upon what ground you tread: upon ground so holy as that all the ground is made of the bodies of Christians, and therein hath received a second consecration. Every puff of wind within these walls may blow the father into the son's eyes, or the wife into her husband's, or his into hers, or both into their children's, or their children's into both. Every grain of dust that flies here is a piece of a Christian. You need not distinguish your pews by figures. You need not say, I sit within so many of such a neighbour, but, I sit within so many inches of my husband's or wife's or child's or friend's grave. Ambitious men never made more shift for places in Court than dead men for graves in churches; and as in our later times we have seen two and two almost in every place and office, so almost every grave is oppressed with twins. And as at Christ's Resurrection some of the dead arose out of their graves that were buried again, so in this lamentable calamity the dead were buried and thrown up again before they were resolved to dust, to make room for more.

But are all these dead? They were in your eyes, and therefore we forbid not that office of the eye, that holy tenderness, to weep for them that are so dead. But there was a part in every one of them that could not die, which the God of life, who breathed it into them from his own mouth, hath sucked into his own bosom. The soul of man is not safer wrapped up in the bosom of God than the body of man is wrapped up in the contract and in the eternal decree of the Resurrection. As soon shall God tear a leaf out of the book of life and cast so many of the elect into Hell fire as leave the body of any of his Saints in corruption for ever. As when my true repentance hath re-engrafted me in my God and re-incorporated me in my Saviour, no man may reproach me and say, Thou wast a sinner, so, since all these dead bodies shall be restored by the power, and are kept alive in the purpose, of Almighty God, we cannot say they are, scarce that they were, dead.

When time shall be no more, when death shall be no more, they shall renew, or rather continue, their being. But yet, beloved, as this state of theirs is not to be lamented, as though they had lost anything which might have conduced to their good by departing out of this world, so neither is it a state to be joyed in, so that we should expose ourselves to dangers unnecessarily in thinking that we want anything conducing to our good which the dead enjoy.

As between two men of equal age, if one sleep and the other wake all night, yet they rise both of an equal age in the morning. So they who shall have slept out a long night of many ages in the grave, and they who shall be caught up in the clouds to meet the Lord Jesus in the air at the last day, shall enter all at once in their bodies into Heaven. No antiquity, no seniority for their bodies. Neither can their souls, who went before, be said to have been there a minute before ours, because we shall all be in a place that reckons not by minutes.

Clocks and sundials were but a late invention upon earth, but the sun itself, and the earth itself, was but a late invention in heaven. God hath been an infinite, a super-infinite, an un-imaginable space, millions of millions of unimaginable spaces in heaven, before the Creation. And our afternoon shall be as long as God's forenoon. For as God never saw beginning, so we shall never see end. But they whom we tread upon now, and we whom others shall tread upon hereafter, shall meet at once where, though we were dead, dead in our several houses, dead in a sinful Egypt, dead in our family, dead in ourselves, dead in the grave, yet we shall be received with that con-solation, and glorious consolation: You were dead but are alive.

From a sermon preached to the Household at Whitehall,
30 April 1626

Some things the several Evangelists record severally: one, and no more. St Matthew, and none but St Matthew, records Joseph's jealousy and suspicion that his wife Mary had been in a fault before her marriage; and then his temper withal, not frequent in that distemper of jealousy, not to exhibit her to open infamy for that fault; and yet his holy discretion too, not to live with a woman faulty that way but to take some other occasion and to put her away privily. In which we have three elements of a wise husband: first, not to be utterly without all jealousy and providence and so to expose his wife to all trials and temptations; and yet not to be too apprehensive and credulous and so expose her to dishonour and infamy; but yet not to be so indulgent to her faults, when they were true faults, as by his connivance and living with her to make her faults his. And all this we have out of that which St Matthew records, and none but he.

St Mark, and none but St Mark, records that story of Christ's recovering a dumb man, and almost deaf, of both infirmities. In which, when we see that our Saviour Christ, though he could have recovered that man with a word, with a touch, with a thought, yet was pleased to enlarge himself in all those ceremonial circumstances of imposition of hands, of piercing his ears with his fingers, of wetting his tongue with spittle, and some others, we might thereby be instructed not to undervalue such ceremonies as have been instituted in the Church for the awakening of men's consideration and the exalting of their devotion, though those ceremonies, prim-arily, naturally, originally, fundamentally, and merely in themselves be not absolutely and essentially necessary. And this we have from that which is recorded by St Mark, and none but him.

St Luke, and none but St Luke, records the history of Mary and Joseph's losing of Christ. In which we see how good and holy persons may lose Christ, and how long. They had lost him and were a whole day without missing him. A man may be without Christ and his Spirit and lie long in an ignorance and senselessness of that loss. And then, where did they lose him? Even in Jerusalem, in the Holy City. Even in this holy place, and now, in this holy exercise, you lose Christ, if either any other respect than his glory brought you hither, or your minds stray out of these walls now you are here. But when they sought him, and sought him sorrowing, and sought him in the Temple, then they found him. If in a holy sadness and penitence you seek him here, in his house, in his ordinance, here he is always at home, here you may always find him. And that we have out of that which St Luke reports, and none but he.

St John, and none but St John, records the story of Christ's miraculous changing of water into wine at the marriage in Cana. In which we see both that Christ honoured the state of marriage, with his personal presence, and also that he afforded his servants so plentiful a use of his creatures as that he was pleased to come to a miraculous supply of wine rather than they should want it.

Some things are severally recorded by the several Evangelists, as all these; and then some things are recorded by all four, as John Baptist's humility and low valuation of himself in respect of Christ which he expresses in that phrase, That he was not worthy to carry his shoes. The Holy Ghost had a care that this should be repeated to us by all four, that the best endeavours of God's best servants are unprofitable, unavailable in themselves, otherwise than as God's gracious acceptation inanimates them and as he puts his hand to that plough which they drive or draw.

Now our text hath neither this singularity nor this universality, it is neither in one only nor in all the Evangelists. But it hath (as they speak in the law) an interpretative universality, a presumptive universality. For that which hath a plurality of voices is said to have all, and this text hath so. For three of the four Evangelists have recorded this text. Only St John, who doth especially extend himself about the divine nature of Christ, pretermits it. But in all the rest, who insist more upon his assuming our nature, and working our salvation in that, the Holy Ghost hath recorded and repeated this protestation of our Saviour's, I came to call not the righteous, but sinners to repentance.

Which words, being spoken by Christ upon occasion of the Pharisees murmuring at his admitting of publicans and sinners to the table with him, at that feast which St Matthew made him, at his house, soon after his calling to the Apostle-ship, direct our consideration upon the whole story, and do not afford but require, not admit but invite, this distribution, that first we consider the occasion of the words and then the words themselves, for of these twins is this text pregnant, and quick, and easily delivered.

We shall see, first, that Christ by his personal presence justified feasting somewhat more than was merely necessary for society and cheerful conversation. He justified feasting, and feasting in an Apostle's house: though a churchman, and an exemplar man, he was not deprived of a plentiful use of God's creatures, nor of the cheerfulness of conversation. And then he justified feasting in the company of publicans and sinners, intimating therein that we must not be, in things of ordinary conversation, over-curious, over-inquisitive, of other men's manners. For whatsoever their manners be, a good man need not take harm by them, and he may do good amongst them. And then, lastly, we shall see the cal-umny that the Pharisees cast upon Christ for this, and the iniquity of that calumny both in the manner and in the matter thereof.

First then, Christ justified feasting, festival and cheerful conversation. For, as St Ambrose says, God, who made the world primarily for his own glory, had made light in vain if he had made no creatures to see and to be seen by that light, wherein he might receive glory; so God, who intended secondarily man's good in the Creation, had made creatures to no purpose if he had not allowed man a use and an enjoying of those creatures. Our mythologists, who think they have conveyed a great deal of moral doctrine in their poetical fables (and so, indeed, they have) had mistaken the matter much when they made it one of the torments of Hell to stand in a fresh river and not be permitted to drink, and amongst pleasant fruits and not to be suffered to eat, if God required such a forbearing, such an abstemiousness, in man, as that being set to rule and govern the creatures, he might not use and enjoy them. Privileges are lost by abusing, but so they are by not using, too.

Of those three opinions, which have all passed through good authors, whether, before the Flood had impaired and

A view of Whitehall Palace from the river. Donne gave many sermons here and at Court. Lambeth Palace can be seen on the south bank. *Below*, the funeral procession of James I from Denmark House

corrupted the herbs and fruits of the earth, men did eat flesh or no, of which the first is absolutely negative, both in matter of law and in matter of fact, no man might, no man did; and the second is directly contrary to this, affirmative in both, all men might, all men did; and the third goes a middle way, it was always lawful, and all men might, but sober and temperate men did forbear and not do it: of these three, though the later have prevailed with those authors and be the common opinion, yet the later part of that later opinion would very hardly fall into proof, that all their sober and temperate men did forbear this eating of flesh, or any lawful use of God's creatures. God himself took his portion in this world so, in meat and drink, in his manifold sacrifices, and God himself gave himself in this world so, in bread and wine, in the Blessed Sacrament of his Body and his Blood; and the very joys of Heaven, after the Resurrection, are conveyed to us also in the marriage supper of the Lamb. God gives plentifully, richly, and will be served so himself.

In all those festivals amongst the Jews which were of God's immediate institution, as the Passover and Pentecost, and the trumpets and tabernacles and the rest, you shall often meet in the Scriptures these two phrases: first, Upon that day you shall humble your souls; and then, Upon that day you shall rejoice before the Lord. Now some interpreters have applied these two phrases to the two days, that upon the eve we should humble our souls in fasting, and upon the day rejoice before the Lord in a festival cheerfulness. But both belong to the day itself: that first we should humble our souls, as we do now, in these holy convocations; and then return and rejoice before the Lord in a cheerful use of his creatures, ourselves; and then send out a portion to them that want. When Christ came to Jairus's house, and commanded away the music and all the funeral solemnities, it was not because he disallowed those solemnities but because he knew there was no funeral to be solemnised in that place, to which he came with an infallible purpose to raise that maid which was dead. Civil recreations, offices of society and mutual entertainment and cheerful conversation, and such a use of God's creatures as may testify him to be a God, not of the valleys only but of the mountains too, not a God of necessity only but of plenty too.

So Matthew began his Apostleship with a feast; and though he, in modesty, forbear saying so, St Luke, who reports the story, says that it was a great feast. He began with a great but ended with a greater, for (if we have St Matthew's history rightly delivered to us) when he was at the greatest feast which

this world can present, when he was receiving and administering the Blessed Sacrament, in that action was he himself
served up as a dish to the table of the Lamb, and added to the
number of the Martyrs then, and died for that Saviour of his
whose death for him he did then celebrate. Abraham made a
great feast that day that Isaac was weaned. Here was Matthew
weaned from the breasts of this world. And he made a feast,
a feast that was a type of a type, a prevision of a vision, of that
vision which St Peter had after, of a sheet with all kind of
meats, clean and unclean, in it. For at this table was the clean
and unspotted Lamb, Christ Jesus himself. And at the same
table those spotted and unclean goats, the publicans and
sinners.

Is there then any conversation with notorious sinners justifiable, excusable? Christ was in himself a dispensation upon
any law, because he was the lawmaker. But here he proceeded
not in that capacity: he took no benefit of any dispensation.
He fulfilled the intention and purpose of the law, for laws
therefore forbade conversation with sinners lest a man should
take infection by such conversation. So the Jews were forbidden to eat with the Gentiles, but it was lest, in eating with
the Gentiles, they might eat of things sacrificed to idols. So
they were forbidden conversation with leprous persons lest,
by such conversation, the disease should be propagated. But
where the danger of infection ceased, all conversation might
be open, and Christ was always far enough from taking any
infection by any conversation with any sinner. He might
apply himself to them, because he could take no harm by
them. But he did it especially, that he might do good upon
them. Some forbear the company of sinners out of a singularity, and pride in their own purity, and say, Stand by thyself, come not near me, for I am holier than thou. But, says
St Augustine, Christ was a lily, though he grew amongst
thorns. A lily is not the less a lily, nor the worse, nor the darker
a lily because it grows amongst thorns. That man is not so
good as he should be that cannot maintain his own integrity
and continue good; or that cannot maintain his charity though
others continue bad. It was St Paul's way: I am made all
things to all men, that I might save some. And in that place
where the Apostle names the persons whom we are to forbear,
amongst them he names idolaters. And, as he does the rest,
he calls even those idolaters brethren. In cases where we are
safe from danger of infection (and it lies much in ourselves to
save ourselves from infection), even some kind of idolaters
are left by St Paul under the name of brethren, and some

brotherly and neighbourly and pious offices belong to them for all that. These faults must arm me to avoid all danger from them, but not extinguish all charity towards them. And therefore it was an unjust calumny in the Pharisees to impute this for a fault to Christ, that he applied himself to these men.

Now in the manner of this calumny, there was a great deal of iniquity, and a great deal in the matter. For, for the manner, that which they say of Christ they say not to Christ himself but they whisper it to his servants, to his Disciples. A legal and juridical accusation is justifiable, maintainable, because it is the proper way for remedy. A private reprehension, done with discretion and moderation, should be acceptable too. But a privy whispering is always pharisaical. The Devil himself, though he be a lion, yet he is a roaring lion. A man may hear him. But, for a privy whisperer, we shall only hear of him. And in their plot there was more mischief.

For when Christ's Disciples plucked ears of corn upon the Sabbath, the Pharisees said nothing to those Disciples, but they come to their Master, to Christ, and they tell him of it. Here, when Christ eats and drinks with these sinners, they never say anything to Christ himself, but they go to his servants and they tell him of it. By privy whisperings and calumnies they would alienate Christ from his Disciples, and his Disciples from him, the King from his subjects by some tales and the subject from the King by other. And they took this for the shortest way to disgrace both their preaching, to discredit both their lives; to defame Christ for a winebibber and a loose companion and to defame his Disciples for profane men and Sabbath-breakers. For discredit a man's life and you disgrace his preaching, lay imputations upon the person and that will evacuate and frustrate all his preaching. For whether it be in the corruption of our nature, or whether it be in the nature of the thing itself, so it is. If I believe the preacher to be an ill man, I shall not be much the better for his good sermons.

Thus they were injurious in the manner of their calumny. They were so too in the matter, to calumniate him therefore because he applied himself to sinners. The wise man in Ecclesiasticus institutes his meditation thus: There is one that hath great need of help, full of poverty, yet the eye of the Lord looked upon him for good, and set him up from his low estate, so that many that saw it marvelled at it. Many marvelled, but none reproached the Lord, chid the Lord, calumniated the Lord, for doing so.

And if the Lord will look upon a sinner, and raise that

bedrid man; if he will look with that eye that pierces deeper than the eye of heaven, the sun (and yet with a look of that eye the womb of the earth conceives); if he will look with that eye that conveys more warmth than the eye of the ostrich (and yet, with a look of that eye, that bird is said to hatch her young ones without sitting); that eye that melted Peter into water and made him flow towards Christ, and rarefied Matthew into air and made him flee towards Christ: if that eye vouchsafe to look upon a publican and redeem a Goshen out of an Egypt, hatch a soul out of a carnal man, produce a saint out of a sinner, shall we marvel at the matter? Marvel so as to doubt God's power? Shall anything be impossible to God? Or shall we marvel at the manner, at any way by which Christ shall be pleased to convey his mercy? Shall we wonder that Christ would live with sinners, who was content to die for sinners? Wonder that he would eat the bread and wine of sinners that gave sinners his own flesh to eat and his own blood to drink? Of if we do wonder at this (as, indeed, nothing is more wonderful), yet let us not calumniate, let us not misinterpret any way that he shall be pleased to take, to derive [impart] his mercy to any man.

But as we tread upon many herbs negligently in the field, but when we see them in an apothecary's shop we begin to think that there is some virtue in them, so, howsoever we have a perfect hatred and a religious despite against a sinner as a sinner, yet if Jesus Christ shall have been pleased to have come to his door, and to have stood and knocked and entered and supped, and brought his dish and made himself that dish, and sealed a reconciliation to that sinner in admitting him to that table, to that communion, let us forget the name of publican, the vices of any particular profession, and forget the name of sinner, the history of any man's former life, and be glad to meet that man now, in the arms, and to grow up with that man, now, in the bowels, of Christ Jesus. Christ left out the righteous, not that there were any such but such as thought themselves so; and he took in sinners, not all effectually that were simply so, but such as the sense of their sins, and the miserable state that that occasioned, brought to an acknowledgement that they were so.

Christ justifies feasting. He feasts you with himself. And feasting in an Apostle's house, in his own house, he feasts you often here. This Christ, with joy and thanksgiving, we acknowledge to be come. To be come actually. We expect no other after him, we join no other to him. And come freely, without any necessity imposed by any above him, and with-

out any invitation from us here. Come, not to meet us, who
were not able to rise without him, but yet not to force us, to
save us against our wills, but come to call us by his ordinances
in his Church. Us, not as we pretend any righteousness of our
own, but as we confess ourselves to be sinners, and sinners led
by this call to repentance. Which repentance is an everlasting
divorce from our beloved sin, and an everlasting marriage
and superinduction of our ever-living God.

*From a sermon preached at the funeral of Sir William Cockayne,
Knight, Alderman of London, 12 December 1626*

God made the first marriage and man made the first divorce.
God married the body and soul in the Creation, and man
divorced the body and soul by death through sin, in his fall.
God doth not admit, not justify, not authorise such superinductions upon such divorces, as some have imagined: that
the soul, departing from one body, should become the soul of
another body in a perpetual revolution and transmigration of
souls through bodies, which hath been the giddiness of some
philosophers to think; or that the body of the dead should
become the body of an evil spirit, that that spirit might, at his
will and to his purpose, inform and inanimate that dead body.
God allows no such superinductions, no such second marriages, upon such divorces by death, no such disposition of soul
or body after their dissolution by death.

But because God hath made the band of marriage indis-
soluble but by death, farther than man can die this divorce
cannot fall upon man. As far as man is immortal, man is a
married man still, still in possession of a soul and a body too.
And man is for ever immortal in both: immortal in his soul
by preservation, and immortal in his body by reparation in
the Resurrection. For though they be separated 'by bed and
board', they are not divorced. Though the soul be at the table
of the Lamb in glory, and the body but at the table of the
Serpent in dust; though the soul be in that bed which is
always green, in an everlasting spring, in Abraham's bosom,
and the body but in that green bed whose covering is but a
yard and a half of turf and a rug of grass, and the sheet but a
winding sheet, yet they are not divorced. They shall return
to one another again, in an inseparable reunion, in the
Resurrection.

To establish this assurance of a Resurrection in us, God
does sometimes, in this life, that which he hath promised for

the next: that is, he gives a resurrection to life after a bodily death here. To the widow of Naim's son he bequeaths new life, and to Jairus's daughter he gives the same legacy. And out of the surplus of his inexhaustible estate, out of the over-flowing of his power, he enables his executors to do as he did. For Peter gives Dorcas this resurrection too. Divers examples hath he given us, of the resurrection of every particular man, in particular resurrections such as we have named, and one of the general Resurrection in the Resurrection of Christ himself.

For in him we all rose, for he was all in all. They that are not fallen yet by any actual sin (children newly baptised) are risen already in him. And they that are not dead yet—nay, not alive yet, not yet born—have a resurrection in him who was not only the Lamb slain from the beginning, but from all beginnings was risen too. And all that shall ever have part in the second Resurrection are risen with him from that time.

Nothing is permanent in temporal things. Riches pros-perously multiplied, children honourably bestowed, additions of honour and titles fairly acquired, places of command and government justly received and duly executed—all testi-monies, all evidences of worldly happiness have a dissolution, a determination in the death of this and of every such man.

There is nothing, no spiritual thing, perfect in this world; nothing, no temporal thing, permanent and durable. And how imperfect is all our knowledge! What one thing do we know perfectly? Whether we consider arts or sciences, the servant knows but according to the proportion of his master's knowledge in that art, and the scholar knows but according to the proportion of his master's knowledge in that science. Young men mend not their sight by using old men's spec-tacles, and yet we look upon Nature but with Aristotle's spectacles, and the body of man but with Galen's, and upon the frame of the world but with Ptolemy's spectacles. Almost all knowledge is rather like a child that is embalmed to make a mummy than that is nursed to make a man; rather conserved in the stature of the first age than grown to be greater. And if there be any addition to knowledge, it is rather a new know-ledge than a greater knowledge, rather a singularity in a de-sire of proposing something that was not known at all before than an improving, an advancing, a multiplying of former inceptions; and by that means no knowledge comes to be perfect. One philosopher thinks he is dived to the bottom when he says he knows nothing but this, that he knows nothing; and yet another thinks that he hath expressed more knowledge than he in saying that he knows not so much as that, that he knows nothing.

Though a man knew not that every sin casts another shovel of brimstone upon him in Hell, yet if he knows that every riotous feast cuts off a year, and every wanton night seven years of his seventy in this world, it were some degree towards perfection in knowledge. He that purchases a manor will think to have an exact survey of the land. But who thinks of taking so exact a survey of his conscience, how that money was got that purchased that manor? We call that a man's means, which he hath. But that is truly his means, what way he came by it. And yet how few there are (when a state comes to any great proportion) that know that, that know what they have, what they are worth? We have seen great wills dilated into glorious uses, and into pious uses, and then too narrow an estate to reach to it. And we have seen wills where the testator thinks he hath bequeathed all, and he hath not known half his own worth.

When thou knowest a wife, a son, a servant, a friend no better but that that wife betrays thy bed, and that son thine estate, and that servant thy credit, and that friend thy secret, what canst thou say thou knowest? But we must not insist upon this consideration of knowledge. For though knowledge be of a spiritual nature, yet it is but a terrestrial spirit, conversant upon earth. Spiritual things of a more rarefied nature than knowledge, even faith itself and all that grows from that in us, falls within this rule which we have in hand: that even in spiritual things, nothing is perfect.

When we consider with a religious seriousness the manifold weaknesses of the strongest devotions in time of prayer, it is a sad consideration. I throw myself down in my chamber, and I call in and invite God and his angels thither. And when they are there I neglect God and his angels for the noise of a fly, for the rattling of a coach, for the whining of a door. I talk on, in the same posture of praying—eyes lifted up, knees bowed down, as though I prayed to God. And if God or his angels should ask me when I thought last of God in that prayer, I cannot tell. Sometimes I find that I had forgot what I was about. But when I began to forget it, I cannot tell. A memory of yesterday's pleasures, a fear of tomorrow's dangers, a straw under my knee, a noise in mine ear, a light in mine eye, an anything, a nothing, a fancy, a chimera in my brain, troubles me in my prayer: so certainly is there nothing, nothing in spiritual things, perfect in this world.

Not in things that belong to faith, not in things that belong to hope, not in things that belong to action, to works, to charity—there is nothing perfect there neither. I would be loth to say that every good is a sin. That were to say that every deformed or disordered man were a beast, or that every corrupt meat were poison. It is not utterly so, not so altogether. But it is so much towards it as that there is no work of ours so good as that we can look for thanks at God's hand for that work; no work that hath not so much ill mingled with it as that we need not cry God mercy for that work. There was so much corruption in the getting, or so much vainglory in the bestowing, as that no man builds an hospital but his soul lies, though not dead, yet lame in that hospital. No man mends a highway but he is, though not drowned, yet mired in that way. No man relieves the poor but he needs relief for that relief. In all those works of charity, the world that hath benefit by them is bound to confess and acknowledge a goodness, and to call them good works. But the man that does them, and knows the weaknesses of them, knows they are not good works. God, out of my confession of the impurity of my best actions, shall vouchsafe to take off his eyes from that impurity, as though there were none. But no spiritual thing in us, not faith, not hope, not charity, have any purity, any perfection, in themselves.

To lament a dead friend is natural, and civil; and he is the deader of the two, the verier carcass, that does not so. But inordinate lamentation implies a suspicion of a worse state in him that is gone; and if I do believe him to be in Heaven, deliberately, advisedly, to wish him here that is in Heaven is an uncharitable desire. For, for me to say he is preferred by being where he is, but I were better if he were again where I am, were such an indisposition as if the prince's servant should be loth to see his master king because he should not hold the same place with him, being king, as he did when he was prince. Not to hope well of him that is gone is uncharitableness. And at the same time, when I believe him to be better, to wish him worse is uncharitableness too.

There is no form of building stronger than an arch, and yet an arch hath declinations which even a flat roof hath not. The flat roof lies equal in all parts, the arch declines downwards in all parts, and yet the arch is a firm supporter. Our devotions do not the less bear us upright, in the sight of God, because they have some declinations towards natural affections. God doth easier pardon some neglectings of his grace, when it proceeds out of a tenderness or may be excused out of good nature, than any presuming upon his grace. If a man do depart in some actions from an exact obedience of God's will, upon infirmity or human affections and not a contempt, God passes it over oftentimes. For when our Saviour Christ says, Be pure as your Father in Heaven is pure, that is a rule for our purity but not a measure of our purity. It is that we should be pure so, not that we should be so pure as our Father in Heaven. Though God look upon the inscription, he looks upon the metal too. Though he look that his image should be preserved in us, he looks in what earthen vessels this image is put, and put by his own hand. And though he hate us in our rebellions, yet he pities us in our grievances. Though he would have us better, he forsakes us not for every degree of illness.

As in spiritual things there is nothing perfect, so in temporal there is nothing permanent. Consider the greatest bodies upon earth, the monarchies, objects which one would think Destiny might stand and stare at, but not shake. Consider the smallest bodies upon earth, the hairs of our head, objects which one would think Destiny would not observe, or could not discern. And yet Destiny (to speak to a natural man), and God (to speak to a Christian) is no more troubled to make a monarchy ruinous than to make a hair grey. Nay, nothing needs to be done to either, by God or Destiny: a monarchy will ruin, as a hair will grow grey, of itself. In the elements themselves, of which all sub-elementary things are composed, there is no acquiescence, but a vicissitudinary transmutation into one another. Air condensed becomes water, a more solid body; and air rarefied becomes fire, a body more disputable and inapparent.

It is so in the condition of men too. A merchant condensed, kneaded and packed up in a great estate, becomes a Lord. And a merchant rarefied, blown up by a perfidious factor, or by a riotous son, evaporates into air, into nothing, and is not seen. And if there were anything permanent and durable in this world, yet we got nothing by it, because howsoever that might last in itself, yet we could not last to enjoy it. If our goods were not amongst movables, yet we ourselves are. If they could stay with us, yet we cannot stay with them. When Goliath had armed and fortified this body, and Jezebel had painted and perfumed this body, and Dives had pampered and larded this body, as God said to Ezekiel when he brought him to the dry bones, Son of Man, dost thou think these bones can live? They said in their hearts to all the world, Can these bodies die? And they are dead.

The Lord of Life was the first that named death: *Morte morieris*, says God, Thou shalt die the death. I do the less fear or abhor death because I find it in his mouth. Even a malediction hath a sweetness in his mouth, for there is a blessing wrapped up in it, a mercy in every correction, a resurrection upon every death. When Jezebel's beauty, exalted to that height which it had by art, or, higher than that, to that height which it had in her own opinion, shall be infinitely multiplied upon every body; and as God shall know no man from his own Son, so as not to see the very righteousness of his own Son upon that man: so the angels shall know no man from Christ, so as not to desire to look upon that man's face, because the most deformed wretch that is there shall have the very beauty of Christ himself, so shall Goliath's armour and Dives' fullness be doubled and redoubled upon us. And everything that we can call good shall first be infinitely exalted in the goodness, and then infinitely multiplied in the proportion, and again infinitely extended in the duration.

And since we are in an action of preparing this dead brother of ours to that state (for the funeral is the Easter Eve, the burial is the depositing of that man for the Resurrection), so shall we dismiss you with consolation, by a like occasional inverting the text, from passion in Martha's mouth, Lord, if thou hadst been here, my brother had not died, to joy in ours: Lord, because thou wast here, our brother is not dead.

St Paul's, Christmas Day 1626

My body is my prison, and I would be so obedient to the law as not to break prison. I would not hasten my death by starving or macerating [oppressing] this body. But if this prison be burnt down by continual fevers, or blown down with continual vapours, would any man be so in love with that ground upon which that prison stood as to desire rather to stay there than to go home? Our prisons are fallen, our bodies are dead to many former uses: our palate dead in a tastelessness, our stomach dead in an indigestibleness, our feet dead in a lameness and our invention in a dullness and our memory in a forgetfulness. And yet, as a man that should love the ground where his prison stood, we love this clay that was a body in the days of our youth—and but our prison then, when it was at best. Of thy prison thou shalt be delivered whether thou wilt or not. Thou must die. 'Fool, this night thy soul may be taken from thee.' And then, what shalt thou be tomorrow? Prophesy upon thyself by that which thou hast done today.

St Paul's, Easter Day, 25 March 1627

Little know we how little a way a soul hath to go to Heaven when it departs from the body. Whether it must pass locally through Moon and Sun and Firmament (and if all that must be done, all that may be done in less time than I have proposed the doubt in), or whether that soul finds new light in the same room and be not carried into any other, but that the glory of Heaven be diffused over all, I know not, I dispute not, I enquire not. Without disputing or enquiring I know that when Christ says that God is not the God of the dead, he says that to assure me that those whom I call dead, live. And when the Apostle tells me that God is not ashamed to be called the God of the dead, he tells me that to assure me that God's servants lose nothing by dying.

Before the King at Whitehall, 1 April 1627

The first thing that God made was light, the last thing that he hath reserved to do is the manifestation of the light of his essence in our glorification. And for publication of himself here, by the way, he hath constituted a Church in a visibility, in an eminency, as a city upon a hill. And in this Church, his ordinance is ordinance indeed: his ordinance of preaching batters the soul, and by that breach the Spirit enters. His Ministers are an earthquake and shake an earthly soul. They are the sons of thunder and scatter a cloudy conscience. They are as the fall of waters and carry with them whole congregations—three thousand at a sermon, five thousand at a sermon, a whole city, such a city as Nineveh, at a sermon. And they are as the roaring of a lion, where the lion of the tribe of Judah cries down the lion that seeks whom he may devour: that is, orthodox and fundamental truths are established against clamorous and vociferous innovations.

God hath made all things in a roundness, from the round superficies of this earth which we tread here to the round convexity of those heavens which, as long as they shall have any being, shall be our footstool when we come to Heaven. God hath wrapped up all things in circles, and then a circle hath no angles: there are no corners in a circle.

This whisperer wounds thee, and with a stiletto of gold. He strangles thee with scarves of silk, he smothers thee with the down of phoenixes, he stifles thee with a perfume of amber, he destroys thee by praising thee, overthrows thee by exalting thee, and undoes thee by trusting thee — by trusting thee with those secrets that bring thee into a desperate perplexity, either to betray another that pretends to have trusted thee, or to perish thyself for the saving of another that plotted to betray thee. And therefore, if you can hear a good organ at church and have the music of a domestic peace at home, peace in thy walls, peace in thy bosom, never harken after the music of spheres, never hunt after the knowledge of higher secrets than appertain to thee. But since Christ hath made you kings and priests in your proportion, take heed what you hear in derogation of either the State or the Church.

From a sermon of commemoration of the Lady Danvers, 1 July 1627

First then, to shake the constancy of a Christian, there will always be scorners, jesters, scoffers and mockers at religion. The period and consummation of the Christian religion, the Judgement Day, the Second Coming of Christ, will always be subject to scorns. And many times a scorn cuts deeper than a sword. Lucian wounded religion more by making jests at it than Arius or Pelagius or Nestorius with making arguments against it. For against those professed heretics and against their studied arguments, which might seem to have some weight, it well beseemed those grave and reverend Fathers of the Church to call their Councils, and to take into their serious consideration those arguments, and solemnly to conclude and determine and decree in the point. But it would ill have become those reverend persons to have called their Councils, or taken into their so serious considerations, epigrams and satires and libels and scurrilous and scornful jests against any point of religion. Scorns and jests are easilier apprehended and understood by vulgar and ordinary capacities than arguments are. And then, learned men are not so earnest nor so diligent to overthrow and confute a jest or scorn as they are an argument; and so they pass more uncontrolled, and prevail further and live longer, than arguments do.

It is the height of Job's complaint that contemptible persons made jests upon him; and it is the depth of Samson's calamity that when the Philistines' hearts were merry, then they called for Samson to make them sport. So to the Israelites in Babylon, when they were in that heaviness that every breath they breathed was a sigh, their enemies called to sing them a song. And so they proceeded with him who fulfilled in himself alone all types and images and prophecies of sorrows, who was, as the Prophet calls him, a man composed and elemented of sorrows, our Lord and Saviour Christ Jesus. For they plaited a crown of thorns upon his head, and they put a reed into his hand, and they bowed the knee before him, and mocked him.

Truly the conniving at several religions, as dangerous as it is, is not so dishonourable to God as the suffering of jesters at religion. That may induce heresy, but this does establish atheism. And as that is the public mischief, so, for the private, there lies much danger in this, that he that gives himself the liberty of jesting at religion shall find it hard to take up at last. As when Julian the Apostate had received his death wound, and could not choose but confess that that wound came from the hand and power of Christ, yet he confessed it in a phrase of scorn, *Vicisti Galilæe*, The day is thine, O Galilean, and no more. It is not, Thou hast accomplished thy purpose, O my God, nor O my Maker, nor O my Redeemer, but, in a style of contempt, *Vicisti Galilæe*, and no more.

As it is said of old cosmographers, that when they had said all that they knew of a country and yet much more was to be said, they said that the rest of those countries were possessed with giants or witches or spirits or wild beasts, so that they could pierce no farther into that country; so, when we have travelled as far as we can with safety—that is, as far as ancient or modern expositors lead us in the discovery of these new heavens and new earth—yet we must say at last that it is a country inhabited with angels and archangels, with cherubins and seraphins, and that we can look no farther into it with these eyes.

Where it is locally, we enquire not. We rest in this, that it is the habitation prepared for the blessed Saints of God: heavens where the moon is more glorious than our sun, and the sun as glorious as he that made it. For it is he himself, the Son of God, the Sun of Glory. A new earth, where all their waters are milk and all their milk honey; where all their grass is corn and all their corn manna; where all their glebe, all their clods of earth, are gold, and all their gold of innumerable carats; where all their minutes are ages and all their ages eternity; where every thing is every minute in the highest exaltation, as good as it can be, and yet super-exalted and infinitely multiplied by every minute's addition — every minute infinitely better than ever it was before.

Elsewhere the Holy Ghost applies himself to the natural affections of men. To those that are affected with riches he says that that new city shall be all of gold and, in the foundations, all manner of precious stones. To those that are affected with beauty he promises an everlasting association with that beautiful couple, that fair pair, which spend their time in that contemplation and that protestation: Behold thou art fair, my beloved, says he; and then she replies, Thou art fair too; noting the mutual complacency between Christ and his Church there. To those that delight in music he promises continual singing, and every minute a new song. To those whose thoughts are exercised upon honour, and titles civil or ecclesiastical, he promises priesthood, and, if that be not enough, a royal priesthood. And to those who look after military honour, triumph after their victory in the Militant Church. And to those that are carried with sumptuous and magnificent feasts, a Marriage Supper of the Lamb.

But here the Holy Ghost proceeds not that way, by improvement of things which we have and love here, riches or beauty or music or honour or feasts, but by an everlasting possession of that which we hunger and thirst and pant after here and cannot compass, that is, justice or righteousness.

What would a worn and macerated suitor, oppressed by the bribery of the rich or the might of a potent adversary, give or do or suffer that he might have justice? What would a dejected spirit, a disconsolate soul, oppressed with the weight of heavy and habitual sin, that stands naked in a frosty winter of desperation and cannot compass one fig leaf, one colour, one excuse for any circumstance of any sin, give for the garment of righteousness? Here there is none that does right, none that executes justice, or not for justice sake. Justice is not justice that is done for fear of an appeal or a commission. In our new heavens and new earth dwelleth justice. And that's my comfort.

*From a sermon preached at the Earl of Bridgewater's house in
London at the marriage of his daughter, 19 November 1627*

There are so many evidences of the immortality of the soul,
even to a natural man's reason, that it required not an article
of the Creed to fix this notion. But the Resurrection of the
body is discernible by no other light but that of faith, nor
could be fixed by any less assurance than an article of the
Creed. Where be all the splinters of that bone which a shot
hath shivered and scattered in the air? Where be all the atoms
of that flesh which a corrosive hath eaten away, or a consumption hath breathed and exhaled away, from our arms and other
limbs? In what wrinkle, in what furrow, in what bowel of the
earth lie all the grains of the ashes of a body burnt a thousand
years since? In what corner, in what ventricle of the sea, lies
all the jelly of a body drowned in the general flood? What
coherence, what sympathy, what dependence maintains any
relation, any correspondence, between an arm that was lost in
Europe and a leg that was lost in Africa or Asia scores of years
between?

One humour of our dead body produces worms, and those
worms suck and exhaust all other humour; and then all dies,
and all dries, and moulders into dust, and that dust is blown
into the river, and that puddled water tumbled into the sea,
which ebbs and flows in infinite revolutions—and still, still
God knows in what cabinet every seed-pearl lies, in what part
of the world every grain of every man's dust lies. And he
whispers, he hisses, he beckons for the bodies of his Saints;
and in the twinkling of an eye that body that was scattered
over all the elements is sat down at the right hand of God in
a glorious Resurrection. A dropsy hath extended me to an
enormous corpulence and unwieldiness; a consumption hath
attenuated me to a feeble leanness; and God raises me a body
such as it should have been if these infirmities had not inter-
vened and deformed it.

Till the Resurrection we must not look for angelic perfec-
tions but bear with one another's infirmities. Now, when we
would tell you what those angels of God in Heaven, to which
we are compared, are, we can come no nearer to telling you
that than by telling you we cannot tell. Only the angels themselves know one another, and one good point in which we
shall be like them then shall be that then we shall know what
they are. We know they are 'spirits in nature'. But what the

nature of a spirit is, we know not. We know they are 'angels in office', appointed to exercise God's will upon us. But how a spirit should execute those bodily actions that angels do in their own motion, and in the transportation of other things, we know not.

We know they are creatures, but whether created with this world or long before, we know not. We know that for their number, and for their faculties also, there may be one angel for every man, but whether there be so or no we know not. We know the angels know, they understand, but whether by seeing all in God or by a clearer manifestation of the species of things to them than to us, we know not. We know they are distinguished into Orders—the Apostle tells us so. But what, or how many, their Orders are, we know not. Let them tell you that can [says St Augustine], so they be able to prove that they tell you true. They are creatures that have not so much of a body as flesh is, as froth is, as a vapour is, as a sigh is; and yet with a touch they shall moulder a rock into less atoms than the sand that it stands upon, and a millstone into smaller flour than it grinds. They are creatures *made*—yet not a minute older now than when they were first made, if they were made before all measure of time began. Nor, if they were made in the beginning of time and be now six thousand years old, have they one wrinkle of age in their face or one sob of weariness in their lungs. They are God's eldest sons. They are super-elementary meteors. They hang between the nature of God and the nature of man and are of middle condition. And (if we may without offence express it so) they are the riddles of Heaven and the perplexities of speculation.

St Paul's, in the evening, 23 November 1628

He that oppresses the poor digs in a dunghill for worms. And he departs from that posture which God in nature gave him, that is, erect, to look upward. For his eye is always down—upon them that lie in the dust under his feet. Certainly he that sears [dries] up himself, and makes himself insensible of the cries and curses of the poor here in this world, does but pre-pare himself for the howlings and gnashings of teeth in the world to come. It is the serpent's taste, the serpent's diet: dust shalt thou eat all the days of thy life. And he feeds but on dust that oppresses the poor. And as there is, evidently, more in-humanity, more violation of nature, in this oppression than in emulation, so may there well seem to be more impiety, and

more violation of God himself, by that word which the Holy
Ghost chooses in the next place, which is Reproach. He that
oppresses the poor, reproaches his Maker.

St Paul's, Christmas Day 1629

Humiliation is the beginning of sanctification; and as without this, without holiness, no man shall see God though he
pore whole nights upon the Bible, so, without that, without
humility, no man shall hear God speak to his soul though he
hear three two-hour sermons every day. But if God bring
thee to that humiliation of soul and body here, he will improve
and advance thy sanctification more abundantly; and when
he hath brought it to the best perfection that this life is capable
of, he will provide another manner of abundance in the life to
come: which is the last beating of the pulse of this text,* the
last panting of the pulse thereof, our anhelation [gasping] and
panting after the joys and glory and eternity of the Kingdom
of Heaven.

What a dim vespers of a glorious festival, what a poor half-
holiday, is Methuselah's nine hundred years, to eternity!
What a poor account hath that man made that says, This land
hath been in my name, and in my ancestors', from the Conquest! What a yesterday is that? Not six hundred years! If I
could believe the transmigration of souls and think that my
soul had been successively in some creature or other since the
Creation, what a yesterday is that? Not six thousand years!
What a yesterday for the past, what a tomorrow for the future,
is any term that can be comprehended in cypher or counters!
But as, how abundant a life soever any man hath in this world
for temporal abundances, I have life more abundantly than he
if I have the spiritual life of grace, so, what measure soever I
have of this spiritual life of grace in this world I shall have
that more abundantly in Heaven. For there my term shall be
a term for three lives—for those three that, as long as the
Father and the Son and the Holy Ghost live, I shall not die.

* John 10.10: 'I am come that they might have life, and that they might have it more abundantly.'

Death's Duel

*Death's Duel, or a Consolation to the Soul against the Dying Life,
and Living Death, of the Body. Delivered in a sermon at
Whitehall, before the King's Majesty, in the beginning
of Lent, 25 February 1630. Being his last sermon,
and called by his Majesty's Household 'The
Doctor's Own Funeral Sermon'.*

Buildings stand by the benefit of their foundations that sustain and support them, and of their buttresses that comprehend and embrace them, and of their contignations [joists]
that knit and unite them. The foundations suffer them not to
sink, the buttresses suffer them not to swerve, and the contignation and knitting suffers them not to cleave. The body
of our building is in the former part of this verse.* It is this.
He that is our God is the God of salvation, of salvations in the
plural, so it is in the original: the God that gives us spiritual
and temporal salvation too. But of this building the foundation, the buttresses, the contignations are in this part of the
verse, which constitutes our text, and in the three divers
acceptations of the words amongst our expositors, Unto God
the Lord belong the issues of death.

For first the foundation of this building (that our God is
the God of all salvations) is laid in this: that unto this God
the Lord belong the issues of death, that is, it is in his power
to give us an issue and deliverance, even then when we are
brought to the jaws and teeth of death, and to the lips of that
whirlpool, the grave. And so in the acceptation, this issue of
death is a deliverance from death, and this is the most obvious
and most ordinary acceptation of these words, and that upon
which our translation lays hold, the issues *from* death. And
then secondly, the buttresses that comprehend and settle this
building—that he that is our God is the God of all salvations
—are thus raised. Unto God the Lord belong the issues of
death, that is, the disposition and manner of our death: what
kind of issue and transmigration we shall have out of this
world, whether prepared or sudden, whether violent or natural, whether in our perfect senses or shaken and disordered
by sickness. There is no condemnation to be argued out of
that, no judgement to be made upon that. For howsoever they

* The text was Psalms 68.20: 'And unto God the Lord belong the issues of death' ('i.e. from
death'— Donne's note).

die, precious in his sight is the death of his Saints, and with him are the issues of death. The ways of our departing out of this life are in his hands.

And so, in this sense of the words, this issue of death is a deliverance in death. Not that God will deliver us from dying, but that he will have a care of us in the hour of death, of what kind soever our passage be. And this sense and acceptation of the words, the natural frame and contexture, doth well and poignantly administer unto us.

And then lastly, the contignation and knitting of this building—that he that is our God is the God of all salvations —consists in this: Unto this God the Lord belong the issues of death, that is, that this God the Lord, having united and knit both natures in one and, being God, having also come into this world in our flesh, he could have no other means to save us, he could have no other issue out of this world, nor return to his former glory, but by death. And so, in this sense, this issue of death is a deliverance by death, by the death of this God, our Lord Christ Jesus. And this is St Augustine's acceptation of the words, and those many and great persons that have adhered to him.

In all these three lines, then, we shall look upon these words, first, as the God of power, the Almighty Father, rescues his servants from the jaws of death; and then as the God of mercy, the glorious Son, rescued us by taking upon himself this issue of death; and then between these two, as the God of comfort, the Holy Ghost, rescues us from all discomfort by his blessed impressions beforehand, that what manner of death soever be ordained for us, yet this our issue in death shall be an entrance into everlasting life. And these three considerations—our deliverance from death, in death and by death—will abundantly do all the offices of the foundations, of the buttresses, of the contignation of this our building: that he that is our God is the God of all salvations, because unto this God the Lord belong the issues of death.

First then we consider that with God the Lord are the issues of death, and therefore in all our deaths, and deadly calamities of this life, we may justly hope of a good issue from him; and all our periods and transitions in this life are so many passages from death to death. Our very birth and entrance into this life is an issue from death, for in our mother's womb we are dead, so as that we do not know we live, not so much as we do in our sleep; neither is there any grave so close, or so putrid a prison, as the womb would be unto us if we stayed in it beyond our time, or died there before our time.

In the grave the worms do not kill us; we breed and feed and then kill those worms which we ourselves produced. In the womb the dead child kills the mother that conceived it and is a murderer, nay a parricide, even after it is dead.

And if we be not dead so in the womb, so as that, being dead, we kill her that gave us our first life, our life of vegetation, yet we are dead so as David's idols are dead. In the womb we have eyes and see not, ears and hear not. There in the womb we are fitted for works of darkness, all the while deprived of light. And there in the womb we are taught cruelty, by being fed with blood, and may be damned though we be never born. Of our very making in the womb David says, I am wonderfully and fearfully made, and, Such knowledge is too excellent for me. For even that is the Lord's doing, and it is wonderful in our eyes. It is he that made us, and not we ourselves, no, nor our parents neither. Thy hands have made me and fashioned me round about, saith Job, and (as the original word is), Thou hast taken pains about me; and yet, says he, Thou dost destroy me. Though I be the masterpiece of the greatest master (man is so), yet if thou do no more for me, if thou leave me where thou madest me, destruction will follow. The womb, which should be the house of life, becomes death itself if God leave us there. That which God threatens so often, the shutting of the womb, is not so heavy nor so discomfortable a curse in the first as in the latter shutting, nor in the shutting of barrenness as in the shutting of weakness, when children are come to the birth and there is not strength to bring forth.

It is the exaltation of misery to fall from a near hope of happiness. And in that vehement imprecation the Prophet expresses the height of God's anger, Give them, O Lord, what will thou give them? Give them a miscarrying womb. Therefore as soon as we are men (that is, inanimated, quickened in the womb), though we cannot ourselves, our parents have reason to say in our behalf, Wretched man that he is, who shall deliver him from this body of death? For even the womb is a body of death if there be no deliverer. It must be that he said to Jeremiah, Before I formed thee I knew thee, and before thou camest out of the womb I sanctified thee. We are not sure that there was no kind of ship nor boat to fish in, nor to pass by, till God prescribed Noah that absolute form of the ark. That word which the Holy Ghost by Moses useth for the ark is common to all kind of boats, *Thebah*, and is the same word that Moses useth for the boat that he was exposed in, that his mother laid him in an ark of bulrushes. But we are

Donne's portrait on the title-page of *Death's Duel*. The portrait was engraved after a drawing on board made by Martin Droeshout shortly before the poet's death. The inscription reads: 'May this shroud of the body be the shroud of the soul; the shroud of Jesus'

sure that Eve had no midwife when she was delivered of Cain;
therefore she might well say, I have gotten a man from the
Lord, wholly, entirely from the Lord: it is the Lord that
enabled me to conceive, the Lord that infused a quickening
soul into that conception, the Lord that brought into the
world that which himself had quickened. Without all this
might Eve say, My body had been but the house of death,
and to God the Lord belong the issues of death.

But then this deliverance from that death, the death of the
womb, is an entrance, a delivering over to another death, the
manifold deaths of this world. We have a winding sheet in our
mothers' womb which grows with us from our conception,
and we come into the world wound up in that winding sheet,
for we come to seek a grave. And as prisoners discharged of
actions may lie for fees, so, when the womb hath discharged
us, yet we are bound to it by cords of flesh, by such a string as
that we cannot go thence nor stay there. We celebrate our own
funerals with cries, even at our birth, as though our three
score and ten years of life were spent in our mothers' labour
and our circle made up in the first point thereof. We beg one
baptism with another, a sacrament of tears, and we come into
a world that lasts many ages, but we last not.

Says our blessed Saviour, speaking of Heaven, There are
many mansions, divers and durable, so that if a man cannot
possess a martyr's house (he hath shed no blood for Christ),
yet he may have a confessor's, he hath been ready to glorify
God in the shedding of his blood. And if a woman cannot
possess a virgin's house (she hath embraced the holy state of
marriage), yet she may have a matron's house, she hath
brought forth and brought up children in the fear of God. In
my Father's house, in Heaven, there are many mansions, but
here upon earth the Son of Man hath not where to lay his
head, says he himself.

How then hath God given this earth to the sons of men?
He hath given them earth for their materials to be made of
earth, and he hath given them earth for their grave and
sepulchre, to return and resolve to earth, but not for their
possession. Here we have no continuing city, nay, no cottage
that continues, nay, no persons, no bodies, that continue.
Whatsoever moved St Jerome to call the journeys of the
Israelites in the wilderness mansions, the word (the word is
Nasang) signifies but a journey, but a peregrination. Even the
Israel of God hath no mansions, but journeys, pilgrimages,
in this life. By that measure did Jacob measure his life to
Pharaoh, the days of the years of my pilgrimage. And though

the Apostle would not say that whilst we are in the body we are dead, yet he says, whilst we are in the body we are but in a pilgrimage, and we are absent from the Lord.

He might have said dead, for this whole world is but an universal churchyard, but our common grave, and the life and motion that the greatest persons have in it is but as the shaking of buried bodies in their graves by an earthquake. That which we call life is but a week of deaths, seven days, seven periods of our life spent in dying, a dying seven times over, and there is an end. Our birth dies in infancy and our infancy dies in youth, and youth and the rest die in age, and age also dies, and determines all. Nor do all these, youth out of infancy or age out of youth, arise so as a phoenix out of the ashes of another phoenix formerly dead, but as a wasp or a serpent out of a carrion, or as a snake out of dung. Our youth is worse than our infancy and our age worse than our youth. Our youth is hungry and thirsty after those sins which our infancy knew not, and our age is sorry and angry that it cannot pursue those sins which our youth did. And besides, all the way, so many deaths — that is, so many deadly calamities — accompany every condition, and every period of this life, as that death itself would be an ease to them that suffer them. Upon this sense doth Job wish that God had not given him an issue from the first death, from the womb: Wherefore hast thou brought me forth out of the womb? O that I had given up the ghost, and no eye had seen me. I should have been as though I had not been.

And not only the impatient Israelites in their murmuring (Would to God we had died by the hand of the Lord in the land of Egypt), but Elijah himself, when he fled from Jezebel and went for his life, as that text says, under the juniper tree requested that he might die and said: It is enough now, O Lord, take away my life. So Jonah justifies his impatience, nay, his anger, towards God himself: Now, O Lord, take, I beseech thee, my life from me, for it is better for me to die than to live. And when God asked him, Doest thou well to be angry for this, and after (about the gourd), Doest thou well to be angry for that?, he replies, I do well to be angry, even unto death. How much worse a death than death is this life, which so good men would so often change for death! But if my case be as St Paul's, that I die daily, that something heavier than death fall upon me every day; if my case be David's case, All day long we are killed; that not only every day but every hour of the day something heavier than death fall upon me; though that be true of me, I was shapen in iniquity, and in sin did my mother conceive me (there I died one death); though that be true of me, I was born not only the child of sin but the child of wrath, of the wrath of God for sin, which is a heavier death: yet with God the Lord are the issues of death, and after a Job, and a Joseph, and a Jeremiah, and a Daniel, I cannot doubt of a deliverance. And if no other deliverance conduce more to his glory and my good, yet he hath the keys of death and he can let me out at that door, that is, deliver me from the manifold deaths of this world, the every day's death and every hour's death, by that one death, the final dissolution of body and soul, the end of all.

But then, is that the end of all? Is that dissolution of body and soul the last death that the body shall suffer (for of spiritual death we speak not now)? It is not. Though this be an issue from the manifold deaths of this world, yet it is an entrance into the death of corruption and putrefaction and vermiculation and incineration, and dispersion in and from the grave, in which every dead man dies over again. It was a prerogative peculiar to Christ not to die this death, not to see corruption.

What gave him this privilege? Not Joseph's great proportion of gums and spices that might have preserved his body from corruption and incineration longer than he needed it, longer than three days, but it would not have done for ever. What preserved him, then? Did his exemption and freedom from original sin preserve him from this corruption and incineration? 'Tis true that original sin hath induced this corruption and incineration upon us. If we had not sinned in Adam, mortality had not put on immortality (as the Apostle speaks), nor corruption had not put on incorruption. But we had had our transmigration from this to the other world without any mortality, any corruption, at all. But yet since Christ took sin upon him, so far as made him mortal, he had it so far too as might have made him see this corruption and incineration, though he had no original sin in himself. What preserved him, then? Did the hypostatical union of both natures, God and man, preserve him from this corruption and incineration? 'Tis true that this was a most powerful embalming, to be embalmed with the divine nature itself. To be embalmed with eternity was able to preserve him from corruption and incineration for ever. And he was embalmed so, embalmed with the divine nature itself, even in his body as well as in his soul, for the Godhead, the divine nature, did not depart, but remained still united to his dead body in the grave.

But yet for all this powerful embalming, this hypostatical

union of both natures, we see Christ did die. And for all this union made him God and man, he became no man—for the union of the body and soul makes the man, and he whose soul and body are separated by death (as long as that state lasts) is properly no man. And therefore as in him the dissolution of body and soul was no dissolution of the hypostatical union, so is there nothing that constrains us to say that, though the flesh of Christ had seen corruption and incineration in the grave, this had been any dissolution of the hypostatical union, for the divine nature, the Godhead, might have remained with all the elements and principles of Christ's body as well as it did with the two constitutive parts of his person, his body and his soul. This incorruption then was not in Joseph's gums and spices, nor was it in Christ's innocency and exemption from original sin, nor was it (that is, it is not necessary to say it was) in the hypostatical union. But this incorruptibleness of his flesh is most conveniently placed in that, Thou wilt not suffer thy holy one to see corruption. We look no further for causes or reasons in the mysteries of religion but to the will and pleasure of God. Christ himself limited his inquisition in that [he said]: Even so, Father, for so it seemed good in thy sight.

Christ's body did not see corruption, therefore, because God had decreed it should not. The humble soul (and only the humble soul is the religious soul) rests himself upon God's purposes and his decrees. But then, it is upon those purposes and decrees of God which he hath declared and manifested, not such as are conceived and imagined in ourselves, though upon some probability, some verisimilitude. So, in our present case, Peter proceeded in his sermon at Jerusalem, and so Paul in his at Antioch. They preached Christ to have been risen without seeing corruption, not only because God had decreed it, but because he had manifested that decree in his Prophet. Therefore doth St Paul cite by special number the second psalm for that decree; and therefore both St Peter and St Paul cite for it that place in the sixteenth psalm. For when God declares his decree and purpose in the express words of his Prophet, or when he declares it in the real execution of the decree, then he makes it ours, then he manifests it to us. And therefore, as the mysteries of our religion are not the objects of our reason, but by faith we rest on God's decree and purpose (it is so, O God, because it is thy will it should be so), so God's decrees are ever to be considered in the manifestation thereof. All manifestation is either in the word of God or in the execution of the decree. And when these two concur and meet, it is the strongest demonstration that can be.

When, therefore, I find those marks of adoption and spiritual filiation, which are delivered in the word of God, to be upon me, when I find that real execution of his good purpose upon me, as that actually I do live under the obedience, and under the conditions, which are evidences of adoption and spiritual filiation, then, and so long as I see these marks and live so, I may safely comfort myself in a holy certitude and a modest infallibility of my adoption. Christ determines himself in that, the purpose of God, because the purpose of God was manifest to him. St Peter and St Paul determine themselves in those two ways of knowing the purpose of God: the word of God before, the execution of the decree in the fulness of time. It was prophesied before, say they, and it is performed now. Christ is risen without seeing corruption.

Now this which is so singularly peculiar to him, that his flesh should not see corruption, at his second coming, his coming to judgement, shall extend to all that are then alive. Their flesh shall not see corruption because (as the Apostle says, and says as a secret, as a mystery, Behold I show you a mystery) we shall not all sleep (that is, not continue in the state of the dead in the grave), but we shall all be changed. In an instant we shall have a dissolution, and in the same instant a redintegration, a recompacting of body and soul, and that shall be truly a death and truly a resurrection, but no sleeping, no corruption. But for us that die now and sleep in the state of the dead, we must all pass this posthumous death, this death after death, nay this death after burial, this dissolution after dissolution, this death of corruption and putrefaction, of vermiculation and incineration, of dissolution and dispersion in and from the grave; when those bodies that have been the children of royal parents, and the parents of royal children, must say with Job, To corruption thou art my father, and to the worm thou art my mother and my sister.

Miserable riddle, when the same worm must be my mother and my sister and myself! Miserable incest, when I must be married to my mother and my sister, and be both father and mother to my own mother and sister, beget and bear that worm which is all that miserable penury; when my mouth shall be filled with dust, and the worm shall feed, and feed sweetly, upon me; when the ambitious man shall have no satisfaction if the poorest slave tread upon him, nor the poorest receive any contentment in being made equal to princes, for they shall be equal but in dust! One dieth at his full strength, being wholly at ease and in quiet; and another dies in the bitterness of his soul, and never eats with pleasure. But they lie down alike in the dust, and the worm covers them. The worm covers them in Job, and in Isaiah, it covers them and is spread under them. The worm is spread under thee, and the worm covers thee. There's the mats and the carpets that lie under, and there's the state and the canopy that hangs over the greatest of the sons of men. Even those bodies that were the temples of the Holy Ghost come to this dilapidation, to ruin, to rubbish, to dust. Even the Israel of the Lord, and Jacob himself, hath no other specification, no other denomination, but that worm of Jacob.

Truly the consideration of this posthumous death, this death after burial, that, after God (with whom are the issues of death) hath delivered me from the death of the womb by bringing me into the world, and from the manifold deaths of the world by laying me in the grave, I must die again in an incineration of this flesh, and in a dispersion of that dust. That that monarch, who spread over many nations alive, must in his dust lie in a corner of that sheet of lead—and there but so long as that lead will last—and that private and retired man that thought himself his own for ever, and never came forth, must, in his dust of the grave, be published and (such are the revolutions of the graves) be mingled in his dust with the dust of every highway and of every dunghill, and swallowed in every puddle and pond. This is the most inglorious and contemptible vilification, the most deadly and peremptory nullification of man, that we can consider.

God seems to have carried the declaration of his power to a great height, when he sets the Prophet Ezekiel in the Valley of Dry Bones and says, Son of Man, can these bones live?, as though it had been impossible. And yet they did. The Lord laid sinews upon them, and flesh, and breathed into them, and they did live. But in that case there were bones to be seen, something visible of which it might be said, Can this thing live? But in this death of incineration, and dispersion of dust, we see nothing that we can call that man's. If we say, Can this dust live? perchance it cannot. It may be the merest dust of the earth, which never did live, nor never shall. It may be the dust of that man's worms which did live, but shall no more. It may be the dust of another man, that concerns not him of whom it is asked. This death of incineration and dispersion is, to natural reason, the most irrecoverable death of all, and yet, Unto God the Lord belong the issues of death, and by recompacting this dust into the same body, and reanimating the same body with the same soul, he shall in a blessed and glorious resurrection give me such an issue from this death as shall never pass into any other death but establish me into a life that shall last as long as the Lord of Life himself. And so have you that that belongs to the first acceptation of these words (Unto God the Lord belong the issues of death): that though from the womb to the grave and in the grave itself we pass from death to death, yet, as Daniel speaks, The Lord our God is able to deliver us, and he will deliver us.

And so we pass unto our second accommodation of these words (Unto God the Lord belong the issues of death): that it belongs to God, and not to man, to pass a judgement upon us at our death, or to conclude a dereliction on God's part upon the manner thereof.

Those indications which the physicians receive, and those predictions which they give for death or recovery in the patient, they receive and they give out of the grounds and the rules of their art. But we have no such rule or art to give a prediction of spiritual death and damnation upon any such indication as we see in any dying man. We see often enough to be sorry, but not to despair, for the mercies of God work momentarily, in minutes, and many times insensibly to by-standers or any other than the party departing, and we may be deceived both ways. We use to comfort ourselves in the death of a friend if it be testified that he went away like a lamb, that is, without any reluctance. But, God knows, that may be accompanied with a dangerous damp and stupefac-tion, and insensibility of his present state. Our blessed Saviour suffered struggles with death, and a sadness even in his soul to death, and an agony even to a bloody sweat in his body, and expostulations with God, and exclamations upon the Cross. He was a devout man who said upon his deathbed, or death turf (for he was an hermit), Hast thou served a good master three score and ten years, and art thou loth to go into his pres-ence? Yet Hilarion was loth. He was a devout man (an hermit too) that said that day he died, Consider this to be the first day's service that ever thou didst thy master, to glorify him in a Christianly and a constant death; and if thy first day be thy last day too, how soon dost thou come to receive thy wages! Yet Balaam could have been content to have stayed longer for it. Make no ill conclusions upon any man's lothness to die.

And then, upon violent deaths inflicted, as upon male-factors, Christ himself hath forbidden us by his own death to make any ill conclusion. For his own death had those impres-sions in it. He was reputed, he was executed, as a malefactor; and no doubt many of them who concurred to his death did believe him to be so. Of sudden death there are scarce examples to be found in the Scriptures upon good men, for death in battle cannot be called sudden death. But God governs not by examples but by rules, and therefore make no ill conclusion upon sudden death, nor upon distempers neither, though perchance accompanied with some words of diffidence and distrust in the mercies of God. The tree lies as it falls. 'Tis true. But yet it is not the last stroke that fells the tree, nor the last word nor gasp that qualifies the soul. Still pray we for a peaceable life against violent death, and for time of repentance against sudden death, and for sober and modest assurance against distempered and diffident death. But never make ill conclusions upon persons overtaken with such deaths. To God the Lord belong the issues of death, and he received Samson, who went out of this world in such a manner (consider it actively, consider it passively, in his own death and in those whom he slew with himself) as was subject to interpretation hard enough. Yet the Holy Ghost hath moved St Paul to celebrate Samson in his great catalogue, and so doth all the Church.

Our critical day is not the very day of our death, but the whole course of our life. I thank him that prays for me when my bell tolls, but I thank him much more that catechises me, or preaches to me, or instructs me how to live. There's my security, the mouth of the Lord hath said it: Do this and thou shalt live. But though I do it, yet I shall die too, die a bodily, a natural death. But God never mentions, never seems to consider, that death, the bodily, the natural death. God doth not say, Live well and thou shalt die well, that is, an easy, quiet death, but live well here and thou shalt live well for ever. As the first part of a sentence pieces well with the last and never respects, never harkens after, the parenthesis that comes between, so doth a good life here flow into an eternal life, without any consideration what manner of death we die. But whether the gate of my prison be opened with an oiled key (by a gentle and preparing sickness), or the gate be hewn down by a violent death, or the gate be burnt down by a raging and frantic fever, a gate into Heaven I shall have, for from the Lord is the cause of my life and with God the Lord are the issues of death. And further we carry not this second acceptation of the words, as this issue of death is God's care that the soul be safe, what agonies soever the body suffers in the hour of death.

But pass to our third part and last part, as this issue of death is a deliverance by the death of another, by the death of Christ.

You have heard of the patience of Job, says St James. All this while you have done that, for in every man, calamitous, miserable man, a Job speaks. Now see the end of the Lord, says that Apostle, which is not that end that the Lord proposed to himself (salvation to us), nor the end which he proposes to us (conformity to him). But see the end of the Lord, says he: the end that the Lord came to, death, and a painful and a shameful death. But why did he die? And why die so? As St Augustine interpreting this text answers that question, because to this God our Lord belonged the issues of death. What can be more obvious, more manifest, says he there, than this sense of these words? In the former part of this verse it is said: He that is our God is the God of salvation. So he reads it, the God that must save us. Who can that be, says he, but Jesus? For therefore that name was given him, because he was to save us. And to this Jesus, says he, this Saviour, belongs the issues of death. Being come into this life in our mortal nature, he could not go out of it any other way than by death. Therefore it is said, says he, To God the Lord belong the issues of death, to show that his way to save us was to die.

And from this text doth St Isidore prove that Christ was truly man (which as many sects of heretics denied as that he was truly God), because to him, though he were *Dominus Dominus* (as the text doubles it), God the Lord, yet to him, to God the Lord, belonged the issues of death. More cannot be said than Christ says of himself: These things Christ ought to suffer. He had no other way but by death. So then, this part of our sermon must needs be a Passion sermon, since all his life was a continual Passion, all our Lent may well be a continual Good Friday. Christ's painful life took off none of the pains of his death, he felt not the less then for having felt so much before. Nor will anything that shall be said before lessen, but rather enlarge, your devotion to that which shall be said of his Passion at the time of the due solemnisation thereof. Christ bled not a drop the less at the last for having bled at his circumcision before, nor will you shed a tear the less then if you shed some now. And therefore be now content to consider with me how to this God the Lord belonged the issues of death.

That God, this Lord, the Lord of life, could die is a strange contemplation. That the Red Sea could be dry, that the sun could stand still, that an oven could be seven times heat and not burn, that lions could be hungry and not bite is strange, miraculously strange, but supermiraculous that God could die. But that God would die is an exaltation of that. But even of that also it is a superexaltation that God should die, must die, and (said St Augustine) God the Lord had no issue but by death and (says Christ himself) all this Christ ought to suffer, was bound to suffer. God is the God of revenges, says David; he would not pass over the sin of man unrevenged, unpunished. But then (says that place), the God of revenges works freely: he punishes, he spares, whom he will. And would he not spare himself? He would not. Love is strong as death, stronger. It drew in death that naturally is not welcome. If it be possible, says Christ, let this cup pass, when his love, expressed in a former decree with his Father, had made it impossible. 'Many waters quench not love.' Christ tried many. He was baptised out of his love, and his love determined not there. He wept over Jerusalem out of his love, and his love determined not there. He mingled blood with water in his agony, and that determined not his love. He wept pure blood, all his blood at all his eyes, at all his pores, in his flagellation and thorns (to the Lord our God belonged the issues of blood), and these expressed, but these did not quench, his love.

He would not spare, nay he could not spare, himself. There was nothing more free, more voluntary, more spontaneous, than the death of Christ. 'Tis true he died voluntarily, but yet when we consider the contract that had passed between his Father and him, there was a kind of necessity upon him. All this Christ ought to suffer. And when shall we date this obligation, this necessity? When shall we say that began? Certainly this decree by which Christ was to suffer all this was an eternal decree. And was there anything before that, that was eternal? Infinite love, eternal love, he pleased to follow this home, and to consider it seriously, that what liberty soever we can conceive in Christ, to die or not to die, this necessity of dying, this decree, is as eternal as that liberty.

And yet how small a matter made he of this necessity and this dying! His Father calls it but a bruise, and but a bruising of his heel (the serpent shall bruise his heel), and yet that was that the serpent should practise and compass his death. Himself calls it but a baptism, as though he were to be the better for it. I have a baptism to be baptised with, and he was in pain till it was accomplished. And yet this baptism was his death. The Holy Ghost calls it joy (for the joy which was set before him he endured the Cross), which was not a joy of his reward after his Passion, but a joy that filled him even in the midst of those torments, and arose from them. When Christ calls his Passion *calicem*, a cup, and no worse (Can ye drink of my cup?), he speaks not odiously, not with detestation of it. Indeed it was a cup, a health to all the world. And, says David, what shall I render to the Lord? Answer you with David, I will take the cup of salvation. Take it, that cup of salvation, his Passion, if not into your present imitation, yet into your present contemplation, and behold how that Lord that was God yet could die, would die, must die, for your salvation.

That Moses and Elias talked with Christ in the Transfiguration both St Matthew and St Mark tell us. But what they talked of, only St Luke. They talked, says he, of his decease, of his death which was to be accomplished at Jerusalem. The word is of his exodus, the very word of our text, his issue by death. Moses who, in his exodus, had prefigured this issue of our Lord, and in passing Israel out of Egypt through the Red Sea had foretold in that actual prophecy Christ's passing of mankind through the sea of his blood, and Elias, whose exodus and issue out of this world was a figure of Christ's Ascension, had no doubt a great satisfaction in talking with our blessed Lord of the full consummation of all this in his death, which was to be accomplished at Jerusalem.

Our meditation of his death should be the more visceral, and affect us more, because it is of a thing already done. The ancient Romans had a certain tenderness, and detestation of the name of death: they could not name death, no, not in their wills. There they could not say, If or when I die, but, When the course of nature is accomplished upon me. To us that speak daily of the death of Christ (he was crucified, dead, and buried), can the memory or the mention of our own death be irksome or bitter? There are, in these latter times amongst us, that name death freely enough, and the death of God, but in blasphemous oaths and execrations. Miserable men, who shall therefore be said never to have named Jesus, because they have named him too often and therefore hear Jesus say, I never knew you, because they made themselves too familiar with him.

Moses and Elias talked with Christ of his death only in a holy and joyful sense of the benefit which they and all the world were to receive by that. Discourses of religion should not be out of curiosity, but to edification. And then they talked with Christ of his death at that time when he was in the greatest height of glory that ever he admitted in this world, that is, his Transfiguration. And we are afraid to speak to the great men of this world of their death but nourish in them a vain imagination of immortality and immutability.

But (as St Peter said there) it is good to dwell here, in this consideration of his death, and therefore transfer we our tabernacle (our devotions) through some of those steps which God the Lord made to his issue of death that day.

Take in the whole day from the hour that Christ received the Passover upon Thursday unto the hour in which he died the next day. Make this present day that day in thy devotion and consider what he did, and remember what you have done. Before he instituted and celebrated the Sacrament (which was after the eating of the Passover), he proceeded to that act of humility, to wash his Disciples' feet, even Peter's, who for a while resisted him. In thy preparation to the holy and blessed Sacrament, hast thou, with a sincere humility, sought a reconciliation with all the world, even with those that have been averse from it and refused that reconciliation from thee? If so (and not else) thou hast spent that first part of this his last day in a conformity with him. After the Sacrament he spent the time till night in prayer, in preaching, in psalms. Hast thou considered that a worthy receiving of the Sacrament consists in a continuation of holiness after, as well as in a preparation before? If so, thou hast therein also conformed thyself to him: so Christ spent his time till night. At night he went into the garden to pray, and he prayed *prolixius*, he spent much time in prayer. How much? Because it is literally expressed that he prayed there three several times, and that returning to his Disciples after his first prayer and finding them asleep said, Could ye not watch with me one hour?, it is collected that he spent three hours in prayer. I dare scarce ask thee whither thou wentest or how thou disposedst of thyself when it grew dark, and after last night. If that time were spent in a holy recommendation of thyself to God, and a submission of thy will to his, it was spent in a conformity to him. In that time and in those prayers was his agony and bloody sweat. I will hope that thou didst pray. But not every ordinary and customary prayer, but prayer actually accompanied with shedding of tears, and dispositively in a readiness to shed blood for his glory in necessary cases, puts thee into a conformity with him. About midnight he was taken and bound with a kiss. Art thou not too conformable to him in that? Is not that too literally, too exactly, thy case? At midnight to have been taken and bound with a kiss? From thence he was carried back to Jerusalem, first to Annas, then to Caiaphas, and (as late as it was) then he was examined and buffeted and delivered over to the custody of those officers from whom he received all those irrisions [mockeries] and violences, the covering of his face, the spitting upon his face, the blasphemies of words and smartness of blows, which that Gospel mentions; in which compass fell that crowing of the cock which called up Peter to his repentance. How thou passedst all that time last night, thou knowest. If thou didst anything then that needed Peter's tears, and hast not shed them, let me be thy cock. Do it now! Now thy Master (in the unworthiest of his servants) looks back upon thee. Do it now!

Betimes in the morning, so soon as it was day, the Jews held a council in the High Priest's hall and agreed upon their evidence against him; and then carried him to Pilate, who was to be his judge. Didst thou accuse thyself, when thou wakedst this morning? And wast thou content to admit even false accusations, that is, rather to suspect actions to have been sin which were not, than to smother and justify such as were truly sins? Then thou spentest that hour in conformity to him. Pilate found no evidence against him. And therefore to ease himself, and to pass a compliment upon Herod, Tetrarch of Galilee, who was at that time at Jerusalem (because Christ, being a Galilean, was of Herod's jurisdiction), Pilate sent him to Herod, and rather as a madman than a malefactor Herod remanded him (with scorns) to Pilate to proceed against him. And this was about eight of the clock.

Hast thou been content to come to this inquisition, this examination, this agitation, this winnowing, this pursuit of thy conscience, to sift it, to follow it from the sins of thy youth to thy present sins, from the sins of thy bed to the sins of thy board, and from the substance to the circumstance of thy sins? That's time spent like thy Saviour's. Pilate would have saved Christ, by using the privilege of the day in his behalf, because that day one prisoner was to be delivered, but they chose Barabbas. He would have saved him from death by satisfying their fury with inflicting other torments upon him, scourging and crowning with thorns, and loading with many scornful and ignominious contumelies. But this redeemed him not; they pressed a crucifying. Hast thou gone about to redeem thy sin by fasting, by alms, by disciplines and mortifications, in the way of satisfaction to the justice of God? That will not serve, that's not the right way. We press an utter crucifying of that sin that governs thee. And that conforms thee to Christ.

Towards noon Pilate gave judgement, and they made such haste to execution as that by noon he was upon the cross. There now hangs that sacred body upon the cross, rebaptised in his own tears and sweat and embalmed in his own blood alive. There are those bowels of compassion which are so conspicuous, so manifested, as that you may see them through his wounds. There those glorious eyes grew faint in their light so as the Sun, ashamed to survive them, departed with his light too. And then that Son of God, who was never from us, and yet had now come a new way unto us in assuming our nature, delivers that soul (which was never out of his Father's hands) by a new way, a voluntary emission of it into his Father's hands. For though to this God our Lord belonged these issues of death, so that, considered in his own contract, he must necessarily die, yet at no breach or battery which they had made upon his sacred body issued his soul. But he gave up the ghost; and as God breathed a soul into the first Adam, so this second Adam breathed his soul into God, into the hands of God. There we leave you in that blessed dependency, to hang upon him that hangs upon the cross. There bathe in his tears, there suck at his wounds, and lie down in peace in his grave till he vouchsafe you a resurrection and an ascension into that Kingdom which he hath purchased for you with the inestimable price of his incorruptible blood. Amen.

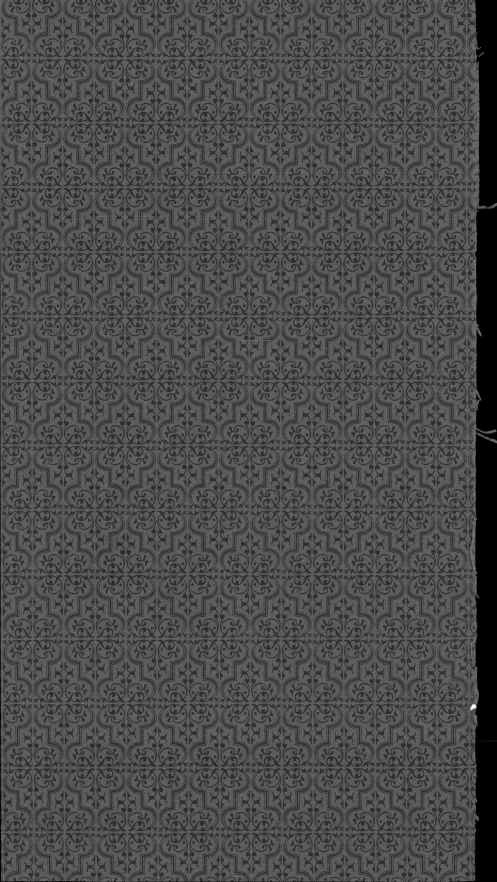